Predicadores

Predicadores

Hispanic Preaching and Immigrant Identity

Tito Madrazo

BAYLOR UNIVERSITY PRESS

Unless otherwise stated, Scripture quotations are from the New Revised Standard Version Bible, copyright 1989, Division of Christian Education of the National Council of the Churches of Christ in the United States of America. Used by permission. All rights reserved.

Jacket design by Kasey McBeath
Cover art: Shutterstock/flovie

Library of Congress Cataloging-in-Publication Data

Names: Madrazo, Tito, 1979- author.
Title: Predicadores : Hispanic preaching and immigrant identity / Tito Madrazo.
Description: Waco : Baylor University Press, 2021. | Includes bibliographical references and index. | Summary: "An ethnographic study of immigrant Protestant congregations in the American South centering primarily on the theology, style, and aims of the pastors' preaching"-- Provided by publisher.
Identifiers: LCCN 2020041153 (print) | LCCN 2020041154 (ebook) | ISBN 9781481313902 (hardcover) | ISBN 9781481313940 (pdf) | ISBN 9781481313926 (epub)
Subjects: LCSH: Hispanic American Protestants--Religion. | Hispanic American churches.
Classification: LCC BR563.H57 M34 2021 (print) | LCC BR563.H57 (ebook) | DDC 251.089/68075--dc23
LC record available at https://lccn.loc.gov/2020041153
LC ebook record available at https://lccn.loc.gov/2020041154

Printed in the United States of America on acid-free paper with a minimum of thirty percent recycled content.

To the many *predicadores/as* whose faithfulness and tenacity inspired this work,
quiero decir gracias con todo mi corazón.

Contents

Acknowledgments   ix

1   Introduction   1

2   *Viajes Concurrentes* / Overlapping Journeys   17

3   *Identidades Multiples* / Multiple Identities   43

4   *La Predicación Misma* / The Preaching Itself   73

5   *Predicadoras* / Female Preachers   113

6   Conclusion   145

Notes   163

Bibliography   181

Index   187

Acknowledgments

If it has accomplished nothing else, the research and writing of this book over the last seven years has certainly reinforced for me how utterly incapable I am of achieving anything on my own. First of all, collaborative ethnography is an exercise in mutuality and trust, and I will be grateful forever for the way in which my collaborators opened their lives and their hearts to me and trusted me with the telling of their stories. Although their true names do not appear in these pages, I hope this work is a true reflection of their commitment to their ministries and their communities.

I am also greatly indebted to the faculty of Duke Divinity School who encouraged me all along the way. Chuck Campbell continually had more faith in me and in this project than I could ever have expected. He, Richard Lischer, Mary McClintock Fulkerson, Edgardo Colón-Emeric, and Kate Bowler shaped my work in so many ways through both their thoughtful questions and the example they provided in their own writing. I have also benefited greatly from the support of my Hispanic Theological Initiative Consortium family and will always be thankful for the guidance of Joanne Rodriguez, Loida Martell-Otero, and Ulrike Guthrie. In addition, special thanks go to Cade Jarrell, David Aycock, and the rest of the amazing team at Baylor University Press for guiding me through the revision and publication process.

My first interest in the lives and practices of immigrants came from the overwhelming admiration I have for my parents, Tito and Sally Madrazo, who brought me to the United States as a young child and always provided me with an example of love and sacrifice that I hope my own children might someday also recognize in me. To those children, my beloved Sophia and Ava, I attribute whatever sanity I still possess as they have kept me grounded and joyful throughout this journey.

And finally, this work is a tribute to my wife, Danielle, whose academic journey inspired my own. Thank you for enduring all things and loving at all times.

1
Introduction

No one arrives at Iglesia Agua Viva[1] by accident. The building in which the church meets is one of a dozen identically nondescript brick boxes slotted along a main traffic corridor in the Raleigh-Durham area behind a Super Walmart.[2] Most of the units are occupied by dry cleaners, nail salons, and the occasional start-up restaurant. As I weave my way through them for the first time, I fail to see any sign of a church, so I stop at a small café and ask if they know of a Spanish-speaking church in the area. They suggest there might be one in the final unit, by the storage buildings.

Emboldened by this new information, I set out again toward the back of the development where most of the buildings are vacant. I park by the only one that has any cars around it, walk up to the nearest door, and read the white lettering on the glass. It signals the presence of a Pentecostal congregation, but nothing about that church's name or the name of its minister suggests that it is a Hispanic[3] community of faith. I turn to walk back to my car when I notice a small sign sticking up out of the flowerbed. In cursive lettering against a blue sky, it reads, *Iglesia Agua Viva*.

I open the door and step into a small entry area with a decorative table. In the corner to my left is a metal folding chair. Having spoken with one of the pastors previously only by phone, I do not want to walk in any further and cause a disruption. I sit down on the chair, from which I can see down a narrow hallway into the main space used for the worship service. A small group of musicians appears to be practicing the songs to be used in that afternoon's worship service. Young people (middle- and high-school age) drift in and out of the main classroom to my right, speaking mostly English and playing on smart phones and tablets. The narrow entrance hallway, which turns immediately right and then left, forces people to come into contact with one another.

Adults, teenagers, and children are constantly greeting one another in Spanish and English and excusing themselves as they navigate the congested space.

The one difficulty for these people milling around prior to the 2:30 p.m. start of the worship service is what to do about me. Only Pastor Esteban is expecting me, so the other members of Iglesia Agua Viva are somewhat startled by my presence there in the entryway. I am dressed as many of them are in khaki slacks, a collared shirt, and a light jacket, but all of them—young and old—treat me as someone out of place. Many of them walk by quickly or wave to make up for the fact that they have been staring. Several say hello with native North Carolina accents (the young) or with less-native accents (their parents). One gentleman in his mid-fifties even goes so far as to let me know his name is "Ma-ark." Though I was born in Venezuela and grew up speaking a substantial amount of Spanish at home, these people recognize me as "other" on this Sunday. I am treated politely, but superficially—previously lively conversations die in my presence.

After a few more minutes, one of the copastors of the congregation, Esteban Pérez, arrives. He of course also recognizes me as an outsider, but because of our previous conversation, he knows who I am and welcomes me warmly with a *doble abrazo* / double embrace.[4] We step into the classroom to my right, and I repeat to him what I had told him on the phone—that I have a scholarly interest in learning more about life and practices in a Hispanic immigrant congregation. Esteban still seems somewhat surprised that participating and observing in his church could be part of genuine academic work, but he also appears to be somewhat flattered. He begins to tell me more about his own experience—immigrating from the Dominican Republic as a young adult with his wife, living in New York, and ultimately settling in the Raleigh area. He had served as a volunteer youth minister at a church in another community for several years before sensing a call to begin a new church in this community. Iglesia Agua Viva had begun four years before and had already met in three different locations. The forty to fifty members include immigrants from seven different Latin American countries.

Esteban suddenly excuses himself. His high-school age son was unable to be there to play the drums, so Esteban is filling in for him. As I follow him through the door of the classroom, I decide to enter the sanctuary and take a less conspicuous spot near the rear. The group that I had heard practicing includes Octavio, a large man of Afro-Caribbean descent who stands as he plays the keyboard; Teodora, one of the church leaders who is directing the singing from the pulpit; and several teenage girls who are standing between them.

As more people enter the worship space from the door at the rear, they leave a wide margin of empty chairs between themselves and me. Gradually, almost all of the chairs are occupied except for the one on my right and the two on my left. The musicians complete their practice, and Teodora begins to speak a word of greeting from the pulpit. Having noticed the young people's widespread use of tablets, I take out my own iPad and begin taking notes as unobtrusively as possible.

Following her welcome, Teodora invites those present to join her in prayer. Some people stand, while others remain seated. Some kneel on the floor facing the back of the room, their elbows on their seats. Teodora introduces various topics of prayer, and members of the congregation fill in the gaps with their own concurrent prayers. During longer stretches of extemporaneous prayer by Teodora, others chime in with brief words of assent or petition like "*Sí, Senor* / Yes, Lord" or "*Por favor* / Please." This time of prayer lasts approximately twenty-five minutes.

When the prayer time ends, Octavio begins to play the keyboard. Esteban comes in on the drums, and Teodora and the three young girls begin leading the singing of contemporary praise songs. One of the middle school boys operates a laptop hooked up to a projector that displays the words on a screen above the drum set. The music shakes the furniture in the small space, but no one but me appears to notice. Everyone sings, and several members of the congregation raise their hands and sway to the merengue-flavored beat. Each song has several movements back from verse to chorus and occasionally to a bridge. The songs are approximately five minutes long each, and Octavio and Teodora lead the congregation in six of them. Octavio plays chords by ear without the use of written music and gives the others visual cues when beginning a new song or when moving back and forth within a given song.

When the singing ends, Esteban stands up from behind the drum set and comes to the pulpit, perspiring heavily. He offers up one more prayer as the remaining musicians go to their seats. When his eyes open, he looks directly at me and begins to talk about who I am and what I am doing there. The people glance at me as he speaks. Then Esteban asks me to come to the pulpit and share a few words about my work. I can see the looks of curiosity in the eyes of the congregation when I address them in fluent Spanish, but I begin to notice something else as well. Immediately after I speak, I can feel that the members of Iglesia Agua Viva are noticeably less stiff in their interactions around me. They now know that I am, at least to some degree, one of them.[5] As Esteban begins his sermon by directing our attention to various passages of Scripture, one of the women steps across the two empty spaces that separate us and offers to let me use her Bible. After the service, "Ma-ark" apologizes to me for not having properly introduced himself as "Marco," and we have a good conversation about his job as a long-haul trucker.

HISPANIC PROTESTANT GROWTH

My first experience at Iglesia Agua Viva (IAV) provided an entrée into the rapidly expanding world of Hispanic Protestantism in the United States. This growth, of course, parallels the similarly striking growth of the total Hispanic population in this country. According to the Pew Research Center's tabulations, the Hispanic population of the United States continues to grow at an incredibly rapid pace, both in absolute terms and as a percentage of the overall population. From 2000 to 2015, the Hispanic population of the United States increased from 35,204,480 to 56,476,777.[6] This increase of more than 21 million, or just over 60 percent, in fifteen years was driven largely by the rapidly expanding native-born population of Hispanics, which grew by roughly 16 million and represented 75.2 percent of the overall growth. Continuing immigration from Latin American countries, in comparison, only accounted for 24.8 percent of the growth in the Hispanic population. Compared to the total population of the United States, the Hispanic segment of society expanded from 12.5 percent in 2000 to 17.6 percent in 2015, increasing their share of the overall population by 40.8 percent in just fifteen years.

In the state of North Carolina, where I conducted my research, the growth of the Hispanic population has been even more stunning. As recently as 1990, the U.S. Census showed only 76,726 individuals identified as Hispanic out of a total state population of 6,628,637. At that point, the Hispanic share of the state population was barely more than 1 percent. Over the subsequent twenty-five years, the Hispanic population demonstrated remarkable growth. Between 1990 and 2015, the number of individuals self-identified as Hispanic increased from 76,726 to 913,895, a growth rate of 1,091.1 percent. Their share of the total North Carolina population has also increased markedly over the course of those years. Between 1990 and 2015, the total population of North Carolina expanded dramatically from 6,628,637 residents to 10,042,802, for a total growth rate of 51.5 percent. Even so, the Hispanic share of the population still grew more than sevenfold over the same period—from 1.2 percent to 9.1 percent. Much of the research on Hispanics and religion has focused on areas like the Northeast, Southwest, Florida, or California with their long-established Hispanic populations, but the phenomenon of immigration "to new areas, largely situated in more religious regions such as the U.S. Southeast, offers a unique opportunity to refocus" the lens through which Hispanic religious practices are viewed and understood.[7]

TABLE 1.1: NORTH CAROLINA HISPANIC POPULATION GROWTH[8]

	1990	2000	2010	2015
Hispanic population	76,726	378,963	800,998	913,895
Hispanic population percentage increase from 1990	—	393.9%	943.9%	1091.1%
Total population	6,628,637	8,049,313	9,535,692	10,042,802
Hispanic population as a percentage of total population	1.2%	4.7%	8.4%	9.1%

Within the larger narrative of Hispanic growth in the United States is the often-underreported increase of the Hispanic Protestant population in both absolute and relative terms. As recently as 1970, Leo Grebler, Joan Moore, and Ralph Guzman, authors of *The Mexican American People: The Nation's Second Largest Minority*, wrote that "statistically, Protestantism is not important in the Mexican American population."[9] This is no longer the case either for Mexican Americans or for the Hispanic population as a whole. The 2007 Pew study "Changing Faiths: Latinos and the Transformation of American Religion" showed that although 68 percent of Latinos in the United States still identify as Roman Catholics, 20 percent of them now identify as Protestant—15 percent as born-again or evangelical Protestants and 5 percent as members of mainline Protestant denominations.[10] These percentages equate to more than 11 million Hispanic Protestants in the United States.

HISPANIC PROTESTANT PREACHERS AND PREACHING

The growing population of Hispanic Protestants has generated significant interest among social scientists who have explored the role of congregations in cultural assimilation and ethnic identity maintenance.[11] Historians have chronicled the growth of the Hispanic Protestant population within specific denominations[12] and regions,[13] and missiologists from various Protestant traditions have taken greater notice of the social concerns of Hispanic communities that represent the growing edge of their denominations in the United States. Yet scholars have paid little if any attention to the preachers or the preaching within Hispanic Protestant congregations such as Iglesia Agua Viva.

What is the nature of preaching in Hispanic Protestant churches? What are its predominant themes and goals? These questions assume a universality to the Hispanic-American experience that simply doesn't exist. Upon which Hispanic population should we base our answer? A well-established Presbyterian congregation in New York composed of descendants of the Puerto Rican diaspora? A United Methodist church in South Texas made up of Mexican Americans who have identified as Protestants for five generations? A storefront Pentecostal church in Florida whose members all came from a parent church in Colombia? These examples only scratch the surface of the variety present within Hispanic Protestantism in the United States.

Many Hispanic scholars readily acknowledge the difficulty of writing about the practices of such a diverse population. Wrestling to identify an overarching Hispanic theology, Luis G. Pedraja acknowledges that the "different perspectives and communities involved in Hispanic theology restrict attempts to simplify or generalize these theologies."[14] José D. Rodriguez offers a similar opinion about the difficulty of defining a unifying Hispanic practice of biblical interpretation: "There seems to be a consensus that, given the diverse nature of our people, there are a variety of reading strategies employed by Hispanics for biblical interpretation."[15] Also attempting to write about Hispanic hermeneutics, Francisco García-Treto elaborates on the diversity present within the category of "Hispanic" as including not only different countries of origin but also disparate "historical experience, economic factors, and political allegiances, as well as the appearance of generational differences and different degrees of assimilation to Anglo culture and facility with English,"[16] which complicate the discussion even further.

In their 2017 book, *Latino Protestants in America: Growing and Diverse*, Mark Mulder, Aida Ramos, and Gerardo Martí highlight the challenges of this diversity, arguing that the greatest current issue in the field of Hispanic Protestant studies "is the pervasiveness of *ethnoracial essentialization*."[17] Throughout their research, they came across "sweeping statements from pastors, church consultants, denominational leaders and seminary professors" that completely overlooked the many important differences within this diverse population.[18] In light of these findings, Mulder, Ramos, and Martí urge researchers "to preserve variety and texture in observing and describing" Hispanic Protestants.[19]

THE ETHNOGRAPHIC APPROACH

How then can a scholar best "preserve variety and texture in observing and describing" Hispanic Protestant preaching? Is there a way in which Hispanic preachers and their sermons can be allowed to speak for themselves within the academic arena? In my opinion, the closest one can come to achieving these ideals is through ethnography, a research methodology originally developed by pioneering cultural anthropologists like Bronislaw Malinowski, Franz Boas, and Margaret Mead. These researchers eschewed structured experiments and highly formal interviews in favor of understanding a particular culture by immersing themselves in it as much as possible. These early forays in ethno-graphic practice established the discipline not as "an experimental science in search of law," but as "an interpretive one in search of meaning."[20] As a research methodology, ethnography is qualitative in its orientation and aims to pro-vide a "thick description" of life and practice within a particular culture. By "thick description," a term first used about ethnography by the anthropologist Clifford Geertz in his 1973 book *The Interpretation of Cultures*, ethnographers mean a portrayal of a given culture that accounts for the webs of meaning underlying surface data. Thin descriptions will not suffice because the eth-nographer, in trying to fathom the nuances of a specific culture, faces "a mul-tiplicity of complex conceptual structures, many of them superimposed upon or knotted into one another, structures which are at once strange, irregular, and inexplicit, and which he must contrive somehow first to grasp and then to elucidate."[21] A thick description takes into account these myriad variables in order to render a culture in its rich complexity.

To collect data and understand their significance, ethnographers embed themselves as participant-observers within the culture they are studying. This hyphenated term highlights the liminal nature of the ethnographer who, tra-ditionally, attempts to participate as an insider in order to understand the significance of symbols and rituals within a particular culture. Yet the eth-nographer's duty to observe—collecting, analyzing, and presenting data in a scholarly fashion—makes him or her an outsider as well. This insider/outsider distinction can also apply to researchers who come from within the particu-lar culture being researched versus those who come from a different culture. Scholars have debated the relative merits of insider versus outsider research and the exact location along the insider/outsider spectrum which researchers should occupy, but almost all scholars agree that it is inevitable that ethnog-raphers experience some degree of liminality during their research.[22] In order for real understanding to occur, "the outsider must to some extent get into the . . . heads, skins, or shoes" of the people comprising the culture he or she is researching, "whereas the insider must get out of his or her own."[23] Ethnogra-phers' awareness and careful consideration of their relationship to the culture or practice being studied allows them to include personal reflections alongside observational data in order to thicken the description of the culture or practice in question.

ETHNOGRAPHY IN THE SERVICE OF PRACTICAL THEOLOGY

Increasingly in recent years, theologians, historians, ethicists, and other religious scholars have been using ethnography as a tool in the service of theological inquiry. For example, in her chapter "Ethnography" in *The Wiley Blackwell Companion to Practical Theology*, Mary Clark Moschella points to the groundbreaking work of Catholic missiologist Robert J. Schreiter, Protestant practical theologian and ethicist Don Browning, and British practical theologian Elaine Graham to establish a theological rationale for the use of ethnography in theological inquiry.[24] More recently, Christian Scharen and Aana Marie Vigen have identified revelation as the core of ethnography in the service of theology. They define the methodology as "a process of attentive study of, and learning from, people—their words, practices, traditions, experiences, memories, insights—in particular times and places in order to understand how they make meaning . . . and what they can teach us about reality, truth, beauty, moral responsibility, relationship and the divine."[25]

Within this definition, ethnography can be both descriptive and normative. It is descriptive by method as a process of attentive study and normative by its very essence as an act of bearing witness. On the final page of *Places of Redemption*, an ethnographic portrayal of Good Samaritan United Methodist Church, Mary McClintock Fulkerson suggests that her work "can be seen as a form of testimony to that which indicates the reality of God."[26] This normative testimony of ethnography fits well within Bonnie Miller-McLemore's conception of practical theology as being "normatively and eschatologically oriented" as it "not only describes how people live as people of faith in communities and society, but it also considers how they might do so more fully both in and beyond this life and world."[27] Ultimately, ethnographic revelations can "pave the way for more faithful action, spiritual growth, and social transformation."[28] Recent ethnographic studies of faith communities have yielded new insight into a wide variety of matters, including the prosperity gospel movement,[29] the nature of evangelical group Bible studies,[30] congregational care for the sick,[31] and even the intersection of faith, capitalism, and community organizing in London.[32]

SOCIAL LOCATION OF THE RESEARCHER

Ethnographers have given significant attention to issues of "reflexivity" within their methodology and to the many ways in which the social location of the researcher "conditions the knowledge that is constructed."[33] My own social location in relation to Hispanic Protestantism is somewhat complicated. I am an immigrant from Venezuela, and even though my family came to the United States before I was able to form any conscious memories of my native country, the culture within my home and family here in the United States was markedly different from that of many of my childhood friends. We spoke both Spanish and English at home, and we often had traveling relatives with us who spoke only Spanish. This difference in language, as well as differences in cultural values, set us apart from the community around us. We also had distinct experiences, such as my being sworn in as a naturalized citizen, the many instances in which I had to explain my "strange" Venezuelan birth certificate, which was written as a narrative in longhand, and the conversations about why my father, who remains a permanent resident alien, could never vote.

On the other hand, I never felt fully at home in extended family gatherings as the one who was unfamiliar with some of the more current, colloquial forms of Spanish used by cousins who had remained in Venezuela. To them, I was the "American" cousin. My features and relatively lighter skin have often led people within Hispanic communities to react with surprise when I speak Spanish fluently in conversation with them. The diversity of my experience led to an inevitable "biformation"[34] that occurs for many, if not all, people in the United States of Hispanic heritage. The more commonly used expression of this biformation within Hispanic communities is *mestizaje*, which takes into account multiple tributaries (as opposed to two) that contribute to Hispanic identity. Miguel A. De La Torre and Edwin David Aponte define *mestizaje* as "an existential awareness of cultural complexity."[35]

My particular social location thus makes me both an insider and an outsider within my field of research. By sharing both language and faith with my collaborators, I am able to gain entry as an insider into their communities and understand at least some of their practices more easily. Insider research, however, has sometimes been critiqued for inherent bias and other epistemological limitations. Summing up the arguments against insider research, John Aguilar writes that "the conduct of research at home often inhibits the perception of structures and patterns of social and cultural life. Paradoxically, too much is too familiar to be noticed or to arouse the curiosity essential to research."[36] My training in the academic community and my experiences outside of predominantly Hispanic communities qualify me as an outsider, but this too presents its dangers. Outsiders have their own forms of obliviousness, such as failing to recognize nonverbal communication as well as the greater disruption caused by their own outsider presence as participant observers.[37] Most problematic is the claim among advocates of the outsider position that their viewpoint is somehow more objective. One potential way to mitigate some of the problems inherent in the identity of the researcher, whether insider or outsider, is to strive for greater mutuality with individual members of the culture being studied. Rather than treating them merely as informants or interlocutors, the researcher may approach them as collaborators in a shared endeavor. This is what I chose to do. What does such collaboration look like? Here, Luke Eric Lassiter's reflection helps us.

COLLABORATIVE ETHNOGRAPHY

In *The Chicago Guide to Collaborative Ethnography*, Lassiter encourages researchers to move from the "incidental and conditional collaboration" that has always existed in ethnography to a more systematic inclusion of collaboration in all phases of the ethnographic project.[38] Lassiter grounds his collaborative model on the concern among anthropologists for a more dialogic approach toward ethnography as well as on his own experiences of incorporating greater mutuality into his research on Kiowa song. Rather than simply sharing a completed work with his collaborators either for their comments or as an act of appreciation, Lassiter conversed with them throughout his project about the very categories and insights he was developing. Their pushback led to dramatic changes not only in the way he presented his findings, but in the findings themselves.[39]

Lassiter's collaborative model for ethnography has four primary commitments. First is an ethical and moral responsibility to consultants that takes precedence over the quest for knowledge and "engenders a complex and ever shifting negotiation between ethnographers and consultants."[40] I understand this commitment to encompass not only preachers but their congregations as well. My primary concern for my collaborators centers on their vulnerabilities surrounding questions of immigration status. Among the preachers I interviewed, several had come to the United States without documentation or had overstayed their visas. Many of the preachers who were now citizens or permanent residents shared stories with me about having been undocumented. Almost all of them spoke of ministering to undocumented immigrants in their congregations.

The anxiety within the Hispanic community as I conducted many of my interviews in the first half of 2017 was at an all-time high. The newly inaugurated president of the United States, Donald Trump, had campaigned on a platform of aggressive action against undocumented immigrants, promising to build a wall across the entire southern border with Mexico and threatening the use of deportation forces against up to 11 million undocumented immigrants. Already in his first week in office, he was pushing his wall-building initiative and promoting a plan to publish a list of the most sensational crimes committed by undocumented immigrants as a way to turn public opinion against them still further. Given the nature of President Trump's rhetoric, many of my collaborators expressed anxiety about the future for them and their families in the United States. Several of them told of hearing rumors that President Trump was going to direct local law enforcement to establish checkpoints to begin apprehending all Hispanic drivers without current driver's licenses or with restricted permits.[41]

Their fears were not without merit. Throughout President Trump's first year in office, arrests of undocumented immigrants as a part of the Enforcement and Removal Operations (ERO) division of the U.S. Immigration and Customs Enforcement (ICE) increased by roughly 30 percent,[42] mainly for minor offenses—or none at all. On December 5, 2017, ICE's acting director, Thomas Homan, indicated that the increase in arrests of non-criminal undocumented immigrants was not an aberration but the new normal for immigration enforcement under the Trump administration. He told reporters, "The president has made it clear in his executive orders: There's no population off the table. If you're in this country illegally, we're looking for you and we're going to look to apprehend you."[43]

The current threats toward undocumented Hispanic immigrants affect not only them but also their families.[44] One pastor shared with me that he and his wife had overstayed their visa when they had first come to the United States from Central America. During their decade-long residence in North Carolina, his wife had given birth to two children, who therefore possessed birthright citizenship. If the pastor and his wife were identified and deported, they would be faced with a wrenching decision—either to take their children with them into the very same situations they had chosen to leave or to leave them in the care of family or friends, with no assurance that they would ever be able to return and see them.

In light of these very real vulnerabilities, I have chosen in this book not to identify by name any of my collaborators or their churches. Instead, I use pseudonyms for all pastors, congregants, and congregations in this study, and provide generalized descriptions of some buildings and geographic locations, but with sufficient ambiguity to prevent identification. I have also allowed my collaborators to see all the material in this study pertaining to them and their congregations to make sure they are sufficiently comfortable that their identities and those of their congregants will not be exposed.

Lassiter's second commitment is that the collaborative ethnographer be absolutely honest with his or her collaborators. To fulfill this commitment, I introduced myself and explained the aims of my research prior to interviewing all collaborators or attending their worship services. I also asked their permission in advance to use specific sermons within this book.

The third commitment of collaborative ethnography is to produce clearer and more accessible writing in order to facilitate "open dialogue about interpretation and representation."[45] Where I have included direct quotations from collaborators, either from interviews, focus group conversations, or sermons, I present first the original Spanish and then an English translation. Because all translation requires some degree of interpretation, I believe it is only right to allow my interpretive choices to be visible to the reader and to my collaborators. Furthermore, although this book engages in larger academic conversations, I have tried to avoid using academic jargon and insider language in such a way that might obscure the character and concerns of my collaborators.

Finally, Lassiter asserts that collaborative ethnography requires collaborative reading, writing, and co-interpretation of ethnographic texts with consultants throughout the research project and beyond. In keeping with this commitment, I regularly interacted with my collaborators, either individually or in small groups, throughout the process of research and writing. Though very time-consuming, this process profoundly altered the trajectory of my work. Early on during my semi-structured interviews, I became aware that my collaborators were far less interested in many of my original questions than I was. For instance, my efforts to tease out their thoughts related to whether their congregations served as sites of cultural assimilation or of ethnic-identity maintenance were not typically very fruitful. They were far more concerned with their congregations' effectiveness in reaching younger generations while still ministering to newly arriving immigrants. After my first three or four interviews, I therefore altered a significant number of my questions and rescheduled meetings with my earliest interviewees. This was one way in which my collaborators reshaped my research agenda. Of even greater significance was the way in which they challenged me to paint a more nuanced picture of the primary focal points within their preaching, a matter which I take up in chapter 4. Their preaching, as well as their understanding of it, resisted simple categorization. At the end of this project, I sat down with all of my collaborators once more, not just to show them how I had used their sermons and stories, but also to discuss the conclusions they had helped me reach. These conversations proved to be very generative and led to further changes within what I had thought was a final manuscript.

SPECIFIC RESEARCH METHODS EMPLOYED

The primary methods used in my ethnographic research were semi-structured interviews, focus groups, and participant observation. Taken together, these three principal methods provided triangulation from various focal points.

In keeping with the principles of collaborative ethnography, all interviews were loosely semi-structured, so that collaborators were able to move the conversation to what they believed to be most important. My collaborators often broadened my perspective of certain aspects of their experiences in such a way that I had to go back and interview some collaborators again in order to round out my understanding. These additional interviews also served as an opportunity for my co-intellectuals to clarify and contextualize earlier responses for me. Although my already established relationship with certain interviewees may have influenced their responses to some degree, I view this as an advantage. Rather than believing that I can achieve a position of absolute neutrality as a researcher, I accept C. A. B. Warren's view that within the interview "the perspectives of the interviewer and the respondent dance together for the moment but also extend outward in social space and backward and forward in time."[46] This dance, which in the sphere of collaborative ethnography is one of acknowledged mutuality, influences both parties as they pursue understanding together.

As the chapters of this book began taking shape, I invited collaborators who had participated in interviews to join me for lunch so that we could talk through the material present in each chapter. I typically read some of the material (or had them read sections primarily in Spanish but also occasionally in English) and asked them to reflect on it. Having multiple collaborators present de-centered me as the researcher and provided an additional bulwark against the possibility that I was misrepresenting my collaborators' input.

The final angle of approach for my research was to conduct participant observation in Hispanic Protestant congregations. Participant observation "involves data gathering by means of participation in the daily life of informants in their natural setting: watching, observing, and talking to them in order to discover their interpretations, social meaning and activities."[47] In addition to interacting with pastors in their "natural setting," I was also able to reflect on the relationship between preachers and their congregations.

Although some of my participant observation comprised single visits to the congregations of pastors who had served as my collaborators, for over four years I maintained an ongoing relationship with one church in particular, Iglesia Agua Viva (IAV). Over the years, we have found other ways to collaborate. I preach in the absence of their pastors on occasion and participate in the life of their congregation regularly. This participation has allowed me to reflect more deeply on the realities they face than I otherwise might have been able to do had my participant-observation been limited to briefer encounters.

SCOPE AND THESIS

Recognizing the many differences among Hispanic Protestant congregations and clergy regarding such factors as denominational affiliation, longevity of residence in the United States, educational backgrounds, and countries of origin, I make no attempt to offer a normative definition of Hispanic preaching in the pages that follow. And yet the lived reality and experiences of my collaborators do offer insight into a significant cross-section of Hispanic Protestant preachers.

Who were my collaborators? Looking back over their journeys and identities, several common themes emerge. All twenty-four of my collaborators except for one were first-generation immigrants preaching to congregations of first-generation immigrants and their children.[48] Since the Hispanic population of North Carolina has grown from 76,726 in 1990 to 913,895 in 2015,[49] at least 837,169 (or 91.6 percent) of Hispanics living in North Carolina in 2015 had either moved to or been born in the state over the preceding twenty-five years.[50] Although it is likely that some of these Hispanic residents moved to North Carolina from other states, a significant number of them are first-generation immigrants or their children. Throughout my participant-observation in local Hispanic congregations, I rarely encountered native-born U.S. citizens over the age of twenty-five.

Twenty of my twenty-four collaborators were also first-generation converts to Protestant Christianity, meaning that they represented the first generation within their families to identify as *cristianos* or *evangélicos*.[51] More than half of them converted to Protestantism prior to their arrival in the United States. Many of them described dramatic conversion experiences "*conociendo a Cristo* / coming to know Christ" for the first time. Finally, all of my collaborators were ministering in very recently established churches. Some of these churches were "plants" sponsored by or connected to larger Anglo American denominations (Assemblies of God, United Methodist, Cooperative Baptist Fellowship), either within existing Anglo American church structures or in rented facilities. Others were completely independent storefront start-ups. None, however, had been in existence longer than thirty years, and most of their congregations were less than ten years old. In many cases, the pastors who served as my collaborators were also the founding pastors of their congregations.

While these similarities denote a certain segment of the Hispanic Protestant population, the differences between my collaborators also locate them within the larger panorama of U.S. Hispanic Protestant experience. Both male and female preachers served as collaborators in this project. They represent several different denominational identities and connections (Assemblies of

God, United Methodist, Cooperative Baptist Fellowship, Iglesia de Dios Pentecostal M.I., and independent). The preachers themselves had varying educational backgrounds, ranging from not having completed elementary school to having earned a graduate degree in divinity. They served congregations in rural, urban, and suburban settings.

Given the points of convergence and divergence between the experiences and identities of my collaborators, I feel confident in saying that this exploration of Hispanic preaching offers insight into the nature of proclamation within new Hispanic Protestant churches composed of and pastored by recent immigrants. In addition to fitting the vast majority of Hispanic Protestant congregations in North Carolina, this description also applies to a large and rapidly increasing number of churches throughout the United States. Both the preachers and their proclamation were deeply influenced by migration stories and bicultural realities. More specifically, many of the preachers in this study experienced their conversion and calling as a form of healing from the wounds attending their migration journeys. The bicultural, bivocational, and bilingual aspects of their lives continually connect their ministries to the everyday realities of immigrant life. Grounded in these elements of their journeys, their preaching focuses on the healing of the wounds experienced by their immigrant audiences. The Hispanic Protestant preaching of my collaborators resists easy characterization as it incorporates elements of both traditional and liberative preaching, but it is always closely connected to the experiences of its hearers. This will become evident in the chapters ahead.

A LOOK AHEAD

Moving forward through this book, chapter 2 focuses on the *Viajes Concurrentes* / Overlapping Journeys undertaken by my collaborators. Hispanic preachers travel down pathways of migration, Protestant conversion, and ministerial calling, often in rapid succession. These concurrent experiences closely tie the vocational practices of the preachers—including their preaching—to the experiences and attendant wounds of migration. Chapter 3 highlights the *Identidades Multiples* / Multiple Identities borne by Hispanic immigrant pastors. Almost all of my collaborators were bivocational, lived within bicultural families, and navigated complex relationships with the Anglo American leadership of their denominations or with both leaders and members of Anglo American congregations with whom they shared facilities. Experiences of *identidades multiples* continually reinforced their identity as immigrants and shaped their preaching and pastoral care.

Chapter 4 builds on the previous two chapters by examining *La Predicación Misma* / The Preaching Itself and the way in which the highly contextual experiences of my collaborators affect their proclamation. The chapter begins by examining a particular vision of what constitutes authentic Hispanic Protestant preaching developed over many years by Justo González and, more recently, Pablo Jiménez. From there, it complicates concepts of authenticity as it focuses on five major homiletical themes that emerged from the sermons of my collaborators and the way in which each of them echoes the immigrant experiences and wounds of the preacher and his or her congregation. Chapter 5 focuses on the *Predicadoras* / Female Preachers among my collaborators and especially the areas of divergence between their lived experiences and those of the male preachers. I explore ways in which liberative readings of Scripture, Pentecostal theology, and the power of personal testimony and faithful service have opened doors for these particular women. Finally, I include a close reading of one of my collaborator's sermons that illustrates the power and the importance of the female voice in Hispanic Protestant pulpits.

In chapter 6, I return to my understanding of the primary purpose of ethnography as an act of bearing witness to the practices of lived faith. I found that the importance of such witnessing increases when the faith communities in question have been marginalized, oppressed, and overlooked—as has been the case for the congregations served by those who collaborated in this study. I also consider the significance of my research for the field of homiletics, the understanding of vocational discernment, the practice of collaborative ethnography, the ongoing evolution of theological education, and the future of the Hispanic Protestant church.

2
Viajes Concurrentes / Overlapping Journeys

S everal years ago, I was part of a gathering of Hispanic pastors in the Raleigh-Durham area. We met together at a conference center nestled deep in a wooded property near Chapel Hill. As a way of building rapport and trust within the group, we each began by sharing how we had received our *llamado* / call to ministry. Among the participants that day was a veteran Baptist minister named Ignacio who used a motorized wheelchair for mobility. He cleared his throat and began to speak:

En mi caso, yo creo que todo tiene que ver con el accidente que tuve. En 1978, cuando mi mamá murió, mi papá nos trajo a los estados unidos porque él ya estaba aquí trabajando en el campo. Y nunca más fui a la escuela. Me fui al trabajo a los once años—a cortar tomate o naranja a escondidas. Pero había una familia para mantener y después de mí, había cinco hijos más. Yo era muy rebelde de joven. Un peleonero.

Y me accidenté en el año 1985 aquí en la Carolina del Norte. Tuve un accidente donde me fracturé la C4 y C5. No sé realmente que pasó en mi accidente. Mi familia no lo sabe. Solamente me encontraron tirado en los baños con el cuello fracturado. No tengo memoria. Sé lo que sucedió ese día antes de que empecé yo a tomar y sé cuando desperté en el hospital.

In my case, I believe everything has to do with the accident I had. In 1978, when my mom died, my dad brought us to the United States because he was already working here in the fields. And I never went to school again. I went to work at eleven years of age—to cut tomatoes and oranges in secret. But there was a family to support and after me, there were five more children. I was very rebellious as a youth. A fighter.

And I had my accident in 1985 here in North Carolina. I had an accident where my C4 and C5 were fractured. I don't really know what happened in my accident. My family doesn't know. Only that they found me thrown in the bathroom with a broken neck. I don't have any memory of it. I know what happened that day before I began drinking, and I know when I woke up in the hospital.

In the University Hospital in Chapel Hill, just a few miles from where he was sharing his story with us, Ignacio had his first encounter with a Protestant Hispanic pastor who told him, "*Dios te ama Ignacio, y Él está cuidando de ti* / God loves you Ignacio, and He is caring for you." But instead of providing consolation, the pastor's words only provoked anger in Ignacio. If God loved him, why had Ignacio suffered this accident? At the time of his injury, Ignacio hadn't quite turned seventeen. He was moved to a rehabilitation facility in Fayetteville, where he realized that he would survive but would never fully recover his mobility.

No quería una vida en silla de ruedas. No quería vivir paralizado. Entonces, empecé a pensar, "En Estados Unidos no me van a dejar morir, pero en mi país, si me pueden dejar morir." Porque allá si no tienes dinero, no hay medicina ni hay cuidado.

Entonces, convencí a mi papá que me llevara a México. Mi papá no quería—decía que aquí está lo mejor. Pero yo respondí, "No, aquí no me curan porque soy hispano, porque no hablo inglés. No me ponen atención, pero en mi país, si me van a poner atención." Pero no era cierto. Lo que yo quería era llegar a México, deteriorarme, y morir. Porque yo decía, "Con diecisiete años toda una vida delante en silla de ruedas—yo no quiero."

I didn't want a life in a wheelchair. I didn't want to live paralyzed. So, I began to think, "In the United States, they are not going to let me die, but in my country, they can let me die." Because there, if you don't have money, there isn't any medicine or any care.

So, I convinced my dad to take me to Mexico. My dad didn't want to—he said that the best [care] was here. But I responded, "No, here they won't cure me because I am Hispanic, because I don't speak English. They don't pay attention to me, but in my country, they will pay attention to me." But it wasn't true. What I wanted was to get to Mexico, deteriorate, and die. Because I said, "Being seventeen years old, with a whole life in front of me in a wheelchair—I don't want it."

Convinced by Ignacio's resolution, his father took him back to Mexico, to the last little town in the state of Mexico on the border with the state of Guerrero, a town called Naranjo. And the first doctor who saw Ignacio in Mexico confronted his father, "*Adónde estuvo tu cabeza? Si él va a recuperar algo, va a ser en los Estados Unidos* / Where was your head? If he is going to recover anything, it will be in the United States." Ignacio's father left him in the care of an aunt, who happened to be the only *evangélica* / Protestant in the entire family. She too tried to tell Ignacio that God loved him, but seeing that this only made him angry, she adopted a different tack. She no longer mentioned God at all, Ignacio said,

Pero empezó a cuidarme como si yo hubiera sido un hijo de ella. Dejó de hablarme de Dios, pero empezó a bañarme como si yo fuera un bebé recién nacido. Me cambiaba como si yo fuera un bebé recién nacido. Me alimentaba como si yo fuera un bebé recién nacido. Empezó a tocarme donde uno no puede resistir. Me tocó con un amor desinteresado.	But she began to care for me as if I had been a child of hers. She stopped talking to me about God, but she began to bathe me as though I were a newborn baby. She changed me as though I were a newborn baby. She fed me as though I were a newborn baby. She began to touch me where one cannot resist. She touched me with a love void of self-interest.
Eso fue lo que me convenció que Dios existía. Yo pensé, "¿Quieres ver a Dios? Allí está Dios." No me habló de Dios. No me habló de Dios. No me habló de Dios. Fui yo que dije, "¿Me puedes llevar a tu iglesia?" "Yo te llevo hijo," me dijo. Y me llevó a su iglesia, pero sus hechos me convencieron más que sus palabras.	That was what convinced me that God existed. I thought, "Do you want to see God? There is God." She didn't talk to me about God. She didn't talk to me about God. She didn't talk to me about God. I was the one who said, "Can you take me to your church?" "I will take you my child," she said. And she took me to her church, but her actions convinced me more than her words.

During that time, Ignacio had another dramatic experience that he characterized as miraculous. Since his accident, he had been wearing a cervical collar to support his head because he lacked both strength and mobility in his neck. He had the ability to move one hand slightly, but his other arm had been immobile for months. Doctors in Chapel Hill, Fayetteville, and Mexico had all told him that the loss of mobility and strength in his neck and arms was permanent. One day, as he sat on a couch in Mexico, a three-year-old playing in his aunt's home jumped up from behind the couch and grabbed Ignacio by the neck. He twisted Ignacio's neck backwards in such a way that Ignacio felt it surely must have broken again. He passed out from the pain and shock and woke up to find his aunt praying and crying over him.

But he also awoke to new feelings of sensation in his arms and neck. He told his aunt that he no longer needed to wear the cervical collar. And he began to feed himself for the first time since his accident. The arm that previously had been barely usable now functioned almost completely. The arm that had been totally immobile now possessed a significant range of motion.

Encouraged by what he characterized as two miracles—recovering significant mobility and experiencing the reality of God's love through his aunt—Ignacio attended church for the first time:

Mi tía iba a una iglesia pentecostés. El letrero dijo, "Iglesia Pentecostés Getsemaní." Y mi tía me llevó a un culto de navidad, y el predicador predicó, y había como 300 personas yo creo. Yo fui el único que pasé enfrente para que el predicador orara por mí. Y cuando él lo hizo, me sentí que mi vida cambió. Estaba muy contento, muy feliz. Quería hablar con mi familia de Dios. Nunca salía a la calle; ahora quería salir a la calle. Ya no lloraba, porque antes pasaba todas las noches llorando. Empecé a sonreír. Me olvidaba que estaba en la silla de ruedas. Y siempre quería ir a la iglesia.

Pero el asunto es que yo pienso que es allí cuando Dios empezó a llamarme porque no me dio tan solo ganas de irme a la iglesia. Yo decía a mi tía, "Puede Ud. hablar al pastor para ver si yo pudiera decir algo." Dijo, "Sí, hijo, eso se llama testimonio." "Pues, diga al pastor que yo quiero dar testimonio." Él dijo que yo podía hacerlo el jueves durante el servicio de oración. El jueves no llegaba gente.

My aunt went to a Pentecostal church. The sign said, "Gethsemane Pentecostal Church." And my aunt took me to a Christmas service, and the preacher preached, and there were about 300 people there, I think. I was the only one who went forward to have the preacher pray for me. And when he did it, I felt that my life changed. I was very content, very happy. I wanted to talk with my family about God. Before, I never went out in the street; now I wanted to go out in the street. I didn't cry anymore, because before I spent every night crying. I began to smile. I forgot that I was in a wheelchair. And I always wanted to go to church.

But the point is that I think that was when God began to call me because He didn't just give me the desire to go to church. I said to my aunt, "Can you talk to the pastor to see if I could say something." She said, "Yes, child, that is called testimony." "Well, tell the pastor that I want to give testimony." He said that I could do it Thursday during the prayer service. On Thursdays, nobody came.

Ignacio knew that the pastor had offered him the Thursday service as a way of mitigating the potential risk of having such a new believer speak in front of larger gatherings of the church, but he spoke at the service anyway and shared that he was happy because God had changed him and that he no longer cared that he was in a wheelchair. Having seen so many church members talk about God with such serious faces and scolding tones, he tried to offer a more hopeful view of the gospel. Gradually, as the pastor saw the earnestness with which Ignacio approached his newfound faith, he offered him the opportunity to lead the prayer service every Thursday.

Toda la gente que no iba antes los jueves empezó a llegar. Era más grande la reunión de jueves que de los otros días. Y el pastor me dijo, "Dios te está llamando. Si a mí me pides trabajo, no te lo voy a dar, porque para mí no sirves para nada. Y ninguno de los hermanos aquí te van a ofrecer trabajo tampoco, porque no nos sirves para nada. Pero Dios es el mejor empleador, y él tiene trabajo para ti. Nunca te olvides de eso Ignacio."

All the people who had not been going on Thursdays before began to come. The Thursday meetings were bigger than on all of the other days. And the pastor told me, "God is calling you. If you ask me for work, I'm not going to give it to you, because you are useless to me. And none of the brothers or sisters here are going to offer you a job either, because you are useless to us. But God is the best employer, and He has work for you. Never forget this Ignacio."

Ignacio had not been asked to share any details about his migration experience—he had done so spontaneously—but as we listened to his story, we all understood that the details of his *llamado* and *migración* were inextricably interwoven. The *viajes concurrentes* / overlapping journeys of migration experience and vocational discernment ground the preaching practices of my collaborators in their experience as immigrants and contribute to the resonance of their ministries and proclamation for their communities. It was within his specific immigrant context and its trauma that Ignacio had discerned God's calling. And his calling would eventually lead him to preach to those whose lives had also been marked by *migración*. After Ignacio finished telling his story, the next participant stood up and shared with us another story of *viajes concurrentes*. By the end of the evening, all of the participants had described journeys in which their *llamado* had been indelibly shaped by *migración*.

This evident connection present in these pastors' vocational pilgrimages bears a strong similarity to Mary McClintock Fulkerson's understanding that "theological reflection is not something brought in after a situation has been described; it is a sensibility that initiates the inquiry at the outset."[1] Among the collaborators who participated in this study, theological reflection arose within the context of migration and initiated the process of inquiry that led to vocational discernment. McClintock Fulkerson further elaborates:

> Theologies that matter arise out of dilemmas—out of situations that matter. The generative process of theological understanding is a process provoked, not confined to preconceived, fixed categories. Rather, as Charles Winquist is reported to have said, creative thinking originates at the scene of a wound. Wounds generate new thinking. . . . Like a wound, theological thinking is generated by a sometimes inchoate sense that something *must* be addressed.[2]

IDENTIFYING THE WOUND

The experience of a wound—the something that must be addressed—is pervasive among first-generation Hispanic immigrants and can take many forms. David Abalos writes about the forebears of today's U.S. Latino population coming "to this country seeking a new life, a better life, at the cost of great personal suffering and risk. They left behind loved ones, a familiar land and culture, to journey into the desert of an unknown land with a strange language and culture."[3] While this is certainly true, the reality of these losses is much less remote for most of my collaborators. When they speak of the wounds of immigration, they are not reflecting on the trauma experienced by their ancestors but relating the pain of their own recent experiences and current situations. For many undocumented immigrants, these wounds begin with the trauma of crossing the border (and often long before in a violent or otherwise fraught situation at home). Seth Holmes writes of the "many mortal dangers" migrants face in the borderlands, including "Mexican and American assailants and kidnappers after their money; heat, sun, snakes, and cacti after their bodies; armed American vigilantes after their freedom; and Border Patrol agents after their records."[4] Awaiting those immigrants who find work in the agricultural industry is another experience of suffering: the intense labor of "picking fruit bent over all day, every day, moving quickly, exposed to pesticides and the weather."[5] Their efforts on behalf of the agricultural industry of the United States inevitably lead to bodies that "ache, decay, and are injured" at rates far higher than the bodies of subsistence farmers in Mexico.[6] Holmes relates the following conversation with field workers as he conducted participant observation among them: "After the first week of picking on the farm, I asked two young female pickers how their knees and backs felt. One replied that she could no longer feel anything (*'Mi cuerpo ya no puede sentir nada'*), though her knees still hurt sometimes. The other said that her knees, back, and hips always hurt (*'Siempre me duelen'*)."[7]

Ignacio had experienced this kind of pain from the time he was eleven years old. He had also been thrust into what he described as an adult world characterized by uncertainty, violence, and substance abuse. These were the physical and structural manifestations of the wounds of immigration that led to his own traumatic injury, which eventually provided the context for his calling into ministry.

Another collaborator who participated in this study described the way in which a physical wound paved the way for his arrival in the United States. David[8] was born in Nayarit, Mexico, in the town of Amapa. For many years, David's father had been coming to North Carolina with a work visa to labor in the tobacco fields. He would spend ten months out of the year in the United States and two months with his family in Amapa. In 2003, David's father had his foot amputated after an accident on the job. This left David's family in limbo as his father would no longer be able to earn money in the fields to send back to Nayarit. Over the course of several conversations, however, David's father convinced the owner of the farming operation to offer his work visa to David instead. David, who had just turned eighteen, shared that things did not go quite as planned:

Cuando tomé el lugar de mi papá, entré a trabajar, pero la operación de mi papá costó mucho dinero y no lo teníamos. Alguien le recomendó que agarrara un abogado para pedir la ayuda del señor (el dueño) para que pagara la operación. Entonces [el abogado] le llamó al señor americano y él se molestó tanto que me corrió. La visa se perdió. Me regresé a México. Después volví con otra persona, pero sin documentos.

When I took my dad's place, I came to work, but my dad's operation cost a lot of money, and we did not have it. Someone recommended that we get a lawyer to ask for help from the gentleman (the owner) so that he would pay for the operation. So, [the lawyer] called the American gentleman and he got so angry that he ran me off. The visa was lost. I returned to Mexico. Later, I returned with another person, but without documents.

For David, the physical wound suffered by his father led to wounds of injustice and eventually contributed to his undocumented status and its accompanying uncertainty and stress.

But the physical injuries suffered by undocumented immigrants in their journeys and labor do not tell the full tale of immigrant wounds. In *The Uprooted*, a chronicling of nineteenth-century immigration to the United States, the historian Oscar Handlin writes of the pervasive wounds of loneliness suffered by newcomers to this country.

Loneliness had also the painful depth of isolation. The man who once had been surrounded with individual beings was here cast adrift in a life empty of all but impersonal things. In the Old Country, this house in this village, these fields by these trees, had had a character and identity of their own. They had testified to the peasant's *I*, had fixed his place in the visible universe. The church, the shrine, the graveyard and the generations that inhabited it had also had their personality, had also testified to the peasant's *I*, and had fixed his place in a larger invisible universe.[9]

Many of my collaborators identified this loss of identity as one of the primary wounds inherent in their experience of immigration, and especially in that of

undocumented immigration. Eduardo, a United Methodist pastor in a small town in central North Carolina, described it like this:

En la experiencia de venir como inmigrante viene trauma. Cuando un inmigrante no tiene documentos, ¿quién es? Al inicio, cuando yo empecé como pastor, me vino alguien buscando una persona con cierto nombre. Y yo dije, "No existe esa persona aquí." Pero el hombre siguió, diciendo, "Es así de esta altura y tal." Y yo pensé, "Tengo idea de esa persona, pero él no se llama así." Y me insistía que esa persona venía aquí, pero yo dije, "No me suena."	Trauma comes in the experience of coming as an immigrant. When an immigrant does not have documents, who is he or she? In the beginning, when I began to work as a pastor, someone came to me looking for a person with a certain name. And I said, "That person does not exist here." But the man continued, saying, "He's this tall and so and so." And I thought, "I have an idea who this person might be, but that's not what he's called." And he insisted that that person came here, but I said, "That does not sound right to me."
Y yo pensaba, ¿Quién es esta persona y como es que yo como pastor no lo conozco? Entonces pregunté a la iglesia y un hermano dijo, "Ese es el nombre que uso para mi trabajo."	And I thought, who is this person and how is it that I, as the pastor, do not know him? So, I asked the church, and a brother said, "That's the name I use for my work."
La situación de un inmigrante cambia todo. La conversación clásica es así: "¿Cómo te llamas? ¿De dónde vienes? ¿Y qué haces o dónde trabajas?" Para un inmigrante que tiene otro nombre, que ha falsificado sus documentos y está trabajando con esas dos cosas aquí, ¿Cómo puede participar en esa conversación? Está negando su identidad. No es nadie aquí.	The situation of an immigrant changes everything. The classic conversation goes like this: "What is your name? Where are you from? And, what do you do or where do you work?" For an immigrant who has another name, who has falsified his or her documents and is working with those two things like that, how can he or she participate in that conversation? He/she is denying his/her identity. He/she is nobody here.

Other collaborators with whom I worked reflected on their and other immigrants' primary wound having been the loss of family and community.[10] One Baptist pastor involved in this project came to the United States from Mexico twenty-eight years ago as an agricultural worker. Since then, he has traveled extensively within the United States, but he has never once gone back to Mexico for fear that he might not be able to return to his home and family in North Carolina. Over nearly three decades, he has missed innumerable family celebrations, weddings, and funerals. His primary interactions with his family

of origin have been phone conversations and money transfers. Even for those immigrants with visas or permanent resident or citizen status, the reality of distance and travel costs greatly complicates the ability to see family members regularly. In speaking about the wound created by the loss of family, another Baptist pastor identified the reconstruction of *"nuestras relaciones, nuestras familias /* our relationships, our families" as *"un asunto muy importante por los hispanos /* a very important matter for Hispanics."

The loss of family is a significant component within the overall loss of community suffered by Hispanic immigrants. Even where community prevails, immigrants find it changed not only by the pressures of the surrounding culture but by the very space in which it exists. Handlin writes that ways "long taken for granted" by immigrants "adjusted slowly and painfully to density of population in the cities, to disorder in the towns, and to distance on the farms."[11] Several of my collaborators spoke of the isolation they experienced due to both density and distance when they first arrived in eastern North Carolina to work in the tobacco fields. They bunked with five or six total strangers in decaying old houses or rusted trailers and found themselves completely unable to communicate with their employers without the use of intermediaries whose translations they did not always trust. Their coworkers came and went frequently, and they again relied on others to navigate certain routine activities like grocery shopping. They no longer felt welcome in the kind of social settings that had formed a significant portion of their communal life. A United Methodist elder with pastoral experience in rural settings shared with me that the search for a community in which they can participate often brought people to his congregation:

Van a la iglesia buscando una comunidad. Van a la iglesia esperando tener espacios para ejercer liderazgo, aunque muchos no saben que tienen esos dones. Yo noté que cuando la iglesia puede crear espacios para identificar y utilizar esos dones, eso es lo que les hace regresar.

They go to the church looking for community. They go to the church hoping to have spaces to exercise leadership, even though many of them do not know they have those gifts. I noticed that when the church can create spaces to identify and utilize those gifts, that is what made them return.

In addition to the loss of identity and community that many immigrants suffer, Hispanic immigrants deal with other ongoing difficulties including harsh working conditions, the fear of deportation, xenophobia, and separation from family. Eduardo spoke of the ongoing difficulty of these continually open wounds:

La comunidad hispana sigue siendo muy lastimada. Aunque los tiempos han cambiado en este país, los latinos en otro sentido son los esclavos de hoy. Son un recurso para los demás. Todas las empresas quieren tener latinos porque trabajan sin horario. Producen bien y no hay que pagarles los beneficios. Les dan su salario del día y se acabó. Y parte del trauma que yo veo es que hay mucha soledad y eso lleva a mucha gente al alcohol y otras cosas.

The Hispanic community continues to be very wounded. Even though times have changed in this country, in another sense, Latinos are today's slaves. They are a resource for others. All the businesses want to have Latinos because they work without a schedule.[12] They produce well, and you do not have to pay them benefits. You give them their wages for the day, and it's over. And part of the problem I see is that there is so much loneliness and that leads many people to alcohol and other things.

CALLING AT THE SITE OF A WOUND

Using McClintock Fulkerson's language, these wounds are the something that must be addressed in the lives of so many Hispanic immigrants today. Many of them seek healing for these wounds through participation in religious communities. Indeed, the wounds themselves often prompt deeper reflection for immigrants on the spiritual dimensions of their lives. As Timothy L. Smith has written, "the acts of uprooting, migration, resettlement, and community-building [become] for the participants a theologizing experience."[13] Daniel Ramírez expands on this concept, writing of the way in which migration caused by "economic exigencies or opportunities or vicissitudes" often "leads to human uprootedness, mobility, and liminality, which, in turn, often shake loose traditional or received ways and beliefs."[14]

For the collaborators involved in this study, addressing their wounds involved responding to a call to ministry—a call they experienced at the site of their wounds. I do not mean to suggest that only Hispanic immigrants experience a call to vocational ministry within the context of their own or others' physical or psychological suffering. This is certainly not the case. Yet there seems to be a greater tendency in Anglo American literature on ministerial calling to leave out these kinds of contextual considerations. John Adam Kern relates the calling of J. M. Thoburn, a veteran missionary to India, who said quite succinctly, "So one day I went into the forest, and under the shade of a maple tree had a quiet season of prayer. While I was praying the Lord came near and said to me, 'Go preach my gospel.'"[15] The call narrative of J. M. Thoburn could have taken place almost anywhere and does not reveal any

explicit connection either to the needs of the people he would eventually serve in India or to the receiving or healing of wounds in his own life.

A century later, James O. Chatham, a well-known Presbyterian author and pastor, wrote a handbook for exploring ministerial vocation called *Is It I, Lord?* Before exploring the realities of ministerial life, Chatham shares several contemporary call narratives, including his own. He tells of pursuing graduate studies in engineering until an encounter with a minister caused him to reevaluate his path:

> Then a strange thing happened. T. Hartley Hall IV, a campus pastor at my college, said to me rather offhandedly one day, "Chatham, when are you going to get out of this engineering stuff and do what you really ought to with your life?"
>
> I don't think I replied. I was stunned. I probably wasn't articulate enough to reply. But that simple comment set off fireworks in my head. T. Hartley thought I could do it. T. Hartley was no casual observer; later, he became a seminary president. He wouldn't make that comment without good reason. I had grown up around the church. I was fascinated with biblical history. I was bailing out of engineering. Should I think about it?[16]

Chatham goes on to share many other stories centered on the discovery of ministerial vocation. Several of them involve people abandoning promising careers or other degree programs for ministry. In nearly all of them, however, Chatham characterizes the vocational journey as a choice brought on to some degree by a crisis of purpose in the lives of individuals. They found their current educational or career path to be unfulfilling. They sensed that God had called them to something different, something more.

My Hispanic collaborators occasionally related similar feelings of ennui prior to the beginnings of their ministry, but the causal elements in their narratives always arose from the wounds inherent in their transnational and migrant identities and, most specifically, in the way they perceived God to have brought healing to those wounds. Some of their wounds, like Ignacio's, were literal wounds requiring physical healing. Other collaborators recognized God's calling through the presence of congregations that served as a balm for their loneliness and loss of identity. Some of them described God working in supernatural ways through the difficulties they faced regarding their immigration status. Still others reflected on their vocational discernment in hindsight as a providential occurrence brought about through the stresses and transience of immigrant life.

SUPERNATURAL HEALING AS A VOCATIONAL CALL

Isaac was born in the Mexican city of San Luis Río Colorado, just across the border from Yuma, Arizona. His father had been the manager of a bank in Mexico but struggled nonetheless to support his family. In the 1980s, he applied for and was granted a visa allowing him to work in Arizona at a gasoline station, which paid him significantly more than his white-collar position in San Luis Río Colorado. Eventually, Isaac's father was able to apply for permanent residency for himself and begin the longer process of seeking official documentation for his family. In the meantime, Isaac began attending school in the United States, crossing the border every day between his middle school campus and his home. Over the course of these years, he came to see himself, to some degree, as both American and Mexican until an accident reminded him of the difficulty of his limited access.

Yo tenía catorce años, y estaba jugando fútbol americano entre amigos. Nos emocionamos un poco, y una tarde yo salí lastimado. No podía caminar bien. Y pensé, "Bueno, se me va a quitar." Resultó que no. Se me había dislocado la cadera. Y yo no me di cuenta hasta dos meses después en un campamento en Baja California de jóvenes. Estábamos jugando otra cosa y me tumbaron. Y cuando caí, ya no pude levantarme.

Tomaron una radiografía y me dijeron, "Tenemos que operar, pero los tornillos que hay que poner en el fémur no los tenemos." Pues mi papá empezó a buscar alternativas en Arizona porque él tenía seguro médico. Y un doctor allá trató, sin abrir, de meter el hueso de nuevo en la cadera. Él nos dijo al principio que iba a ver si podía. Total que no pudo y esa misma noche me llevaron en ambulancia al hospital de niños en San Diego, California donde había un cirujano que me iba a operar.

I was fourteen years old, and I was playing American football with friends. We got a little excited, and one afternoon, I left injured. I was not able to walk well. And I thought, "Well, it will go away." But it did not. I had dislocated my hip. I did not realize it until two months later in a youth camp in Baja California. We were playing something else, and they knocked me down. And when I fell, I could not get back up again.

They took an x-ray and told me, "We need to operate, but we do not have the screws that we need to put in the femur." Well, my dad began to look for alternatives in Arizona because he had health insurance. And a doctor there tried, without opening me up, to get the bone back into the hip again. He told us at the beginning that he was going to see if he could do it. In the end, he could not, and that same night they took me in an ambulance to the children's hospital in San Diego, California, where there was a surgeon who was going to operate on me.

Y era una situación complicada. Yo tenía la pierna derecha más corta y apuntando para afuera. Y el doctor dijo, "Tenemos que operar, quebrar la pierna y poner placas para que no tengas problemas después." Pero el seguro ya no cubría y mi familia no tenía dinero para esa operación. Entonces regresamos a San Luis Río Colorado.

And it was a complicated situation. My right leg was shorter and was pointing outward. And the doctor said, "We need to operate, break the leg and put in plates so that you do not have problems later on." But our insurance did not cover any more, and my family did not have money for that operation. So, we returned to San Luis Río Colorado.

Isaac and his friends had just enough access to life in the United States to want to play American football, but not enough in order to have the proper safety equipment. His family had just enough access to hospitals and health insurance in the United States to see what was possible, but not to afford it. Isaac remained in his family's home for several days, until his father decided to seek the counsel and spiritual support of their local Methodist minister.

Un día mi papá me dijo, "Vamos a visitar al pastor." Y fuimos a la casa del pastor y no estaba el pastor ni su esposa, pero estaba su mamá. Y saludamos a ella, pero ya nos íbamos cuando esta hermana nos dijo, "No se vayan—¿su hijo es el muchacho que tuvo esa lesión, no? ¿Por qué no pasan y vamos a hacer oración?" Y papá le contó la situación a ella—que estaba tratando de conseguir el dinero para pagar la operación y conseguir seguro que pudiera cubrir más.

Y esa hermana dijo, "Mire Señor, tu hijo no va a necesitar que le operen. Dios tiene el poder para sanar a su hijo. ¿Ud. cree que Dios tiene el poder para sanar a su hijo?" Y él dijo que sí. Y pensé, "Esta mujer está loca." Pues yo no creía. Pero ella me sentó en una silla en la mitad de la sala. Y sin hacer mucho escándalo, tomó mis piernas así y si ella dijo algo con su boca yo no lo escuché, pero yo pude ver una pierna más corta que la otra y medio chueca. Y sentí mucho calor en mi cuerpo y entre

One day, my dad told me, "Let's go visit the pastor." And we went to the pastor's house and the pastor and his wife were not there, but his mother was. And we greeted her, but we were already leaving when this sister[17] said to us, "Don't go—your son is the boy who had that injury, right? Why don't you come in and we can have prayer?" And dad told her about the situation—that he was trying to come up with the money to pay for the operation and find insurance that could cover more.

And that sister said, "Look, mister, your son isn't going to need to be operated on. God has the power to heal your son. Do you believe that God has the power to heal your son?" And he said that he did. And I thought, "This woman is crazy." Well, I didn't believe. But she sat me down in a chair in the middle of the living room. And without making much of a fuss, she took my legs like this and if she said anything with her mouth I couldn't hear it, but I

lágrimas yo vi que la pierna enderezó y creció, y yo no necesitaba la operación.

Y bueno yo fui otra vez al cirujano en California y a buscar otra opinión en el distrito federal. Y tomaron radiografías y me revisaron. Y dijeron, "No sabemos qué pasó, pero la naturaleza hizo su trabajo." Y yo dije, "Fue Dios; no fue la naturaleza." Y eso es lo que pasó.

could see that one leg was shorter than the other and half twisted. And I felt a lot of heat in my body, and through my tears I could see that my leg straightened and grew, and I didn't need the operation.

And, well, I went again to the surgeon in California and to seek out another opinion in Mexico City.[18] And they took X-rays and examined me. And they said, "We don't know what happened, but nature did its job." And I said, "It was God; it wasn't nature." And that is what happened.

Those were Isaac's first opportunities to bear witness to what he described as the supernatural intervention of God in his life, but certainly not his last ones. Soon afterward, Isaac's pastor invited him "*a predicar y compartir mi testimonio con los jóvenes y con la iglesia* / to preach and share my testimony with the youth and with the church."[19] Testimonies of healing have played a significant role in the evangelism of Hispanic people on both sides of the U.S.-Mexican border.[20] This was the manner in which Isaac learned to preach—reflecting theologically on his own experiences and growing comfortable speaking in front of people. His wound, complicated by his migratory status, and his experience of healing provided him with his first message and an open platform to preach, first in his church and then in other Methodist churches in the state of Sonora. Through these experiences, those communities of faith and their leaders would increasingly affirm Isaac's pursuit of a ministerial vocation in the United Methodist Church. Isaac's early testimonies/sermons focused primarily on the healing—both physical and spiritual—that an individual could experience through Christ. His preaching was traditionally evangelistic, while also taking seriously the situation of those living in the borderlands. Isaac's story—which he has shared with countless congregations over the years—highlights the disparities he faced as a young man. Although Isaac never denied the need for more equitable access to healthcare or for greater social justice, it seemed to him in his early years in the borderlands that those things were beyond the reach of his efforts. The more accessible form of liberation and of healing came through supernatural means. This is what he had experienced, and it was what he explained to audiences with whom his message resonated.

CALLING IN THE HEALING PRESENCE OF CONGREGATIONAL LIFE

Esteban and Diana arrived in New York City in 1991 as undocumented immigrants from the Dominican Republic. They were both teenagers, had recently married, and had plans to study. They confessed that they had no idea how difficult it would be to enroll in an accredited institution given their immigration status and their nearly total unfamiliarity with the English language. They had been ready to matriculate at the University of Santo Domingo prior to their immigration, but in New York they said, "*Quisimos echar adelante y no pudimos* / We wanted to get ahead and could not." Soon after their arrival, they discovered that Diana was pregnant with their first child. Esteban scrambled to find better-paying work to keep up with the bills.

In the midst of this season of frustration, isolation, and uncertainty, Esteban and Diana turned to the church. In the Dominican Republic, they had been part of *La Iglesia Pentecostal de Dios Movimiento Internacional* / the Pentecostal Church of God International Movement, but in New York they began attending a nondenominational church led by a pastor with credentials through the Assemblies of God. Diana reflected on the important role that the congregation played in their lives:

Cuando encontramos una iglesia, eso fue algo maravilloso. Ahora, conocimos personas que estaban en las mismas condiciones que nosotros. Conocimos gente que nos ayudó con muchas cosas. A pesar de que yo tenía diecisiete años y Esteban diecinueve, había en nosotros algo, una madurez en cierto sentido, cuando nos enfocamos en algo y queremos alcanzar eso—tanto en lo espiritual tanto como en lo secular—lo hacemos. Hubo cosas que en lo secular no pudimos porque fue muy duro, pero en lo espiritual, inmediatamente encontramos iglesia.	When we found a church, that was something marvelous. Now we met people who were in the same conditions as us. We came to know people who helped us with many things. In spite of the fact that I was seventeen and Esteban was nineteen, there was something in us, a maturity in a certain sense, that when we focus on something and want to achieve it—whether it was something spiritual or secular—we do it. There were secular things that we could not do because it was very hard, but spiritually speaking, we immediately found a church.

Esteban introduced himself to the pastor of the congregation and told him that he had been a musician in his church in the Dominican Republic. The current drummer in the church's praise band was the son of the pastor, and he was still learning his way around the instrument, so the pastor invited Esteban to work with him. This served as their entry point into a community that soon enveloped their growing family entirely:

En la iglesia nos ayudaron a encontrar el apartamento cerca de Prospect Park en Brooklyn. Lo más lindo fue que en el edificio entero donde vivíamos estaban los hermanos de la iglesia donde íbamos. Fue como el libro de los Hechos, donde la iglesia primitiva se ayudaba mutuamente. Fue una ayuda tan grande. Nos ayudaron a conseguir muebles. Nos daban las instrucciones para todo.

Yo estaba a los 4 meses en mi embarazo. Nos dieron un "baby shower" para nuestra hija. No hacían eso en la República Dominicana. La iglesia era de gran ayuda en nuestra situación como inmigrantes. Nos sentimos acogido.

In the church, they helped us to find an apartment close to Prospect Park in Brooklyn. The most beautiful part of it was that in the whole building where we lived were the brothers and sisters of the church where we were going. It was like the book of Acts, where the primitive church helped each other mutually. It was a very great help. They helped us find furniture. They gave us instructions for everything.

I was four months pregnant. They gave us a baby shower for our daughter. They didn't do that in the Dominican Republic. The church was a great help in our situation as immigrants. We felt embraced.

The congregation in Brooklyn became a surrogate family for Esteban and Diana. Their experience echoes the findings of Kathleen Sullivan, who conducted a case study of immigrant religious experience at the Iglesia de Dios in the Mimosa Park barrio of Houston. One of Sullivan's interviewees, an elderly Guadalajaran widow, said, "Church has become my life, and that is why I am happy to live only a few blocks away. This is like my second home, and all who come here are my family."[21] Esteban had actively served his church in the Dominican Republic, but Diana had not been quite as involved. Now she began to see the possibilities of congregational life in a radically different sense. She found mothers to guide her in her new journey of parenthood. The identity she and Esteban had hoped for, as college students and white-collar workers, had never materialized. There were, however, opportunities to work hard and achieve goals within the spiritual career opening before them in this extremely receptive congregation. Over the next few years, Esteban and Diana would take advantage of every one of these opportunities that came their way.

Comenzamos espiritualmente a entregarnos aún más. Comenzamos allí—él era el baterista, y yo era secretaria de las damas. Empezamos a enseñar a los niños. Yo manejaba el van. Y también yo hacía una célula de los ancianos.

We began spiritually to give of ourselves even more. We began there—he was the drummer, and I was the secretary of the ladies. We began to teach the children. I drove the van. And I also led a cell group of senior adults.

It was in the context of leading this cell group that Diana got to know María, an older woman who had planted many congregations in the Dominican Republic over many years spent as a missionary. One day María took Diana aside and told her, "*En ti hay propósito; en ti hay algo muy especial que Dios va a usar* / In you, there is a purpose; in you there is something special that God is going to use."

After serving in and living among their congregation for a little over a decade, Esteban and Diana relocated to a small town outside of Raleigh, North Carolina. They found the experience to be radically different for recently arrived Hispanic immigrants in this new environment. Rather than living in buildings filled with immigrants and being able to shop in bodegas where Spanish was the most prevalent language, Hispanic immigrants in their area of North Carolina were much more isolated. Esteban and Diana commuted more than thirty minutes each way to attend a Hispanic congregation in a distant Raleigh suburb. When they first went there, their plan was to take things easy and not get overly involved. Eventually, however, they felt God leading them to live out the calling they had first sensed in their Brooklyn congregation. They subleased their location in a strip mall from an Anglo American Pentecostal church and started Iglesia Agua Viva as an attempt to offer to newer immigrants the kind of embrace and sense of purpose they had experienced.

CALLED IN THE FACE OF DEPORTATION

Just as several of my collaborators first understood their calling, at least in part, through an experience of supernatural healing, many of them also described God's intervention in their migration as part of their journey of vocational discernment. Ignacio, whose story served as the prelude to this chapter, described his return to the United States as another miraculous circumstance. Ignacio had been sharing his testimony at *Iglesia Pentecostés Getsemaní* / Gethsemane Pentecostal Church every Thursday night for several months when his brother came from the United States to bring him back. Only Ignacio did not want to go:

Yo ya sabía lo que era vivir en los estados unidos donde yo me accidenté. Yo no tenía papeles. Mi hermano si tenía papeles. Entonces, dije a Dios, "Si esto es de tí, me vas a cruzar al otro lado. Pero por el puente. Yo no quiero que me lleven por el rio." Porque mi hermano ya me había dicho, "No te	I already knew what it was to live in the United States where I had had my accident. I didn't have documents. My brother did have documents. So, I said to God, "If this is from you, you are going to get me across to the other side. But on the bridge. I don't want them to carry me across by the river." Because

preocupes—traigo dinero y ya hablé con un coyote que te va a pasar." Pero yo no quería coyote. Yo ya había pasado a los Estados Unidos varias veces usando coyote y yo sé que son bien crueles.

Hablé con mi hermano y le dije, "Mira hermano, ahora soy cristiano, y quiero hacer las cosas como Dios las hace. Yo no quiero cruzar por coyote." Se me quedó viendo en el hotel y dijo, "Yo no puedo creer que tú te has hecho aleluya. ¿Cómo crees que te podamos pasar entonces si tú no tienes papeles?"

my brother had already said, "Don't worry—I brought money and I already talked with a coyote who will get you across." But I didn't want a coyote. I had already crossed into the United States several times using a coyote, and I know that they are very cruel.

I talked to my brother and told him, "Look brother, I am a Christian now, and I want to do things the way God does things. I don't want to cross with a coyote." He kept looking at me there in the hotel and said, "I cannot believe that you have become an *aleluya*.[22] How do you think we can pass then since you don't have papers?"

In spite of his brother's anger, Ignacio insisted that if God wanted him to cross back into the United States, then he would be able to cross on the bridge and that the officials at the Border Control Station would allow him to pass. Eventually, his brother agreed to Ignacio's plan, but he was worried, not only for Ignacio, but also for himself in case the Border Patrol accused him of human smuggling. When they arrived at the Border Control Station, the officer asked for papers from Ignacio's brother and from the four people sitting in the back seat of the truck. Then he walked around to the passenger side where Ignacio was sitting.

El hombre vino y se paró al lado mío, pero no habló conmigo. La ventana estaba bajada y yo estaba ahí pero el empezó a hablar con mi hermano. Dijo, "El sol está caliente. Veo que la placa es de Norte Carolina. Vayan con cuidado—hay ciertas áreas donde no hay gasolineras. Y cargan agua porque es bien caliente y van lejos. Que tengan feliz día. Pasen."

Y mi hermano dijo, "Debe ser una trampa. Nos van a dejar pasar para después decir que yo soy coyote." Le dije "No. Es Dios." Cuando estábamos por llegar a San Antonio, me dijo mi hermano, "Me estás convenciendo que Dios existe."

The man came and stopped at my side but didn't talk to me. The window was down, and I was right there, but he began to talk to my brother. He said, "The sun is hot. I see that your license plate is from North Carolina. Proceed with caution—there are certain areas where there aren't any gas stations. And carry water because it's hot and you've got a long way to go. Have a nice day. You can pass."

And my brother said, "It must be a trap. They're going to let us pass so that later they can say that I'm a coyote." I said, "No. It's God." When we were almost to San Antonio, my brother said to me, "You're starting to convince me that God exists."

Crossing the border without documentation became an important element of Ignacio's testimony, legitimizing not only his presence in the United States but also the ministerial purposes that God had for him.[23] Belief that God might act supernaturally on behalf of those attempting to cross into the United States or those facing deportation was widespread among the congregations served by all of my collaborators, whether Baptist, United Methodist, or Pentecostal. Testimonies of God's activity on behalf of the undocumented inspired hope within congregants and credentialed the witness as one who had indeed experienced divine intervention through faith.[24] Nowhere was this more evident in the course of my participant observation than in the case of Juan. I first heard Juan's name during one of my early interactions with Iglesia Agua Viva. During the lengthy (twenty- to thirty-minute) extemporary prayers offered at the beginning of the Sunday services and the Thursday Bible studies, Juan's name was mentioned regularly as someone in need of both strength and freedom. I guessed that he was in jail but could not be sure, and I did not yet feel sufficiently accepted by the community to ask. One Thursday night, the woman leading the prayer began offering up expressions of thanksgiving that Juan was going to be set free. The entire congregation joined in with her, sharing similar expressions of gratitude for what they called *el milagro* / the miracle of Juan's deliverance.

A few weeks later, another member of the congregation introduced me to Juan in the hallway outside the sanctuary. It seemed too abrupt to ask him why everyone had been praying for him or whether he had been in jail, so I decided on the more innocuous question of how he made a living. The following conversation/interview arose out of his response:

"*¿Dónde trabajas?* / Where do you work?"

It was a casual question that I asked as I was leaning against the wall in the hallway, but my attempts at small talk immediately plunged us into deeper waters with Juan's answer:

En ninguna parte ahora, pero estoy buscando trabajo. Acabo de pasar cuatro meses en la cárcel.	Nowhere currently, but I am looking for work. I just spent four months in jail.

I had already guessed that Juan had recently been released from jail, but I did not know how long he had been there or for what reason. Although I suspected that his imprisonment might be related to his immigration status, I had been hesitant to bring up the topic as a newcomer to the community who had not yet established deep bonds of trust. I did not want to expose feelings of shame or fear over documentation status or police detainment in such a way that might damage my growing relationship with the members of IAV. What I found in Juan's case, however, was an eagerness to share a story he understood as the miraculous intervention of God on his behalf.

Juan is a mechanic by trade. He takes in cars (usually from other Hispanic immigrants) and works on them at his home, typically receiving cash payment upon completing the work. Several months prior to our conversation, one of his clients arrived to pick up his vehicle but refused to pay the agreed-upon price. Juan withheld the car, and the client accused him of theft. A detective from the local police department came and questioned him aggressively. The experience was particularly scary for Juan because he only understood a small fraction of the questions being asked. In spite of his anxiety, Juan attempted to answer them all and did his best to appear compliant.

Nevertheless, the detective arrested him that day on suspicion of theft. Ultimately, the district attorney's office declined to press charges related to that original complaint, but in the course of the investigation Juan's undocumented status was revealed, and he was transferred to an Immigration and Customs Enforcement detention facility. Throughout our conversation, Juan referred to it as *el centro de deportación* / the deportation center. Pastor Esteban visited Juan during that time and assured him that in the end, his situation would be used to glorify God. Encouraged by Esteban's words, Juan began to preach to approximately fifteen of his fellow detainees on a regular basis.

During the four months of his detention, Juan and his fellow members of IAV continued to pray for his deliverance. Much of Juan's interaction with the ICE authorities came in conversations with a woman he referred to as *la deportadora* / the deporter. I assumed she was simply one of the immigration agents working there, but, according to Juan, all the other detained individuals also called her *la deportadora* because detainees who met with her were usually sent back to their countries of origin soon after. After Juan had spent several months at the center, the *deportadora* told him that he was going to be released in a few weeks but that he would have to leave the country—to go back to Argentina without his wife and children. From there, she said, he could begin to work his way back through the "proper," grindingly slow legal channels. Juan even signed paperwork confirming his deportation. At this point, despair set in. Juan says he lost forty pounds in a few weeks as he thought about being separated from his wife and two children. His despair was so great that he was considered suicidal. Immigration agents placed him in a straitjacket and mandated psychological exams. The *deportadora* continued to tell him that there was nothing on earth that could prevent his deportation, so Juan began to pray specifically for something beyond earth to help.

Two days later, the *deportadora* returned to explain that Juan would not be deported after all. She was speaking in English during their conversation, and Juan could not totally understand her message. Another prisoner named Jaime translated as the other fifty-five men in the cell block tried to listen in. Jaime began to cry as he explained that Juan would get to stay in the country and apply for a social security number and a resident work visa. The *deportadora* explained that this was a very unusual decision, and that she could not fully explain how this particular turn of events had come about. But Juan chimed in with an answer.

Me dijiste una vez que nada en este mundo podía prevenir mi deportación. Tuviste razón. Nada en este mundo lo hizo. Dios lo hizo. Es un milagro. Dios ha estado obrando en mi vida, y puede obrar en tu vida también.	You told me once that nothing in this world could prevent my deportation. You were right. Nothing in this world did it. God did it. It's a miracle. God has been working in my life, and He can work in your life too.

Everyone in the unit knew what had happened, and that afternoon, forty of the fifty-five detainees came to hear Juan preach. Several of them wanted to accept Christ. This was a Thursday, and Juan was told that he would probably be released on Monday. His birthday was Saturday, and he began to pray that he might get to spend his birthday with his family. He had missed several family birthdays during his detention, and he wanted his family to be able to celebrate this one together. Without any explanation for the change in plans, Juan was released at 9:00 a.m. on Saturday and celebrated his birthday at home with his family. Pastor Esteban gave Juan the opportunity to preach at church that Sunday. Since then, he has become a regular contributor on a local Christian AM radio program as well as a guest preacher in churches as far away as Texas.

As in the case of Isaac's supernatural healing, Juan's experience of divine deliverance provided him with both the platform and the message that launched his preaching ministry. Like Isaac's earliest preaching efforts, Juan's proclamation also defies simple categorization. His testimony features an unblinking portrayal of the injustice he had suffered and the emotional and physical toll of his detainment. He regularly equates his own social location with the experiences of marginalized individuals in Scripture, often describing his experience as analogous to the experience of Paul and Silas in the jail in Philippi.[25] Part of his message—the belief that God has once again shown himself to be on the side of the oppressed and the marginalized—could be characterized as liberationist. The invitation Juan offers, however, is not to greater social action, but to individual repentance and deeper personal faith. Like Isaac's experience of calling and earliest forays into ministry, Juan's experiences reveal the complexity often present in the preaching of first-generation Hispanic Protestants.

THRUST INTO THE LINE OF SERVICE

Por otra parte, ya no es el sacerdote—el profesional de la Palabra de Dios—quien se dirige a las gentes y sirve de vehículo al mensaje; sino el zapatero, el minero, el vendedor de empanadas; en una palabra, los personajes de la vida cotidiana. El que habla, podría ser uno de los que pasan; y el que pasa, podrá muy bien algún día ser el predicador.[26]

On the other hand, it is no longer the priest—the professional of God's Word—who addresses the people and serves as a vehicle for the message; but rather the shoemaker, the miner, the seller of empanadas; in a word, the characters of everyday life. The one who speaks could be one of those who passes by; and the one who passes by, could very well be the preacher one day.

Christian Lalive d'Epinay, a Swiss anthropologist, wrote these words in his groundbreaking work *Refugio de las Masas / Haven for the Masses*, a study of the explosive growth of the Pentecostal church in Chile. Writing in 1969, d'Epinay sought to understand the underlying factors of Pentecostalism's rise in South America. Among his findings, he noted the importance of pastoral identity. Instead of being guided by highly trained priests who often came from different cultural or socioeconomic backgrounds, Pentecostal congregations had very different ideas about who could serve *de vehículo al mensaje / as a vehicle for the message*. It was everyday folk—the shoemaker, the miner, and the seller of empanadas—who already had intimate knowledge of their community and neighbors who served as *predicadores* within these congregations. Also notable in d'Epinay's observation is the rapidity, at least rhetorically, with which this transition from laity to clergy took place. One day, these people were common laborers in the community. The next, they had become its preachers.

Many of my collaborators described their first forays into ministry happening with this same sense of suddenness and unexpectedness. In fact, they often spoke of their first ministerial stints as unwilling responses to an absence of pastoral leadership within their local congregations. The ongoing wounds of migration often include transiency and a paucity of formal education among Hispanic immigrants, as well as a lack of interconnectedness between congregations. Churches looking for new pastors are often on their own. Even in those cases, as in the United Methodist church, where there is greater denominational support, it can still be exceedingly difficult to find a new pastor with some degree of ministerial skill who will not be a doctrinal mismatch for a particular congregation. The candidate pool from which they are drawing in an area of such recent migration is not particularly deep. Some congregations find themselves reaching farther than they would have imagined for new pastoral leadership. Two of my collaborators, Álvaro and Linda, first came to Raleigh from Puerto Rico in order to preach during a series of revival services. Several people from a nearby community attended the services and pulled them aside afterward, begging them to relocate to Raleigh to begin a new church in their suburb, which had no Hispanic congregations at that time. Álvaro and Linda, a husband and wife pastoral team, had been happily serving a congregation in Puerto Rico for several years at that point, but sensed God speaking to them through this heartfelt request and planted a new church in the Raleigh area nearly twenty years ago.

Given the real difficulties in finding pastoral leadership that led some churches to import ministers like Álvaro and Linda, many Hispanic churches—Baptist, United Methodist, and Pentecostal—have begun the process of identifying and training new ministers from the earliest stages of their members' church involvement. Ernesto, a Baptist pastor from a small town an hour and a half from Raleigh, told of the way his ministerial training began immediately after his conversion to Protestant Christianity:

En ese año que yo me convertí a Cristo en el 99, la iglesia donde yo me convertí a Cristo nos empezó a enseñar, a discipular, y empezabamos a tomar un estudio de homilética. Entonces, empecé a tomar esos estudios con el pastor de la iglesia. Entonces, nueve meses después de yo convertirme a Cristo, prediqué mi primer sermón. No era solo compartir testimonio. Fue un sermón.	In that year that I converted to Christ in 1999, the church where I converted to Christ began to teach us, to disciple us, and we began to take a study in homiletics. Then I began to take those studies with the pastor of the church. Then, nine months after I converted to Christ, I preached my first sermon. It wasn't just sharing testimony. It was a sermon.
Yo seguí con los estudios y de vez en cuando el pastor me pedía que yo predicara a la congregación, especialmente cuando el salía de vacaciones o salía fuera del país. Me decía, "Quiero que me ayudes cierto domingo o tales domingos a predicar."	I continued with the studies, and from time to time the pastor asked me to preach to the congregation, especially when he would leave on vacation or travel outside the country. He would tell me, "I want you to help me on a certain Sunday or certain Sundays by preaching."

Ernesto's experience was a very common one for many of my collabora-tors. Due to their size and the income of their congregants, most Hispanic congregations in this area lack the financial support to hire multiple staff members. This presents pastors with the dilemma of finding guest preach-ers when they travel—which can be often as they attempt to maintain con-nections with family members in various other states and countries. Train-ing new members in ministerial tasks from the very beginning of their involvement in the congregation affords the ministers an opportunity to cultivate their own substitute preachers and teachers while also helping to influence their doctrinal positions so that they are roughly congruent with those of the pastor.

Of course, not all substitute needs are for a single Sunday or even a few Sun-days in a row. Agustín, an ordained United Methodist elder who has pastored several different congregations within a ninety-mile radius of Raleigh, became engaged as a substitute pastor in an indefinite sense not long after coming to the United States. Agustín originally arrived with a tourist visa with the stated goal of improving his English. His plan was to stay with his uncle, Enrique, who was a Hispanic United Methodist pastor leading several congregations in and around Raleigh.

Cuando llegué, mi tío estaba estab-leciendo iglesias metodistas aquí en esta zona, tratando de alcanzar a in-migrantes de la primera generación, la mayoría que eran católicos nominales, entonces eran muy nuevos en la fe. Inmediatamente me invitó a ayudar-le, entonces tuve la oportunidad de involucrarme en el ministerio dando estudios bíblicos.	When I arrived, my uncle was estab-lishing Methodist churches here in this area, trying to reach first-generation immigrants, the majority of whom were nominal Catholics and therefore very new in the faith. He immediately invited me to help him, so I had the opportunity to become involved in the ministry giving Bible studies.

Although Agustín had previously been part of a Methodist congregation in Mexico, he had spent the previous four or five years in a Pentecostal church in the Mexican state of Sonora. His uncle did not see this as an obstacle to his involvement as a Bible study teacher in several fledgling Hispanic United Methodist congregations. Agustín spoke openly of using the discipleship materials from his Pentecostal congregation as resources in his teaching. His role, however, was about to expand once again, this time from helper to pastor:

Ese mismo año, [mi tío] se enfermó y tuvo que dejar de pastorear. Y prácticamente, tomé muchas de las responsabilidades de él. Tomé el entrenamiento con la iglesia metodista de los misioneros laicos. Después me dieron la oportunidad de pastorear una iglesia [al este de Raleigh]. Sin formación teológica, sin formación pastoral, empecé a pastorear. Los servicios duraban media hora—yo quería terminar rápido porque me sentí incapaz. Fui encontrando más confianza, y pedí ayuda de otros pastores.

That same year, [my uncle] became sick and had to give up pastoring. And, practically, I took on many of his responsibilities. I took the Methodist church's lay missionary training. Afterward, they gave me the opportunity to pastor a church [east of Raleigh]. Without theological formation, without pastoral formation, I began to pastor. The services lasted half an hour—I wanted to finish quickly because I felt incapable. I went along discovering more confidence, and I asked for help from other pastors.

Agustín, as well as many of my other collaborators who found themselves similarly thrust into the line of service, discovered migration-related wounds in the lives of their congregants. These communal wounds resulted from congregations that found themselves bereft of pastoral leadership or unable to experience wholeness due to the difficulties of their collective immigrant realities. Likewise, the healing offered through the rapid progression of an individual from layperson to minister also served as a balm for the community as a whole.

Whereas Agustín was thrust into ministry through the grave illness of a previous pastor, pastoral vacancies often arise out of more mundane concerns. Because the vast majority of Hispanic pastors in the Raleigh-Durham area are bivocational, they often need to move in order to obtain or maintain a secular job that provides a larger portion of their family's income. This pastoral transiency often leaves lay members with the responsibility of becoming interim and even permanent pastors seemingly overnight. Leo, a Baptist pastor of a congregation near Durham, related his first experience in pastoral leadership as being a complete shock:

Estábamos en una iglesia de las Asambleas de Dios en Dothan, Alabama por un tiempo. El pastor me motivaba mucho para prepararme a predicar. Un día me dijo de repente que él tenía que ir de la iglesia. Él estaba regresando a Florida y me dejó encargado con la iglesia. Yo estaba como interino por más de un año. Después llegaron otros pastores, y ellos también tenían que irse. Yo estaba allí como pastor interino otra vez por catorce meses.

We were in an Assemblies of God church in Dothan, Alabama, for a while. The pastor was really motivating me to prepare myself to preach. One day, he told me suddenly that he had to leave the church. He was returning to Florida, and he left me in charge of the church. I was there as an interim for more than a year. Afterward other pastors came, and they also had to leave. I was there as interim another time for fourteen months.

Leo and his wife eventually moved to North Carolina to be closer to their grown children. After settling in, they joined a nearby Hispanic Baptist church where Leo, upon sharing some of his experience in church leadership, was immediately assigned teaching responsibilities. Within a few years, he was sent out to plant his new congregation near Durham.

Ernesto, Agustín, Leo, and many other Hispanic immigrant preachers have experienced the kind of sudden change described by Christian Lalive d'Epinay. Seemingly overnight, they go from being the ones who pass by to being the ones who preach. This rapid beginning to their ministry indicates that these preachers received a kind of organic, ecclesially based transmission of pastoral theology and ministerial practices from their previous pastors and even from the congregations that first called them. The location of these churches in the United States and the pervasiveness of English-language resources that have been translated into Spanish means that there is most likely some Anglo American theological and homiletical influence as well. The primary influence on the lives of these preachers, however, came from the Hispanic immigrant pastors who mentored them and often created space for their ministry, both through their guidance and through their eventual departure.[27]

HEALING THE WOUNDS

The process of vocational discernment for my collaborators almost always involved thinking theologically and acting faithfully in response to the wounds that they and their communities had suffered through migration. The foregoing stories attest that these wounds can be physical, emotional, psychological, or relational, but in some way, my collaborators' experiences of divine calling arose from the healing they had experienced from these wounds and/or the healing they hoped to offer to their wounded communities. Sometimes the healing in question occurred as a supernatural experience of physical healing or divine deliverance, and sometimes it came through the ongoing and uplifting presence of a local congregation. Sometimes the healing even came about unexpectedly as my collaborators unwittingly found themselves on the front lines of ministry and discovered their own calling to be healers of their community's many wounds. In whatever way their journeys of migration and their attendant wounds intersected with their journeys of vocational discernment, there is no doubt that these were *viajes concurrentes* that would together shape the arc of these preachers' ministries and proclamation and guide them to heal similar wounds in the lives of their future congregants.

3
Identidades Multiples / Multiple Identities

The twentieth-century German theologian Helmut Thielicke, in his classic work *A Little Exercise for Young Theologians*, recounts the story of a hypothetical young theologian/pastor as a way to convey the church's occasional suspicion of theological education. Thielicke's protagonist begins as a lay leader in his local congregation whose well-received scriptural discourses are aided less by commentaries than by his lively faith and his close relationships with his fellow parishioners. Yet when the young man returns from his first semester of theological education, these same parishioners find him drastically changed. His response to the Bible study of an old acquaintance is no longer that of earnest excitement. Instead, he offers his friend a detached critique that employs inscrutable theological jargon. After several more semesters of study, the student once more returns home and this time leads a Bible study himself. The result is entirely different from those he led prior to pursuing his theological education:

> Under a considerable display of the apparatus of exegetical science and surrounded by the air of the initiated, he produces paralyzing and unhappy trivialities, and the inner muscular strength of a lively young Christian is horribly squeezed to death in a formal armor of abstract ideas.[1]

The failure of the young man arises not just from his exposure to these new abstract ideas, but from the way in which his adoption of these ideas has separated him from the community which formed him initially. Thielicke's admonition is that "true theologians" must "think within the community of God's people, and for that community, and in the name of that community."[2]

The same can be said for "true" pastors as well. In *Black Preaching: The Recovery of a Powerful Art*, Henry H. Mitchell draws connections between the effectiveness of black preaching and the connection its practitioners enjoy with their communities and congregations. The effective preacher, according to Mitchell, must "affirm and work *within* the culture of the congregation."[3] Mitchell critiques both African American and Anglo American preachers who adopt the intellectual posture of Thielicke's hypothetical young theologian and reject their congregation's traditional practices and vernacular language. He declares, "No amount of concern for educational levels or correctness of belief should be allowed to lure the preacher into frontal engagement with the fundamental wisdom of the communal life of a group or race."[4] There are, perhaps, occasions when overt confrontation is necessary, when the fundamental wisdom of certain groups may be so corrupted by sin as to be gravely wrong, as in the case of groups espousing racist or violent ideologies. In general, however, Mitchell argues that preachers should follow the example of Martin Luther King Jr. and others of his generation who tapped into the cultural resonance of spirituals and gospel songs in their messages. Mitchell contends that a message "that rides in on the surrounding culture . . . partakes of the power and lasting quality of that culture."[5] Black preaching, in Mitchell's estimation, has maintained this cultural connection because it has always embodied two key principles. The first is that preaching should always clothe itself in the vernacular of the hearers, employing accessible vocabulary and idioms. Mitchell points to the historical lack of access to institutional theological education as a contributing factor to the black preacher's continued use of his or her congregation's lexicon. The second principle present in traditional black preaching is the importance it gives to preaching to people's current needs. Black preachers, having alternately suffered and overcome alongside their congregants through slavery, Jim Crow, the Great Migration, the civil rights movement, and modern movements such as Black Lives Matter and the struggle against mass incarceration, have always been acutely aware of the needs of their audience.

In the previous chapter, I shared many of my collaborators' immigration narratives, stories that indelibly mark them and shape the arc of their preaching ministries. These experiences provide a key point of connection between them and their congregations. But immigration, as a journey, is far more than simply catching a flight across the Caribbean or crossing a river by night. It is more than just an initial period of adjustment to the confusing conglomeration of cultures in a constantly evolving New York neighborhood or to the perpetual transience of life as a migrant worker. The ongoing immigrant experiences of my collaborators are marked by the constant awareness and continual negotiation of their transnational, bicultural, and bivocational identities.

These *identidades multiples* / multiple identities make my collaborators liminal figures within U.S. society but also increase the number of shared connections between them and their congregations. Even for several of my collaborators who immigrated at an early age or the one who was born into an immigrant family in the United States, the ongoing reality of *identidades multiples* provides the cultural connections necessary to understand and employ culturally appropriate language in sermons that address the real needs of Hispanic immigrant communities. In this way, Hispanic immigrant preachers work within the culture of their congregations with much the same effectiveness and power that black preachers have wielded for generations. Their multiple identities also anchor their preaching to the lived experiences of their communities. These preachers are so grounded in the ongoing realities of their own immigrant lives and immigrant congregations that their sermons continually touch on the particular wounds and needs of immigrant communities.

THE LIFE OF A HISPANIC PASTOR

Cecilio Arrastía, the well-known Cuban-American pastor who also wrote one of the first Spanish-language homiletical texts in the United States, laments within that text the difficulty that most pastors have in setting aside time exclusively for the preparation of their sermons:

Otras exigencias ineludibles del pastorado toman un tiempo precioso de la labor de estudio concentrado con miras a la producción de, por lo menos, cincuenta y dos piezas homiléticas al año.[6]	Other inescapable exigencies of the pastorate take precious time from the work of concentrated study with an eye toward the production of, at least, fifty-two homiletical pieces a year.

Among these exigencies, Arrastía includes a long list of duties that most pastors would recognize:

Administración de la iglesia, consejería pastoral, visitación a enfermos y a sanos, participación en programas de la comunidad, en acontecimientos y comités denominacionales, todo esto y mucho más.[7]	Administration of the church, pastoral counseling, visitation of the sick and the healthy, participation in community programs, in events and denominational committees, all this and much more.

All of these complexities lead to multiple ministerial identities that are part of the reality of ministry for most pastors regardless of their ethnicity and the primary language in which they preach.

There are, however, other challenges of *identidades multiples* that are more unique to the paradigm of Hispanic ministry in the United States, especially for those ministers who are first-generation immigrants ministering to other recent immigrants. In a sermon focused on encouraging his congregation to be better stewards of their time, Pastor Esteban of Iglesia Agua Viva painted a vivid mental picture of *el pastor orquesta* (literally "the pastor-orchestra," but functionally "the pastoral one-man-band"). According to Esteban, the "*pastor orquesta*" in many Hispanic congregations finishes his sermon only to find half a dozen people awaiting him with immediate pastoral counseling needs. He does his best to attend to each of them while also sweeping the floor of the church and thoroughly cleaning the bathrooms so as to avoid conflict with the Anglo church with which his congregation shares facilities. During the week, he struggles to fulfill his duty as pastor while also juggling his roles as husband, father, and sixty-hour-per-week employee at a secular job. And maybe, just maybe, on a good week, he might have time for a little exercise to keep his body in shape for the rigors of his schedule. Esteban offered this true-to-life description of many Hispanic pastors as both an example to be followed in terms of industry and also a reprimand to congregants who were leaving too much for their pastor to do through their own lack of commitment and involvement. As difficult as these kinds of challenges are for many Hispanic pastors, they are also part of what anchors them within the shared ethos of their community and allows their preaching to be contextually relevant and effective. The remainder of this chapter will explore several of the multiple identities inherent in the lives and work of my collaborators and underline the way in which they reinforce immigrant identity and foster greater understanding of the communities they serve. My collaborators lived out multiple identities through their bivocational work, the bicultural reality of their ministry, the necessity of navigating complex denominational circumstances related to their ethnicity, and their commitment to service-based ministry.

BIVOCATIONAL BEING

During my time as a participant-observer at Iglesia Agua Viva, I first became aware of Esteban's other job when a female member of the congregation who worked for the Mexican food company Barcel brought a box full of Takis (rolled corn tortilla chips) in snack-sized packages for the congregation to enjoy. This led to some good-natured ribbing between her and Esteban about the relative merits of Takis and Fritos. When I asked him, half-jokingly, about his strong feelings related to corn chips, Esteban explained that he had a full-time job as a driver for Frito-Lay in the greater Raleigh area. His delivery route typically required no fewer than sixty hours of work each week, and Esteban would usually leave his house before six o'clock in the morning and return after six in the evening. This schedule sometimes prevented Esteban from leading Bible study during their Thursday evening services. Diana, who worked as a teacher's aide at a local high school, covered these duties instead. Her schedule was also busy enough for her to remark that, "*De vez en cuando estoy amaneciendo preparando un sermón* / occasionally I am up until dawn preparing a sermon." Esteban often arrived partway through the Thursday evening services wearing his embroidered Frito-Lay polo shirt with a Frito-Lay jacket over the top in colder months. During his long hours on the job, Esteban regularly thought through and even practiced his Sunday sermons in the solitude of his driver's cab. His delivery truck also served as a mobile counselor's office from which he would provide pastoral care by phone to many of his parishioners.

This kind of hectic schedule was the reality for many of my collaborators, who reflected on what it meant for them to be bivocational ministers. David, for example, worked in a large mining operation doing insulation work. There were not many Hispanic workers in other areas of the mining operation, but all the workers who dealt with insulation were Hispanic because, in David's opinion, the work was "*muy duro y muy sucio* / very hard and very dirty." He described the strain of balancing work and ministry like this:

Normalmente trabajo cuarenta horas a la semana, pero en estos últimos meses han estado cambiando mucho, y he trabajado sesenta o a veces setenta horas semanales. Tengo tres o cinco minutos después del trabajo para bañarme y cambiarme y comer en el carro yendo a la iglesia. A veces es muy pesado, pero yo siempre estoy muy agradecido con Dios por las fuerzas que me da.	Normally, I work forty hours a week, but in these last months, they have been changing a lot, and I have worked sixty or at times seventy hours a week. I have three or five minutes after work to bathe and change clothes and eat in the car going to church. Sometimes it is very difficult, but I am always very grateful to God for the strength he gives me.

David and his wife have several young children whom they often bring along as they carry out church responsibilities. So far, David said, they have been able to balance everything without their children feeling any resentment toward the church, but another of my collaborators, Antonio, shared with me that his bivocational workload had nearly cost him his family.

Es muy difícil para un pastor bivocacional que tiene que trabajar afuera, mantener una familia, darles tiempo a ellos, y también administrar una iglesia. Es difícil hermano. Al empezar, la iglesia no requiere mucho tiempo. A medida que la iglesia va creciendo, va requiriendo más tiempo y más tiempo. Al principio es solo un estudio bíblico y listo. Después, hay un servicio formal. Después, empiezas a visitar, ya no a cinco sino a diez, ya no a diez sino a veinte [familias].

It is very difficult for a bivocational pastor who must work outside [of the church], maintain a family, give time to them, and also administer a church. It is difficult, brother. In the beginning, the church doesn't require much time. As the church grows, it requires more and more time. At the beginning, it is just a Bible study and that is it. Later, there is a formal service. Then you start to visit no longer five but ten, no longer ten but twenty [families].

As the new congregation established by Antonio continued to grow and generate more demands on his time, he found himself having to choose between being present for the many activities of the church and attending events for his children.

Terminaba mi trabajo, llegaba a la casa a las cinco o seis de la tarde, me bañaba rápido y dije "vámonos" a los hijos porque teníamos que ir a la iglesia. Cuando mi hija mayor estaba en el "middle school," estaba en la lista de los estudiantes que sacaron puros "As" y le dieron un trofeo y todo. Hicieron algo especial en la escuela, pero no asistimos. En "high school" tuvo también eso, lo mismo. Y no asistimos.

I used to finish my work, arrive at the house at five or six in the evening, bathe rapidly, and I said, "Let's go" to the kids because we had to go to the church. When my oldest daughter was in middle school, she was on the list of students who made straight As and they gave her a trophy and everything. They did something special in the school, but we did not attend. In high school, they had that also, the same thing. And we did not go.

This was a consistent pattern for Antonio's family during the nearly ten years that he pastored a church in a small town about an hour outside of Durham. Since the town in which the church was located was thirty minutes from the town where Antonio lived—and often much farther still from the work sites for his job as a highway construction worker—Antonio and his family spent much of their time either at the church or in transit to and from its activities. One of these journeys provided the context for the following conversation.

Un día cuando dejamos la iglesia regresando para acá, mi hija la mayor iba a cumplir veintiún años. Y yo le dije a mi hija, "Hay un programa en migración que cuando sus hijos cumplen los veintiún años, ellos te pueden arreglar [tu estatus migratorio]." Entonces yo le dije, "Mija, ya vas a cumplir veintiún años—¿no te parece que sería buen tiempo para ayudarnos en esto?"

Y nunca había sentido ese coraje que ella tenía guardado, pero me dijo, "Yo muchas veces he buscado que tu tengas tiempo para mí. Y no has tenido tiempo. ¿Porque no le pides esto a tu iglesia para que ellos te arreglen, porque allá has dedicado todo tu tiempo?"

One day when we were leaving the church returning here, my oldest daughter was about to turn twenty-one years old. And I said to my daughter, "There is an immigration program that when your children turn twenty-one, they can fix it for you [your immigration status]." Then I said to her, "My daughter, you are about to turn twenty-one—doesn't it seem like a good time to help us with this?"

And never before had I felt the anger[8] that she had harbored, but she told me, "Many times, I have looked for you to have time for me. And you have not had time. Why don't you ask this question of your church so that they can help you fix it, because that is where you have dedicated all your time?"

The ensuing crisis in his family caused Antonio to give up the pastorate of the congregation he had founded and guided for almost ten years. When he and I spoke, he had instead taken up the position of associate pastor in a larger Hispanic congregation. This kind of position, rare among the churches with which I interacted, allowed him much more flexibility. Antonio reflected back on his years of balancing full-time work and full-time ministry:

Yo hice demasiado—hice lo que no debería de haber hecho. Me costó muchas lágrimas. Me costó regresar atrás y casi volver a comenzar con mi familia. Honestamente, quité mucho tiempo de mi familia por la obra.

I did too much—I did what I should not have done. It cost me many tears. It cost me moving backward and almost starting over with my family. Honestly, I took too much time from my family for the work.

All of my collaborators who were physically capable of doing other work—Ignacio being the lone exception—had done so, balancing ministry and secular employment to the best of their ability. They were custodians and teachers' aides, construction workers and car salesmen. For some of them, like Antonio, the overall workload became too overwhelming, but their status as bivocational ministers also yielded certain benefits within their ministerial context. Esteban and Diana shared an experience with me in which they overheard several of their congregants talking about Esteban having arrived late for an activity of the church. One of them lamented the fact that he did not have more time to dedicate to the church because of his other job. The other person then launched into a tirade against some of the Protestant ministers he had observed in his country of origin who seemed to live off the generosity of the church without working particularly hard in either sacred or secular endeavors. Defending Esteban's efforts as the opposite of what he saw as the freeloading ways of those ministers, he exclaimed, "*¡Por lo menos mi pastor trabaja! /* At least my pastor works!" Esteban's busy schedule gave him credibility among his parishioners; it also enabled him to see the world through their eyes. Like many of my other collaborators, he worked in a blue-collar or manual labor profession and understood the grueling nature of the kind of work in which many of his congregants were engaged. Many of my collaborators also understood the discrimination inherent in the kinds of jobs available for the Hispanic immigrant community, especially for its undocumented members. These bivocational realities grounded their thinking and preaching within the frame of reference of their communities.

In the opinion of several of my collaborators, being bivocational also protected Hispanic immigrant clergy from what they saw as the over-professionalization of many of the Anglo American ministers with whom they interacted. Agustín shared the following reflection with me on the matter:

Pienso que pastores latinos están con la tensión—por un lado, uno puede asimilar al estilo anglo y es más sencillo, con el ritmo del trabajo. ¿Pero es eso lo que necesita la iglesia? ¿Es eso lo que necesita la comunidad latina también? ¿Es eso lo que Dios quiere?	I think that Latino pastors exist with the tension—on one hand, one can assimilate to the Anglo style and it is easier, with the rhythm of work. But is that what the church needs? Is that what the Latino community needs as well? Is that what God wants?
Lo que yo he experimentado aquí es que se profesionaliza tanto la labor del pastor y del predicador que se puede caer en eso. ¿Voy a asimilar a esta manera de trabajar o voy a preservar esta vocación—la manera en que los hispanos vean la vocación? No es una profesión si no un verdadero llamado de Dios.	What I have experienced here is that the work of the pastor and preacher is so professionalized that it can fall into that. Am I going to assimilate to this manner of work or am I going to preserve this vocation—the way in which Hispanics view the vocation? It is not a profession but rather a true call of God.

Being bivocational, in Agustín's opinion, was as much about the community's identification with the minister as it was about the minister being able to understand and communicate the truth of Scripture from the community's point of view. In either case, it was a key component of the connection between the Hispanic preacher and his or her hearers.

BICULTURAL REALITIES AT HOME AND IN THE CHURCH

Por lo general, la identidad se vuelve tema candente para todos nosotros porque todos somos, en un grado u otro, biculturales y bilingües. En buena medida, esto es lo que nos define. Al tiempo que algunos entre nosotros hablan muy poco español, y otros hablan muy poco inglés, nuestra identidad como hispanos en los Estados Unidos tiene mucho que ver con esa realidad bilingüe.[9]

In general, identity becomes a hot topic for all of us because we are all, to one degree or another, bicultural and bilingual. To a large extent, this is what defines us. While some of us speak very little Spanish, and others speak very little English, our identity as Hispanics in the United States has much to do with that bilingual reality.

Justo González wrote these words to capture the common sense of biculturalism shared by Hispanics in the United States. Ultimately, this sense transcends use of and fluency in Spanish, but language is still often a marker of this biculturalism as well as one of the primary ways in which Hispanics recognize their otherness. This sense is only magnified when immigrants consider the language differences between members of different generations within their own families and communities of faith. González writes of the difficulties faced by younger Hispanics as a constant tension between language's utility and its affective power:

Es posible que algunos de nuestros hijos ya hablen muy poco español. Pero aun para ellos esa lengua tiene todavía el poder afectivo del idioma que se escuchó en la cuna. Otros prefieren hablar en español: pero si han de funcionar en la sociedad en que viven se verán obligados a comunicarse en inglés, por escaso que sea su conocimiento de esa lengua.[10]

It is possible that some of our children already speak very little Spanish. But even for them that language still has the affective power of the language that was heard in the cradle. Others prefer to speak in Spanish: but if they are to function in the society in which they live they will be obliged to communicate in English, however little their knowledge of that language may be.

The immigrant identity of my collaborators was constantly reinforced by their own personal reflections on their bicultural status and by the reality of ministering to congregations that were also continually negotiating their own bicultural and bilingual identities, especially across generational lines.

In Iglesia Agua Viva, the adults generally spoke to one another in Spanish. The children and teenagers mostly spoke in English, many of them with the lilt of a North Carolina accent. This linguistic bifurcation extended into the ministry of the church as well: the worship services and adult Bible studies were conducted exclusively in Spanish, but the children's Sunday School was always taught in English. Esteban and Diana, who had immigrated to the United States as young adults, struggled to express themselves as effectively in English and often turned to their own young adult children, who were fully bilingual, to lead these ministries.

Leo, a Baptist minister whose Hispanic congregation shared space with a larger Anglo congregation, spoke about the importance of his Hispanic church conducting its worship services primarily in Spanish:

Tenemos una iglesia hispana porque queremos continuar con nuestra cultura, podemos adorar y alabar al Señor, desarrollar todo bien en español y podemos entendernos bien.	We have a Hispanic church because we want to continue with our culture, we can worship and praise the Lord, develop everything well in Spanish, and we can understand each other well.

In spite of Leo's assertion about the importance of ministry in Spanish, he acknowledged the difficulty and often unexpected complexity presented by younger generations whose primary language was English:

Ha sido un reto con ellos. Tenemos una familia con un niño que nació aquí y otro que lo trajeron de allá. El muchacho que nació allá habla más inglés que el muchacho que nació aquí. El que nació aquí se interesa más en hablar español.	It has been a challenge with them. We have a family with one child who was born here and another that they brought from over there. The boy who was born over there speaks more English than the boy who was born here. The one who was born here is more interested in speaking Spanish.

In order to communicate effectively with a bilingual congregation, Leo described stepping outside of his comfort zone both in public speaking and in private conversation. His feeling was that the younger generation would one day have its own bilingual congregation, but for the time being, as long as they were part of his Spanish-dominant ministry, his responsibility was to find ways to reach across the language barrier:

Cuando yo les hablo a ellos, tengo que esforzarme a hablar más palabras en inglés. Hablo en una forma "mixteada" con ellos. Algunos dicen que está aburrido participar en un servicio porque no entienden mucho. Quiero que ellos se entusiasmen en las cosas del Señor, entonces tengo que buscar métodos para que se entusiasmen.

When I speak to them, I have to make an effort to speak more words in English. I speak in a "mixed" form with them. Some say that it is boring to participate in a service because they do not understand much. I want them to be enthusiastic about the things of the Lord, so I have to look for methods so that they become enthused.

The attempt to communicate well in English was a challenge for Esteban, Diana, Leo, and the majority of my collaborators, but one pastor with whom I interacted faced a different kind of difficulty. Rafael, a Pentecostal pastor about whom I will share more details later in this chapter, was born into an immigrant family in New York and was fully bilingual. Although he used English comfortably in his secular work experience, Spanish had been the primary language for all of his religious communities and seemed to enable his proclamation differently. In English, he described the difference like this:

> I have a hard time preaching and praying in English. When someone asks me to pray, I say, I'm going to pray in Spanish. I find that my messages are more embodied in Spanish. Although my congregation is mixed—there are folks that don't understand Spanish. And I wind up finding myself preaching in both languages at the same time.

When I asked him how this primarily Spanish, but occasionally bilingual, preaching was received by those in the congregation who were English dominant, he explained that the power of the Holy Spirit transcended the language barrier, much as it did on the day of Pentecost in the second chapter of the book of Acts. "Even if they don't speak much Spanish," Rafael insisted, "they get filled with the same word anyway."

Eva, a United Methodist minister, spoke about the challenge of preaching to a community in flux not solely in terms of its dominant language but also regarding its touchstone cultural experiences.

Yo trato de tener en mi mente que no sólo estoy predicando a gente que están fuera de su hogar porque no todos están en esa situación. Hay muchos jóvenes que nacieron aquí. Este es lo único que conocen. No hablan español.

I try to have in my mind that I am not just preaching to people who are away from their home because not everyone is in that situation. There are many young people who were born here. This is all they know. They do not speak Spanish.

Yo pienso que todos como seres humanos enfrentamos los retos de la vida—la depresión, el abuso—son cosas comunes. Pero en realidad enfocarnos en la situación migratoria no es algo que podemos hacer todos los domingos porque no es la situación de todos en la congregación.	I think that everyone as human beings faces the challenges of life—depression, abuse—they are common things. But in reality to focus on the immigration situation is not something that we can do every Sunday because it is not everyone's situation in the congregation.

The encounter for a first-generation immigrant preacher with a congregation, or at least a portion of it, for whom sermons related to immigration difficulties no longer resonate in the same way, has been a difficult one for Eva and for many of my collaborators. Several of them spoke about it reinforcing their own feelings of being "strangers in a strange land," even among their own people.

Ernesto, a Baptist pastor, offered a first-person example of dealing with this difficulty within his own family, in a way very similar to that which Justo González discussed. Ernesto faced this challenge as his own children began attending school. The immersion in an English-dominant environment brought about rapid and permanent changes in his youngest daughter's language usage:

El último año, mi hija pequeña entró en kindergarten y ella, antes de ir a la escuela hablaba bien el español, pero después de seis meses de estar en la escuela, dejó el español y ahora cuando nos habla, habla más en inglés.	Last year, my youngest daughter entered into kindergarten, and before going to school she spoke Spanish well, but after six months of being in school, dropped Spanish, and now when she speaks to us, she speaks more in English.

Ernesto and I were sitting in a booth off in a corner of a Mexican restaurant close to his house as we had this conversation. He had been talking animatedly about his children up to this point, but he appeared almost crestfallen as he shared with me how quickly the institutional influence of public education had altered his daughter's cultural and linguistic identity. His shoulders stooped, and he looked down at the table between us. He let a deep sigh escape and then regathered his breath and momentum to speak about the way that these changes presented the church with both challenges and opportunities:

Entonces, yo pienso que en el futuro en la iglesia donde yo estoy, vamos a tener que traducir el sermón. Puede ser que un joven traduciendo un sermón va a recibir su propio llamado como lo recibieron los pastores echados al fuego.	So, I think that in the future in the church where I am, we will have to translate the sermon. It may be that a young person who is translating a sermon will receive his or her own calling as the pastors who were thrown in the fire received theirs.

Ernesto was referring back to the circumstances which I related in the previous chapter, circumstances by which he had been called into ministry. Just as the scarcity of ministers had led to Ernesto being thrust into a pastoral role suddenly and unexpectedly, a new generation of Hispanic pastors might also discover a calling by serving as a bridge of communication between first-generation immigrant pastors and a second-generation immigrant church.

The bilingual and bicultural reality of the environments in which my collaborators live and minister requires them to deal constantly with questions related to their own identity as immigrants within a very different context. Within the dominant culture, their own more immediate environments of home and church are constantly shifting due to assimilation and acculturation by members of their biological and ecclesial families. Justo González writes about the way in which being bilingual and bicultural requires a perpetual renegotiation of one's own identity:

Empero también es necesario señalar que para muchos hispanos su carácter bilingüe y bicultural, al tiempo que nos provee un sentido de identidad, también hacen la cuestión de identidad mucho más compleja que para la población monolingüe y monocultural. . . . Esto nos lleva a plantearnos con urgencia y hasta con dolor la pregunta de quién soy yo o quiénes somos nosotros.[11]	Nevertheless, it is also necessary to point out that, while for many Hispanics their bilingual and bicultural character provides us with a sense of identity, it also makes the question of identity much more complex than it is for the monolingual and monocultural population . . . This leads us to consider with urgency and even with pain the question of who I am or who we are.

NAVIGATING COMPLEX CHURCH AND DENOMINATIONAL RELATIONSHIPS

Thus far in this chapter, I have focused primarily on the way in which Hispanic ministers' bivocational work and bicultural home and ministry contexts lead to their experience of multiple identities. Another considerable factor in this experience is the way in which their ministry requires them to interact with Anglo congregations and denominations in which their ministries are often embedded or upon which they may depend for logistical or financial support. Justo González writes about the way in which these interconnections frequently lead Hispanic preachers to address radically different audiences:

Los predicadores hispanos en los Estados Unidos no les predican solamente a audiencias y congregaciones latinas, sino que buena parte de nuestra predicación se dirige a la iglesia en general, y frecuentemente tiene lugar en contextos en los que la mayoría de la congregación no es hispana.[12]	Hispanic preachers in the United States do not just preach to Latino audiences and congregations, but rather a significant part of our preaching is directed to the church in general, and it frequently takes place in contexts in which the majority of the congregation is not Hispanic.

A further complication to the scenario that González presents is that Hispanic ministers who occasionally preach to majority non-Hispanic congregations often come as representatives of a group that is not even the "historic" minority in their region in the United States. Of course, what González describes in the realm of preaching is also true in the bigger picture of Hispanic ministry. Hispanic preachers must be masters of two contexts: their own and the larger Anglo-dominated congregations and denominations with which they interact. These relationships cause Hispanic preachers to reflect constantly on the reality of their own identities as they interact and advocate with Anglo Americans in whose presence they are sometimes regarded as, and often feel themselves to be, "others."

Gastón Espinosa provides some additional context for the complex relationships navigated by many of my collaborators. His work focuses on the relationships between Anglo and Latino leadership within various Pentecostal movements—relationships that were often so fraught with misunderstanding and negative racial overtones that they led to schisms within thriving denominations. One such schism took place with the Assemblies of God as its work extended into South Texas and Mexico in the early twentieth century. Seeking greater autonomy, a group of Latino AG leaders began pushing for the Anglo missionaries to "follow through on their pledge to hand over the leadership to Mexicans so they could create a Mexican-run district" within the AG.[13] When their petitions continued to be overlooked and their desires for increased self-governance were thwarted, many Hispanic leaders eventually moved from reformation to revolt, splitting from the Assemblies of God to form the Latin American Council of Christian Churches (CLADIC) under the leadership of Francisco Olazábal. The CLADIC was "the first completely indigenous and legally incorporated Latino Pentecostal (indeed Protestant) denomination in the United States."[14] Although this division certainly decreased the scope of

Latino work within the AG in the near term, in the long term Hispanic AG missionaries continued to evangelize and win new converts to their movement who would gradually struggle for and eventually attain self-determination within the broader denomination.

Espinosa also chronicles similar struggles taking place among early Pentecostals in Puerto Rico. Pentecostalism arrived on the island through the ministry and influence of a native *puertorriqueño* named Juan Lugo who had moved to Hawaii during his childhood, where he heard the gospel preached by Assemblies of God missionaries who had participated in the Azusa Street revivals. Lugo was eventually ordained as a minister and missionary in the Assemblies of God and returned to Puerto Rico in 1916, where he held the first Pentecostal worship service in the island's history. In just over two decades, Pentecostalism became the largest Protestant movement on the island.[15] The Puerto Rican Pentecostal movement traveled a very different road from the Mexican Assemblies of God ministers in the American Southwest. From very early on, with the advice of representatives of the Assemblies of God, they established their own incorporated church, *La Iglesia Pentecostal de Dios* / The Pentecostal Church of God, which the Assemblies of God recognized as a foreign national church within its larger movement. Later on, they would face an uphill climb as they sought to gain recognition and acceptance as a district belonging to the Assemblies of God, only to discover that both their existing relationship and further incorporation would have a negative effect on their ability to set their own domestic priorities and coordinate foreign missions. In 1957, the Pentecostal movement founded by Juan Lugo would officially reorganize as *La Iglesia de Dios Pentecostal Movimiento Internacional* / The Pentecostal Church of God, International Movement. This new appendage to its name recognized the fact that it now existed in competition with the Assemblies of God, stretching beyond the confines of the island of Puerto Rico, to send missionaries across the world.

In his work surveying the history of Hispanic Methodists, Presbyterians, and Baptists in Texas, Paul Barton also writes about Hispanic ministers navigating Anglo hierarchies, particularly in the areas of education and credentialing. In the early 1900s, Hispanic Methodists in Texas who sensed a call to preach were often directed to ministerial training centers like the Wesleyan Institute. Upon their graduation, they were expected to enter into ministry, but "these schools did not meet the normal educational requirements of their denomination," thus permanently relegating them to a ministerial underclass within the Methodist hierarchy.[16] The first Methodist ministers who pushed for the opportunity to attend Southern Methodist University to pursue graduate degrees met with resistance as the Anglo establishment feared that they would eventually opt for careers other than ministry. Gradually, however, their attainment of graduate degrees provided them with a platform from which they could advocate more effectively for their congregations and even rise to positions of greater power within their denomination, transcending the narrower confines of the predominantly Hispanic Rio Grande Annual Conference. These struggles, and eventual gains, were not limited only to Methodists:

> A similar dynamic occurred among Presbyterians and Baptists. As more Mexican-American Presbyterian and Baptist ministers received advanced degrees, their education enabled them to interact with their Anglo-American counterparts on the basis of educational equality.[17]

The struggles of Hispanic movements that Espinosa and Barton examined within their respective denominations are certainly much broader than the difficulties my collaborators discussed with me. None of the ministers with whom I interacted were on the verge of creating their own denominations, although several had shifted denominations due to difficulties they faced or opportunities with which they had been presented. Among my Pentecostal collaborators, several had reached out to build their own ministerial networks or *concilios* / councils. Many of them also encountered difficulties advancing their vocational goals or their visions for their congregations as they faced significant power differentials between themselves and the Anglo American pastors or denominational representatives with whom they worked. For a significant portion of my collaborators, the complexity of their relationships with Anglo American congregations and denominations was most often a reflection of the degree to which they shared space in facilities with Anglo American congregations and the relative complexity of the denominational hierarchy in which they were situated. Those congregations that owned or rented their own facilities tended to have fewer interactions with Anglo American congregations. This was true of half the congregations served by my Pentecostal collaborators and half the congregations served by my Baptist collaborators. Among my United Methodist collaborators, only two of them currently served Spanish language congregations, which were the only congregations using their facilities, and these facilities still belonged to the North Carolina Annual Conference of the United Methodist Church,[18] which had sometimes unusual expectations for these Hispanic ministers that I will discuss later in this section.

Even for pastors whose Hispanic congregations owned or rented their own facilities, working with the larger dominant culture on behalf of their congregation was a routine task. Collaborators in this study often were called on to help translate for their congregants in medical contexts, to help them navigate legal problems, and especially to assist them with complex situations related to their immigration status. During my years of research, nearly all of my collaborators were helping congregants who faced deportation. This involved raising funds (both from Hispanic and Anglo congregations) to help pay for attorneys, coordinating prayer vigils, helping congregants move from their last-known addresses that law enforcement officials had on file, and working with larger Anglo churches who were willing to provide sanctuary for individuals whose other options had been exhausted. Most of my collaborators were fairly well-versed on immigration law from having helped previous parishioners or family members through their own crises. They also made it a point to refresh their knowledge and stay up-to-date in order to assist the next congregant who would find himself or herself in need. One Pentecostal preacher named Ana, who was an ordained minister in the Iglesia de Dios Pentecostal M.I.,[19] was an active member of the Evangelical Immigration Table. Through this organization, she networked regularly with representatives from the Council for Christian Colleges and Universities, the Ethics & Religious Liberty Commission of the Southern Baptist Convention, the National Association of Evangelicals, the Wesleyan Church, and several other organizations to advocate on behalf of immigrant communities. When describing the importance of her work, Ana said:

Podemos mantener la congregación informada. Si los pastores están mal informados no pueden guiar bien a la gente. Como pastores, tenemos que ayudar a la gente a ubicarse.	We can keep the congregation informed. If the pastors are poorly informed, they cannot guide the people well. As pastors, we must help people locate themselves.

Through her work with the Evangelical Immigration Table, Ana was contributing to lobbying efforts in Washington on behalf of immigration reform. She also was providing information to her congregation and to various other Pentecostal pastors in the area regarding new changes to immigration law so they could guide their people well.

Sharing facilities with Anglo congregations added responsibilities for many of my collaborators. At Iglesia Agua Viva, Esteban and Diana attended the larger Anglo congregation's monthly church council meetings in order to make sure their church activities were placed on the calendar and that they would have access to the necessary facilities for hosting them. They and several other collaborators spoke of staying behind after services and cleaning the restrooms themselves in order to make sure the Anglo congregation would not find anything out of order and change their minds about their facility-sharing arrangements. Although Ignacio's church had grown large enough to secure its own building by the time I came to know him, he had spent many years under the same roof as a Southern Baptist congregation. One day, he and several female congregants happened upon several Anglo members of that congregation who were discussing the upcoming wedding of one of their daughters. The mother of the bride-to-be expressed disgust that her daughter's wedding reception would take place in a fellowship hall that also hosted events for "those Mexicans," at which point she indicated Ignacio and the women who were with him. Ignacio said that once the Anglo women had left, the women from his congregation cried and cried about what had been said about them and swore they would never return to Ignacio's congregation as long as it met in that facility. Ignacio appealed humorously and effectively to their sense of solidarity and asked them to reconsider, saying:

¿Me van a dejar solo con esa mujer? ¡Y yo en silla de ruedas! No, por favor, necesito que se queden para protegerme.	Are you going to leave me alone with that woman? And me in a wheelchair! No, please, I need you to stay to protect me.

As someone who had planted many churches, Ignacio also experienced the difficulties of navigating facility sharing at the denominational level. Originally, Ignacio had worked through the Baptist State Convention of North Carolina, the state-level organization of the Southern Baptist Convention, to help make connections with Anglo congregations that might be willing to share their facilities with Hispanic church plants. The effectiveness of this affiliation, in Ignacio's opinion, gradually waned:

Cuando estábamos con el SBC, al principio el director de misiones fue un hermano, a pesar de que él es gringo, cuando él estaba en el área de misiones, de "church planting," hizo un trabajo extraordinario. El venía y empujaba lo que tenía que empujar con su trabajo por los hispanos.	When we were with the SBC, in the beginning the director of missions was a brother who, in spite of being a "gringo," when he was in the area of missions, of "church planting," did an extraordinary job. He came and pushed what needed to be pushed with his work for the Hispanic people.

Pero una vez que se salió el y empezaron a haber otros, llegó un punto donde me sentí solo en realidad. Me sentí cansado porque si yo le decía antes, "Mira, tengo un líder y con este líder voy a mandar dos o tres familias más, pero necesito tu influencia—que vayas a tocar la puerta de la iglesia." Y le daba el nombre. Y él iba, y en dos, tres meses me abría la puerta allí.

Pero después, ya no tuve ese apoyo. Tenía líder, tenía la gente, pero no tenía a quien podía tocar la puerta. Me tenían en espera seis, ocho meses. Una vez estaba esperando un año, y no me dieron una respuesta.

But once he left and there began to be others, a point arrived where I felt alone in reality. I felt tired because if I had said before, "Look, I have a leader and with this leader I am going to send two or three more families, but I need your influence—that you go to knock on the door of the church." And I gave him the name. And he went, and in two, three months he had opened the door for me there.

But afterward, I no longer had that support. I would have a leader, I would have the people, but I did not have someone who could knock on the door. They had me waiting six, eight months. One time, I was waiting for a year, and they did not give me an answer.

This frustration continued for Ignacio for several years until he met a woman who worked for the Cooperative Baptist Fellowship of North Carolina.[20] She asked him about his ministry, and he described the work in which he had been involved, sending out church planters across central and eastern North Carolina. When he shared his recent frustrations, their conversation took an interesting, and ultimately very fruitful, turn:

Ella me dijo, "Tu dime donde abrir puertas y lo haremos." Yo dije, "No me digas eso porque te voy a poner a trabajar." Pero ella insistió. Entonces, yo respondí, "Ah, pues, quiero abrir aquí, quiero abrir allá." Miré el apunto que tenían en misiones y como usaron recursos para abrir nuevas obras y dije yo, "Aquí me quedo."

She told me, "You tell me where to open doors and we will do it." I said, "Do not say that to me because I will put you to work." But she insisted. Then, I responded, "Ah, well, I want to open here, I want to open there." I looked at the focus that they had on missions and how they used resources to open new works, and I said, "I am staying here."

Ignacio's observations about his experiences with both the SBC and CBF revealed the importance of good relationships with Anglo denominational functionaries. Ignacio's desire to plant new congregations, even with pastors willing to serve them and congregants willing to relocate their families in order to help form their critical mass, was not enough without having an Anglo denominational representative who could "knock on the door" for him.

Ignacio used this expression to include everything from making initial contact with an Anglo congregation, to gauging their openness toward sharing their facility with a Hispanic church plant, to helping to develop a mutually beneficial framework for the two congregations as they ministered in such close proximity. The SBC's diminishing capability in this regard coupled with the willingness of a CBF representative to step in as a liaison prompted Ignacio's congregation and the entire network of congregations he had helped to plant to find a new denominational home.

As significant as denominational connections and obligations were for Ignacio and his fellow Baptists, my United Methodist collaborators had the most complex relationships with their denomination. The greater hierarchy of the United Methodist Church facilitated unique opportunities for several of my collaborators, but also presented them with certain difficulties. At the time of our first interview, Teresa had spent the previous two years working in a part-time position as an associate pastor of a small Hispanic United Methodist congregation. After the departure of the previous senior pastor, she was about to assume his role. Both he and she, however, carried more complex burdens than the pastoral leadership of a single congregation.

Hay dos iglesias angloamericanas cerca de nuestra iglesia, y nos juntaron por falta de recursos monetarios. Fue para apoyarnos, financieramente y como forma de recurso. Ellas son más estructuradas para tener eventos, pero nosotros tenemos la fuerza bruta, y tenemos más jóvenes y más energía.	There are two Anglo American churches close to our church, and they joined us together because of a lack of financial resources. It was to support us, financially, and as a form of resource. They are more structured to have events, but we have the brute force, and we have more young people and more energy.

This arrangement also was a way to share pastoral resources. The previous senior pastor of Teresa's congregation had served as the lead pastor of all three churches, while an Anglo minister had a position as copastor of the two Anglo churches. Teresa, in addition to her work as associate pastor of the three-church conglomerate, also directed a cleaning company/ministry that I will discuss later on. Teresa's ministry had her serving in all three churches regularly, and occasionally all three on the same Sunday:

Hay veces también cuando me toca dar doble servicio o triple servicio y tengo que llevar los niños a todos los servicios y se cansan. Un servicio es a las nueve. Otra a las once, y la nuestra es a las 11:30. Lo que pasó ayer es que tuvieron que cambiar el servicio [a las once], para que yo pudiera predicar al principio y después salir corriendo para llegar antes de que empezara la hora por la predicación en nuestra iglesia. Lo hemos hecho antes, pero a veces es un poco difícil.	There are also times when two services or three services are up to me, and I have to take the kids to all the services, and they get tired. One service is at 9:00. Another is at 11:00, and ours is at 11:30. What happened yesterday is that they had to change the service [at 11:00], so that I could preach at the beginning and afterward leave running to arrive before the preaching time began at our church. We have done it before, but sometimes it is a little difficult.

Teresa's circumstances often left her in a difficult position culturally as well as logistically. For some of her Anglo parishioners, Teresa served as a flesh and blood representative of what might otherwise be the totally unknown community of Hispanic immigrants or of DACA recipients. In addition to preaching to the Anglo congregations, Teresa also facilitated interaction between the three communities of faith. In this role as a liaison between Anglo and Hispanic congregations, she saw reconciliation between the groups she served as a substantial part of her role. As she spoke with me about this ministerial imperative, she shifted back and forth between Spanish and English, an auditory manifestation of the constant internal code-switching her role necessitated:

Lo que quiero hacer es crear espacios donde ambos grupos pueden contar su historia en grupos pequeños para que en verdad se pueden conocer. Así no se pueden decir, "Are *your* people coming?" Estamos tratando de cambiar una cultura mental. No es que son racistas o que lo hacen a propósito. No saben.	What I want to do is to create spaces where both groups can tell their story in small groups so that they can truly know each other. That way they cannot say, "Are *your* people coming?" We are trying to change a mental culture. It is not that they are racist or that they do it on purpose. They don't know.

As Teresa was driving back and forth between rural congregations separated by dozens of miles, another United Methodist minister named Manuel was pastoring a Hispanic congregation embedded in a large suburban campus occupied by several other congregations, each aimed at its own niche audience. I met with Manuel in his office, a 1950s brick home that had been absorbed by the growing church campus and now served as an office for him and several other auxiliary ministries of the largest congregation, a First United Methodist Church that had long been a flagship of the once small town that was metamorphosing into a thriving suburb. Manuel had come from the American Baptist tradition and had served in a nonprofit organization prior to coming on staff with this particular United Methodist church as a director of Hispanic outreach with a three-quarter-time position. Gradually, the position became more pastoral, and Manuel began first a monthly prayer service, then a weekly worship service. As the ministry grew, his position was increased to full time, but his workload extended well beyond the demands of just shepherding his growing flock. As the pastor of one congregation within the larger constellation on that campus, he was constantly coordinating with the leadership of the larger Anglo groups.

This included a team-oriented approach to preaching. Rather than following the selected texts of the lectionary as did many other United Methodist churches in the area, Manuel and the other pastors worked together to develop and preach their own sermon series throughout the year.

La iglesia grande determina mucho. Los pastores trabajan juntos para desarrollar series. Se supone que van a ser relevantes para todos. Desarrollamos la serie juntos; luego la aplicación es local.	The big church determines a lot. The pastors work together to develop series. It is assumed that they will be relevant for everyone. We develop the series together; then, the application is local.

The assumptions made regarding the relevance of sermon series depended, knowingly or not, on Manuel's ability to provide linguistic and cultural translations of themes for his parishioners. When all of the congregations were going through a sermon series focusing on pivotal moments in the journey of faith, Manuel used his Mother's Day sermon to talk about a pivotal moment in his mother's life that would be contextually accessible for his congregants:

Entonces yo puedo hablar desde el punto de vista de mi mamá. Y eso va a ser diferente que en un contexto Anglo—cuando ella fue arrestada, mi historia de migración, y eso va a ser muy diferente por mi contexto. Se va a sentir muy diferente el sermón, aunque tenga el mismo tema. Eso es lo que hacemos.	Then I can talk from the point of view of my mom. And that will be different than in an Anglo context—when she was arrested, my immigration story, and that will be very different because of my context. The sermon will feel very different although it has the same theme. That is what we do.

Although the selection of sermon series and themes was generally the prerogative of the Anglo leadership, and left Manuel to find analogous points and culturally appropriate examples, there were also times when the life experiences of the members in Manuel's congregation informed the worship of the Anglo parishioners. Manuel led a workshop on storytelling with twenty members of his congregation. These members focused on telling their own immigration stories. First, they practiced for one another; then, they hosted an event for the Hispanic parishioners. Afterward, they identified some of the storytellers, based on both their giftedness and the poignancy of their stories, to share about their journeys with the Anglo churches. It was Manuel's hope that this form of sharing would lead to greater understanding and mutuality in the communication between the different groups sharing the same campus.

Some misunderstandings, however, were related less to communication than to what Manuel saw as the goals of his ministry. The community in which Manuel ministered had undergone drastic socioeconomic changes during his time there. As the Raleigh-Durham metro area continued to expand, the once-small town in which he ministered became an upscale suburb. Home prices and rents continued to skyrocket, pricing many Hispanics out of the area. Manuel had come to see one of the primary goals of his ministry, even more than growing his own congregation, as preparing Hispanic lay leaders who would serve in other congregations or community efforts elsewhere. To that end, he had established a local training institute for "*misioneros laicos / lay missionaries*."[21] Manuel saw the success of this program as a contributing factor to occasional conflict with the larger Anglo congregation in which his ministry was embedded:

Ha sido un reto. Hemos formado muchos líderes, pero todos se van. Eso es una bendición, pero no hemos creado una base sólida para crecer acá. No siempre es muy fácil en nuestra relación con la iglesia madre porque ellos quieren que crezca la iglesia local. Formar líderes es más atractivo para mí, pero no para ellos. Pero ahí estamos trabajando.	It has been a challenge. We have formed many leaders, but they all go away. That is a blessing, but we have not created a solid base to grow here. It is not always easy in our relationship with the mother church because they want us to grow the local church. Forming leaders is more attractive for me but not for them. But that is where we are working.

Adding to the stress Manuel faces in directing this ministry is the fact that his lay missionaries program blurs the lines between the local Anglo church and the larger Anglo-led North Carolina Annual Conference of the United Methodist Church:

Esto ha traído a mi personalmente como líder algunos "misunderstandings" porque es un programa de la conferencia en medio de una iglesia local. Pero para tener un programa, hay que tener infraestructura para tener éxito, y la conferencia no tiene la infraestructura para apoyarnos, y esta iglesia la tiene.	This has brought me personally as the leader several "misunderstandings" because it is a program of the conference in the middle of a local church. But in order to have a program, it must have infrastructure in order to be successful, and the conference does not have the infrastructure in order to support us, and this church has it.

From the denominational perspective, the conference approves of the goals of Manuel's training initiative, which equips leaders who will serve in the leadership of other congregations, ministries, and community endeavors. Yet they lack the facilities, the budget, and the centralized organization of a local church that Manuel needs. The local church has these resources but does not always see eye to eye with Manuel regarding the larger vision of his work. So Manuel continues walking this ministerial tightrope, receiving salary and support from a local church and broader authorization from the regional conference for his work. This balancing act is a continual reminder of Manuel's immigrant identity and that of his community as they lack resources and authority of their own for much of what they see as necessary and life-giving work. So far, he has turned out sixty graduates from his program, and the enrollment has grown larger with each passing year, but Manuel is not sure what the future holds for his efforts. Reflecting on the ongoing obstacles he faces, Manuel observed:

La iglesia metodista, en el ministerio hispano, tiene muchas más limitaciones. No hay tanta autonomía para que los ministerios locales respondan de manera relevante.	The Methodist church, in its Hispanic ministry, has many more limitations. There is not as much autonomy for local ministries to respond in a relevant manner.

As difficult as Manuel's ministerial circumstances were, Isaac navigated what I found to be the most complex situation among my United Methodist collaborators. He had been in charge of pastoring a small and declining Anglo congregation about an hour away from Raleigh while also growing a new Hispanic church plant in the same facility. Isaac's experience growing up in San Luís Rio Colorado and crossing back and forth across the U.S.-Mexican border each day as he attended school had uniquely prepared him for this pastoral dual identity, but he confessed that the challenges could still be somewhat overwhelming. Isaac had already been working as a church planter from a larger, more prosperous United Methodist Church in the same city. Through that position, he had begun by offering ESL classes to the Hispanic community and gradually forming a nascent congregation, what the UMC refers to as a "missional community."

Y al fin de ese año abrió la oportunidad con esta iglesia. Estaba en un proceso de asesoría para revitalización en la conferencia anual. Decidieron que si no hacían algo diferente que en diez años cerraría sus puertas. Y también vieron que en la comunidad alrededor de la iglesia había muchos afro-americanos y muchas familias hispano-latinas. Entonces, me trajeron para alcanzar a la comunidad, y traer el grupo de hispanos que estaba reuniendo en casas.	And at the end of that year, the opportunity with this church opened up. They were in a process of assessment for revitalization in the annual conference. They decided that if they did not do something different, the church would shut its doors in ten years. And they also saw that in the church's surrounding community there were many African American and many Hispanic-Latino families. Therefore, they brought me to reach the community and to bring the group of Hispanics that was meeting in houses.

Isaac's work, however, is not just to grow this new Hispanic congregation, but also to pastor the dwindling Anglo congregation at the same time. Every Sunday, he prepares and preaches sermons in English for the older congregation while also nurturing the newer Hispanic congregation. On the third Sunday of each month, both congregations are invited to participate in a joint bilingual service, but Isaac still offers English language services on those Sundays as well. Even though Isaac is still providing the same quantity of worship services and pastoral care to the Anglo congregation, he perceives a certain tension among them due to their declining numbers and the unusual arrangement over which he presides.

La iglesia anglo-sajona está muriendo, literalmente. En los últimos dos años he tenido diez funerales. Al principio teníamos cuarenta en asistencia; ahora el promedio es de veinte o veinticinco personas. Y la congregación hispano-latina tiene un promedio de veinticinco personas más o menos. Y eso está trayendo conflicto también. La gente anglosajona siente que está perdiendo su iglesia. Pero la verdad es que Dios está trayendo nueva vida.	The Anglo-Saxon church is dying, literally. In the last two years, I have had ten funerals. At the beginning, we had forty in attendance; now the average is about twenty or twenty-five people. And the Hispanic-Latino congregation has an average of twenty-five people, more or less. And that is bringing conflict as well. The Anglo-Saxon people feel that they are losing their church. But the truth is that God is bringing new life.

Isaac was grateful for the opportunity the United Methodist Church gave him in his community. Few, if any, Hispanic church planters received a full-time salary for planting just one congregation, so this arrangement allowed him to support his young and growing family while also continuing to grow the congregation he had previously started. Yet his role as pastor of two congregations with different ethnicities, different languages, and different trajectories was a difficult one in which he found himself constantly explaining the words, actions, and motivations of each group to the other. The difficulty of his ministry setting extended to his preaching as well:

Es difícil predicar del mismo texto a dos comunidades tan distintas en el mismo lugar. Yo estoy usando el leccionario. Lo estoy haciendo para que me dé más enfoque en un lugar tan complejo. Pero si es difícil.	It is difficult to preach from the same text to two communities in the same place that are so distinct. I am using the lectionary. I am doing it because it gives me more focus in such a complex place. But it is difficult.

Ultimately, the difficulty of navigating complex ecclesial and denominational arrangements and hierarchies forced many of my Hispanic collaborators into what several of them saw as the unenviable position of being perpetual spokespersons. They were constantly justifying their work and explaining the unique needs of their communities to Anglo people in positions of power while also having to relay the results of those conversations to the people whom they served. They found themselves caught in precarious positions when the goals of their supporting organizations did not align with their own vision. They occasionally dealt with racism and indifference but were forced to continue reaching out to Anglo leadership in order to access the funding and networking that were still beyond the reach of their communities. All of these interactions gave rise to their feelings of having multiple identities in their ministerial contexts.

SERVICE-BASED MINISTRY

Like my first trip to Iglesia Agua Viva, my arrival at Ministerio Cristiano Vino Nuevo was delayed by several wrong turns. I have found that the GPS application on my phone is not well calibrated for finding the spaces that Hispanic congregations often rent within larger, and typically older, commercial developments. Vino Nuevo also did not provide much in the way of exterior signage. What it lacked in identification on the outside, however, it more than made up for on the inside, where Vino Nuevo was a world unto itself. Operating within a ten-thousand-square-foot rental space, Vino Nuevo's physical footprint attempted to offer all things to all people. A wide hallway led past a large room that typically hosted youth events. The room had only a few tables and chairs lined up against one wall, but it was well equipped with a ceiling-mounted projector and elaborate systems for both sound and lights that supported outreach-oriented parties for youth, as well as community activities for which the space was often rented by outside groups.

Beyond this space was the pastor's office, which was both the hub and visual embodiment of the multifaceted ministry which he helmed. The walls were covered with posters advertising services including tax preparation, immigration assistance, job counseling, and medical services, all offered in conjunction with the church. The low couches along two walls were covered with stacks of literature from these various community-oriented offerings. A corner workstation held the pastor's computer, as well as the equipment he used to run several radio programs. Musical instruments were scattered throughout the office, and a small bookcase filled with volumes on ministerial organization and inspiration occupied the far wall. Carlos B. Córdova writes about Hispanic ethnic enclaves in large cities like San Francisco, Los Angeles, and Houston providing immigrants with "a wide variety of services: legal, educational, immigration, medical, dental, accounting, income tax consulting, counseling, employment training, and referrals," but Vino Nuevo provided nearly all those services within the walls of the church.[22]

Vino Nuevo's pastor, Rafael, seemed destined to occupy such a space. Born in the Bronx to first-generation immigrant parents from Puerto Rico, Rafael had moved to Puerto Rico at the age of eighteen to study at the Universidad de Turabo. His vocational journey had included stints of traveling as a professional percussionist and vocalist as well as a career with the New York Police Department, from which he had retired before moving to the Raleigh area. After having grown up in a Puerto Rican ethnic enclave, he was surprised by the lack of services available to the Hispanic population in the Raleigh area and began his current endeavor not as a church, but as a community service office and food bank.

> I opened it up and folks would come in and say, "Hey Pastor!" And I'm a drummer running a community center. People would come in at the food bank, and I would tell them about the Lord. We were feeding two or three families and then by the end of the year forty to fifty families. We were giving them community services, showing them how to fill out applications. Teaching them about immigration reform. Whatever they asked, we taught them. We didn't want to leave any stone unturned.[23]

Only gradually did Rafael come to see himself in the way that many of the beneficiaries of the food bank did: as a pastor whose ministry spanned the full spectrum of social and spiritual needs present in his community. The preaching component of Rafael's multifaceted ministry was the last one to launch and, at the time of our conversation, still reached fewer people than the much larger medical clinic that provided the bulk of Rafael's income. Rafael spent twenty hours per week administering the work of the clinic and split the rest between the more traditional work of pastoring a congregation (organizing services, preparing sermons, visiting congregants) and the other community offerings of Vino Nuevo. Rafael explicitly rejected a message centered around the prosperity gospel, but nonetheless affirmed the importance within his ministry of what he described as "social restoration":

> A lot of what happens to people that come to our ministry is that people are in need, but they're in need socially. Their spiritual life flourishes once their social life flourishes. Once they realize that they can be someone in society, their spiritual life shoots up. There's a correlation there. That's the restoration that we want. I want you to be well out there so that you can be well in here.[24]

Rafael's service-based ministry was one born of necessity in multiple senses. Vino Nuevo's offerings were tailored very specifically to the needs of the Hispanic immigrant community in the greater Raleigh area. It also met the needs of Rafael and his family by providing income in the form of a part-time salary as clinic administrator and additional payments received for tax preparation and other consulting he provided. Rafael's congregation alone could not have provided a full-time salary sufficient to support him otherwise. These services, in addition to their financial impact, were also formative for Rafael's sense of pastoral vocation. They provided the context for his calling, in which recently arrived immigrants saw in Rafael someone whose acts of service authorized him as one who might also preach. The services Rafael offered also grounded his pastoral ministry in the reality of the hardships endured by Hispanic immigrants and undergirded his gospel of restoration, both social and spiritual.

Teresa, whom I have already discussed once in this chapter regarding her navigation of complex church relationships, also oversaw a socially oriented ministry as part of her work with her congregation. Her ministry, classified as a "mission" rather than a "church" in large part due to its inability to be financially self-supporting, had established a cleaning service to provide job opportunities and bring in more revenue. In addition to the work Teresa had done over the previous two years as an associate pastor, she had also served as the manager of this company operating within her congregation's larger "mission."

Teresa saw this as a personal and vocational challenge for herself but also as a great source of help for its employees:

Estos últimos dos años, he manejado una compañía que tiene la iglesia. Parte de mi responsabilidad ha sida eso—hacerla crecer. Es un negocio y llevo la contabilidad—cosas que nunca había hecho. Se abrió para la gente de la iglesia, especialmente para madres solteras o gente con low-income, para que pudieran ayudar a sustentar a sus familias. Así no tenían que trabajar horas súper largas. La empresa tiene dos empleadas. Cada empleada trabaja dos días o tres días a la semana.	These last two years, I have run a company that is held by the church. That has been part of my responsibility—to make it grow. It's a business, and I take care of the accounting—things I've never done before. It was opened for church people, especially for single mothers or low-income people, so they could help support their families. That way they did not have to work super long hours. The company has two employees. Each employee works two days or three days a week.

Managing the administration, marketing, scheduling, and accounting for this company—all of which required skills that Teresa had to acquire along the way—certainly served as an additional burden for her to carry. Once again, however, these experiences made her more acutely aware of the difficulties faced by many of the entrepreneurs within her congregation. She also worked closely with two single mothers for whom she provided scheduling, transportation, and financial advice as they learned to manage the money they were making through the cleaning service.

CONCLUSION

Each aspect of the *identidades multiples* that my collaborators embody reinforces the "otherness" that they can never escape as immigrants. From their bivocational work schedules to the bicultural natures of their churches and families, from the complex interethnic denominational power structures they navigate to the multiplicity of needs they attempt to meet within their communities, their role as ministers places them in a kind of perpetual limbo. This constant tension, however, also strengthens their connection with the lived reality of their congregants—unlike Thielicke's young preacher. The *identidades multiples* of my collaborators provide them with culturally appropriate language, images, and experiences to make their preaching resonate deeply within their Hispanic immigrant congregations. The interconnected immigrant realities of both the preacher and the hearer inform the preaching that we will explore more thoroughly in the next chapter.

4

La Predicación Misma / The Preaching Itself

aving explored the overlapping journeys undertaken by *predicadores* and the multiple identities they bring with them and assume, I turn specifically now to the preaching that issues directly from those journeys and identities. To find descriptions of Hispanic Protestant preaching, one must often look past typical scholarly monographs and focus on more practically oriented preaching manuals. In addition to explorations of preaching practices, these books also tend to convey judgments—or at the very least assumptions—of what constitutes "good" or "genuine" preaching in Hispanic Protestant contexts. Two recent works on Hispanic preaching written both by and for Hispanic Protestants were coauthored by Justo González and Pablo Jiménez. *Púlpito: An Introduction to Hispanic Preaching* appeared in English in 2005 and *Manual de Homilética Hispana: Teoría y Práctica desde la Diáspora* arrived a year later in Spanish. Both books begin with four nearly identical chapters focused on Hispanic homiletical theory followed by a selection of sermon exemplars. The introduction of *Púlpito* promises a "comprehensive introduction to Hispanic preaching" reflecting the "trademark characteristics of Latino and Latina religiosity and theology."[1]

By the third chapter of both books, however, González narrows in on one particular strain of Hispanic preaching that he considers more desirable:

La segunda línea divisoria separa a aquellos predicadores hispanos que se contentan con las interpretaciones tradicionales de las Escrituras y de la doctrina, y aquellos otros que se sienten impulsados por las circunstancias en que ellos y sus congregaciones viven	The second dividing line separates those Hispanic preachers who content themselves with the traditional interpretations of scripture and of doctrine, and those others who feel compelled by the circumstances in which they and their congregations live to look for

a buscar nuevas interpretaciones. . . . La predicación del primero de estos grupos es semejante a la que todos hemos conocido por generaciones.[2]	new interpretations. . . . The preaching of the first of these groups is similar to what all of us have known for generations.

Gónzalez later specifies that the traditional interpretations he is critiquing are those "*que les enseñan a leer la Biblia en términos de religiosidad privada y de moral individual* / that teach them to read the Bible in terms of private religiosity and individual morality."[3] González acknowledges that the group of preachers who rely on traditional interpretations of Scripture probably makes up the majority of Hispanic Protestant preachers, but he views this as unfortunate for their communities. González attributes the shortcomings of traditional preaching to a deficient pedagogy that encourages repetition, neglects the hermeneutical task, and fails to take seriously the scriptural text itself.[4] Most critically, González chastises traditional preachers for not "taking the situation of their people seriously" from the pulpit.[5] In González' opinion, however, this failure is not entirely the fault of these preachers. Rather, he sees them as the unwitting victims of a kind of hermeneutical colonization. In *Manual de Homilética Hispana*, he compares the interpretive practices of Hispanic preachers to looking at a landscape:

A muchos se nos ha enseñado a mirar al paisaje desde una perspectiva que no es la nuestra. Se nos ha dicho lo que la Biblia dice, y también se nos ha dicho, quizá más sutilmente, que eso es todo lo que dice. Luego, indirectamente se nos ha disuadido de leer la Biblia y sus doctrinas desde nuestra propia perspectiva, llegando a interpretaciones verdaderamente nuestras. El resultado ha sido una predicación poco auténtica. Es como si un pintor colocado en el fondo de un valle intentase pintar el paisaje desde la cima de una montaña.[6]	Many of us have been taught to see the landscape from a perspective that is not ours. We have been told what the Bible says, and we have been told, perhaps more subtly, that that is all it says. Then indirectly we have been dissuaded from reading the Bible and its doctrines from our own perspective, arriving at interpretations that are truly ours. The result has been not very authentic preaching. It is as if a painter located at the base of a valley tried to paint the landscape from the top of a mountain.

More authentic Hispanic preaching, according to González, must be based on a theology that is truly "ours." Such theology (and preaching) necessarily affirms the worth of Hispanic individuals who too often "hear that we are not what we ought to be, that our language is not correct, that our culture is not conducive to democracy, that we have much to learn from the dominant culture, that our people are poor through their own fault, and so on."[7] In addition to focusing on affirmation, González identifies the Hispanic theology underlying his preferred kind of preaching as a theology of solidarity (as opposed to one based on individualism), and one of eschatological subversion that calls the church into a future of social and political change. In the following chapter of *Púlpito*, Jiménez focuses on hermeneutical practices among Hispanic preachers and declares that marginalization is the point of entry for Hispanic preachers. This hermeneutical orientation allows such preachers to correlate "the social location of the Latino community and the social location of the Bible" and ultimately to produce a reading of resistance.[8]

I first read this description of authentic Hispanic preaching just as I was beginning my research among Hispanic immigrant congregations and was immediately drawn to its call for solidarity and affirmation. I also have a great deal of respect for both of the authors in question.[9] I fully believe that their description of authentic Hispanic preaching accurately reflects their own experiences as well as their hopes for Hispanic communities in the United States. The reality I was encountering on the ground, however, was more complex. I struggled to find the dividing line suggested by González between traditional and more liberative preaching. Many of the sermons preached by my collaborators focused on traditional interpretations of scripture, foregrounding private religiosity and individual morality, yet they also affirmed the worth of their hearers, incorporated themes of solidarity among immigrant communities, and even called for societal change.[10] In every situation, both the sermons I heard and the preachers who delivered them were closely connected to the circumstances of their Hispanic immigrant audiences.

Among my collaborators, the feeling of being indoctrinated by Anglo American theology and hermeneutics was not present at all. The majority of them converted to Protestant Christianity as part of their engagement within wholly Hispanic congregations, either in the United States or in their respective countries of origin. Without access to traditional forms of theological education in the United States, most of them had been prepared for ministry entirely within the context of the churches that had also been active in their conversions. They understood their perspective on preaching and biblical interpretation to be "theirs"—that is to say, authentic to their identity as Hispanic immigrants, even in those areas in which their perspective did not align with González' vision. The implication that traditional Hispanic preaching is the result of colonization denies the agency of many Hispanic immigrant ministers and the reality of the journeys they have taken. Daniel Ramírez pushes back against this kind of diminishment of Hispanic agency in his historical study of Pentecostalism in the borderlands. While taking the reality of colonizing forces seriously, Ramírez still asserts that the rapid expansion of Pentecostal denominations in the borderlands should be viewed as "more a tactic of religious subalterns than a strategy implemented by missionary hegemons."[11] Similarly, the shaping of my collaborators' hermeneutics is best viewed more as an on-the-ground effort of other Hispanic preachers than as a colonizing technique—whether deliberate or incidental—of Anglo American theology.

Recent scholarship has also taken issue with claims of authenticity in a broader sense. Historian and postcolonial theorist Deborah Root asserts that the "notion of cultural authenticity carries with it a notion of inauthenticity against which the former is evaluated."[12] This evaluation, whether explicit or implicit, presupposes a normative set of factors upon which to base such a judgment. There is also a question as to which individuals are permitted to advance claims of authenticity and inauthenticity. Root criticizes the way in which idealized notions of authenticity have been used as political tools to "legitimize or delegitimize actual people and communities."[13] In contrast to concepts of authenticity and inauthenticity being imposed upon particular groups, Root argues that any practice, regardless of the way it might be categorized by others, "can still manifest integrity among the people who respect and treat it as such."[14]

The sermons and stories I have included in this book were universally recognized by their audiences as manifesting integrity—as being "theirs"—both in the theology they espoused and in the connections they made to their hearers' lived realities. Taken as a whole, they argue for a broader and more complex understanding of what constitutes "authentic" Hispanic Protestant preaching.

PRIMARY PREACHING THEMES

As part of my interviews with my collaborators, I asked each of them to describe what they felt made preaching important and to share with me their dominant preaching themes. During these exchanges, they typically spoke first and most strongly of wanting their hearers to have an encounter with Jesus Christ resulting in an experience of spiritual conversion. Álvaro, a Pentecostal pastor, put it like this:

Hay que llevarlos a la transformación de su mente para que ellos tengan una identidad. La identidad de quién es Jesús y quién soy yo en Cristo Jesús. Esa identidad cambia la vida de la persona. Si no tenemos ese cambio, nos quedamos en un círculo vicioso.	One must bring them to the transformation of their minds so that they have an identity. The identity of who is Jesus and who I am in Christ Jesus. That identity changes a person's life. If we do not have that change, we stay in a vicious circle.

Álvaro went on to explain how this new identity resulting from conversion could also lead to renewal in the family, a greater sense of purpose in life, and the general uplifting of the Hispanic community, but he wanted me to understand that all of those other possibilities began and were grounded in a life-changing encounter with Jesus. Ernesto echoed Álvaro's understanding of preaching in his interview:

Quiero que la gente entienda claramente el plan de salvación, que se arrepienta de su pecado porque es donde la biblia nos guía. Hay gente que han pasado años en la iglesia y parece que realmente no han entendido la palabra sobre la salvación. Entonces, yo les digo, "Asegúrense que Uds. han sido salvos. Asegúrense que sus pecados han sido perdonados." El boleto ya está pagado. Quiero que conozcamos más a Dios. Que entendamos más de Dios. Que estemos más unidos a ese Dios que tiene tanta misericordia para nosotros.	I want people to understand clearly the plan of salvation, that one repents of his or her sin because that is where the Bible guides us. There are people who have been in the church for years, and it seems that they really do not understand the word about salvation. Therefore, I tell them, "Be sure that you have been saved. Be sure that your sins have been forgiven." The ticket is already paid. I want us to know God more. To understand God more. To be more united to that God who has so much mercy for us.

In addition to soliciting more free-flowing responses like those given by Álvaro and Ernesto in my interviews with them, I also asked my collaborators to respond to a series of affirmations about preaching and give each a score between one and ten, representing the degree to which the statement reflected their understanding of preaching. A score of ten represented complete agreement, whereas a score of one represented total rejection of the particular statement. The following are the composite scores based on all of their responses:

TABLE 4.1: AFFIRMATIONS RELATED TO PREACHING

Affirmation Related to Preaching	Composite Score
La predicación debe centrarse en la salvación. Preaching should focus on salvation.	9.54
La predicación debe ayudar a la gente a preservar su propia cultura como latinos o inmigrantes de diferentes países. Preaching should help people preserve their own culture as Latinos or immigrants of different countries.	3.94
La predicación debe centrarse en mejorando el hogar. Preaching should focus on improving the home.	9.36

La predicación debe enseñar puntos doctrinales. Preaching should teach points of doctrine.	8.01
La predicación debe centrarse en la prosperidad económica. Preaching should focus on economic prosperity.	4.76
La predicación debe motivar la gente a vivir una vida santa. Preaching should motivate people to live a holy life.	9.05
La predicación debe centrarse en la sanidad física. Preaching should focus on physical healing.	6.17
La predicación debe ayudar a la gente a asimilar a la vida en este país. Preaching should help people assimilate to life in this country.	3.10
La predicación debe centrarse en la justicia social. Preaching should focus on social justice.	5.17

The numeric values that my collaborators ascribed to these questions indicate the priority they place on individual experiences of salvation and the importance of holiness in the lives of their congregants. The table also emphasizes the importance of family and the teaching of doctrine, and I return to these topics later in this chapter. Taken in conjunction with their responses to more open-ended interview questions, my collaborators all described their preaching as oriented toward proclaiming a gospel of salvation based on God's grace and leading to the regeneration of its hearers. This finding concurs with the assertion by Jonathan E. Calvillo and Stanley R. Bailey that Hispanic Protestant religiosity focuses "on personal transformation as a community heavily characterized by the conversion experience."[15]

A reflection of this orientation toward preaching also appears in an earlier work by Pablo Jiménez entitled *Principios de Predicación*. This book, a didactic preaching text intended for use in introductory homiletical courses, stems from Jiménez' work teaching precisely these kinds of courses in both the Seminario Bíblico Latinoamericano in San José, Costa Rica and the Reverendo Juan Figueroa Umpierre Biblical Institute in Puerto Rico.[16] In his first chapter exploring the theology underlying preaching, Jiménez connects preaching most strongly to the concept of evangelism:

La humanidad necesita escuchar y aceptar el mensaje del evangelio porque vivimos en una condición pecaminosa. Los seres humanos, a pesar de haber sido creados para vivir en comunión con Dios, hemos caído en una triste condición de pecado. Más que hechos aislados, el pecado es una fuerza espiritual que lleva al ser humano a alejarse de Dios. El pecado nos coloca bajo el poder destructivo de las fuerzas de la maldad y de la muerte. Por eso, la persona que vive lejos de Dios tiende a destruirse a sí misma, tiende a hacerle daño al resto de la humanidad, tiende a dañar a la creación y hasta puede llegar a hacerles daño a las personas que más ama.[17]

La predicación del evangelio anuncia que, por medio de la obra salvífica de Jesucristo, los seres humanos hemos sido liberados del poder destructor de las fuerzas del mal, del pecado y de la muerte. Por lo tanto, podemos afirmar que el anuncio de la gracia de Dios debe ser precedido por una clara explicación de la condición humana. Se hace necesario denunciar el pecado para así exponer la gracia de Dios plenamente. La denuncia y la condena del pecado es el paso preliminar en el camino que nos llevará a disfrutar de la gracia de Dios.[18]

Humanity needs to hear and accept the message of the gospel because we live in a sinful condition. Human beings, in spite of having been created to live in communion with God, have fallen into a sorrowful condition of sinfulness. More than isolated actions, sin is a spiritual force that leads humans to distance themselves from God. Sin places us under the destructive power of the forces of evil and of death. That is why the person who lives far from God tends to destroy himself (or herself), tends to harm the rest of humanity, tends to harm creation, and can even harm the people he or she loves most.

Preaching of the gospel announces that, by way of the salvific act of Jesus Christ, human beings have been liberated from the destructive power of the forces of evil, of sin and of death. Thus, we can affirm that the announcement of the grace of God should be preceded by a clear explanation of the human condition. It is necessary to denounce sin in order to fully expound the grace of God. The denunciation and condemnation of sin is the first step in the path that brings us to enjoy the grace of God.

Later on in his chapter, Jiménez mentions that "*otras teologías contemporáneas* / other contemporary theologies" understand salvation to extend to "*todas las áreas de la vida, incluyendo la política, la economía, el orden social, la opresión a los grupos minoritarios y la discriminación contra la mujer* / all areas of life, including politics, the economy, the social order, oppression of minorities and discrimination against women."[19] Although Jiménez does not disparage any of these more socially liberative aims of theology or preaching, he also does not include them within his main discussion of preaching's salvific orientation. According to his description, spiritual salvation for the individual comes first, and only then is followed by its outworking into the other arenas that Jiménez lists.

It is this balance of a strong focus on personal salvation along with a highly contextualized understanding of that salvation extending into all areas of life that more closely approximates the preaching of my interlocutors. Marginalization in a social or political sense is not the entry point for my collaborators, but it is certainly an important element of their context, and their preaching often reflects their experience of immigration and adjustment in a new country. Their preaching truly is "a witness of faith produced by a process subjecting our people to continuous suffering and violence,"[20] yet they do not adopt a classically liberationist position focusing on prophetic witness and social change. Instead, their preaching begins with a focus on a transformational encounter with Christ and then branches out into all the ways in which the life and community of faith can heal the wounds of migration.[21] Again and again, my collaborators directed their homiletical energies toward proclaiming those attributes of God they found most meaningful during their immigration or ongoing reality as strangers in a strange land. When migration left them with a deep sense of personal loneliness, *conociendo a Cristo* / knowing Christ brought them a steadfast companion. When the context of migration seemed to present insurmountable obstacles for them, these preachers experienced the often-miraculous providence of God in practical and tangible ways. When they were separated from their people and culture, God provided them with a reconstituted people. Having entered into a world with very different rules and cultural values, Scripture's moral doctrine provided stability. And, finally, a focus on family renewal brought healing from their journeys' many wounds. These five themes echoed through the numerous sermons to which I listened over the course of several years, with many sermons incorporating more than one of them. These themes were also deeply connected to the immigration stories and bivocational realities my collaborators recounted during our initial interviews and ongoing conversations.

In the remainder of this chapter, I explore in greater detail each of the aforementioned themes: (1) Christ as savior and friend; (2) God as miracle worker on behalf of the marginalized; (3) God as gatherer of his people; (4) God as lawgiver and provider of structure in the midst of chaos; and (5) God as healer of the family. My examination of each theme will include insights and biographical detail from my collaborators in addition to my own analysis of representative sermons preached by my collaborators during my time of participant-observation.

CHRIST AS SAVIOR AND FRIEND

Paul Barton cites the hymn "Jesus Is All the World to Me" as an example of the significance for Anglo American Protestants of "a personal relationship with Jesus Christ." He argues that this emphasis was effectively "transmitted to Spanish-speaking converts" at least in part because it was analogous to the kind of "personal relationship that Spanish-speaking Catholics typically had with Nuestra Señora de Guadalupe and other saints."[22] I found the idea of a personal relationship with Christ to be highly significant for all of my collaborators, even those who had grown up in agnostic or atheistic homes prior to their conversion to Protestant Christianity. Rather than merely serving as a replacement for previous devotion to *la virgen* and other saints, the importance of this personal relationship seemed to be grounded in the inherent trauma of the immigration experience and the ongoing reality of living in a community where one is other. More than anything else, the opportunity to have a personal relationship with Christ resonated deeply with many of my Hispanic immigrant collaborators due to their poignant experiences of isolation and anonymity in the United States. Timothy L. Smith writes that "an extensive personalizing of religious faith" is a common feature of immigrant faith communities that should be understood in the light of the immigrant experience rather than as a turn toward a more "private or individualistic" American understanding of religion.[23]

Recall that in chapter 3, I included Ernesto's recollections on his rapid introduction to ministerial tasks upon his conversion to Protestant Christianity as broadly reflecting my collaborators' experiences. Like many of the other pastors in this study, Ernesto also experienced extreme isolation as part of his story. For Ernesto, however, this loss of connection to family and community began long before his journey to the United States:

Yo nací en la ciudad de México. Mis padres eran de seis horas al norte de la ciudad en el estado de Hidalgo, pero yo nací en la ciudad de México. A los dos años mi mamá me llevó al estado de Hidalgo para vivir con mis abuelos. Mi mamá me dejó con mis abuelos.	I was born in Mexico City. My parents were from six hours north of the city in the state of Hidalgo, but I was born in Mexico City. When I was two years old, my mom brought me to Hidalgo in order to live with my grandparents. My mom left me with my grandparents.

Ernesto's experience of being raised by grandparents or other family members was echoed by nearly half of my collaborators. Some of these separations were caused, like Ernesto's, by the relocation of one or both parents in order to earn more and better support their families. Unable to provide suitable housing for young children in these new environs, parents entrusted their children to the care of someone else. Although several collaborators spoke of their parents resettling in Mexico City or another urban center in their country of origin, it was far more common that one or both parents migrated to the United States. In these cases, my collaborators often did not see their parent or parents for many years. Sometimes their parents were eventually able to make arrangements for them to come to the United States as well. At other times, changes in life circumstances forced these awkward reunions, as was the case for Ignacio, who joined his father in the United States after a prolonged separation only because his mother, who had been caring for him in Mexico, passed away unexpectedly.

In addition to being left in the care of his grandparents, Ernesto was to experience further crisis within his family:

Mi padre con mi madre no se entendió y se separaron. Después mi madre volvió a casarse con otro hombre, pero no me integró con la familia. Entonces yo me crié con mis abuelos hasta los dieciséis años. Regresé a la ciudad de México a los dieciséis años ya para trabajar y empecé a vivir con mi madre, pero mi madre ya se había quedado viuda. El esposo de ella falleció en el temblor que hubo en el 1985 en el DF. Ella quedó viuda con seis hijos y a la edad de dieciséis años yo me mudé a vivir con ella y ayudarle.	My father did not get along with my mother, and they separated. Afterward, my mother married another man, but she did not integrate me with the [new] family. So, I grew up with my grandparents until I was sixteen. I returned to Mexico City when I was sixteen, this time in order to work, and I began to live with my mother, but [by that time] my mother had already been left a widow. Her husband died in the earthquake that happened in 1985 in Mexico City. She was left a widow with six children and at the age of sixteen, I moved to live with her and help her.

Divorce was also a common experience within my collaborators' families of origin. Sometimes these divorces were precipitated by substance abuse by a parent or by the stress of trying to hold together marriages across great distances or national borders. Ernesto's experience of being an outsider to a new family of stepsiblings was also the experience of other collaborators and of many congregants within the churches they pastored. Some of them, having recently arrived in the United States, attempted to reunite with parents who had already been here a decade or more only to find themselves displaced by unknown stepsiblings and unwelcome by unknown stepparents or even by their biological but unfamiliar parents.

In spite of Ernesto's experience of rejection, he moved in with his mother and helped provide for his half-siblings for several years before leaving to try and build a life for himself in the United States.

Al llegar a la carolina del norte, no conocí a nadie. Habían unas pocas personas de México, de mi estado o de otros estados. El contratista era de Guerrero. El coyote nos dejó con él, y él ya tenía arreglos con varios rancheros a trabajar. Ellos proveyeron casas viejas o trailers donde cinco o seis hombres podían vivir.	When I arrived in North Carolina, I did not know anyone. There were a few people from Mexico, from my state or from other states. The contractor was from Guerrero. The coyote left us with him, and he already had arrangements with various ranchers for us to work. They provided old houses or trailers where five or six men could live.

From the age of two until early adulthood, Ernesto lived as a liminal member of his own family. Unrecognized by his biological father and unaccepted by his stepfather, Ernesto only reunited with his birth mother when she needed him to help her provide for the half-siblings who barely knew him. Immigrating to the United States only heightened his experience of being unknown. He was passed from a barely familiar coyote into the hands of a perfect stranger who contracted him as a laborer in the agricultural operations of ranchers and farmers for whom he provided functional value, nothing more. Ernesto bunked with other unknown men whose only connection to him was that a few of them might have been from the same state or country.

This narrative of extreme isolation provides the necessary context for understanding the homiletical focus in one of Ernesto's sermons on the blessing of being able to know and be known by Christ. Ernesto's text for the sermon was from the fifth chapter of the Gospel of Mark, focusing on the liberation of a demon-possessed man by Jesus. He titled the sermon, "*La Necesidad del Testimonio* / The Necessity of Testimony." As Ernesto was preaching this message at the beginning of a new calendar year, he reflected briefly on the goals his congregants might be setting for the year ahead. He suggested that perhaps they might desire to be better *testigos* / witnesses on behalf of Christ in the coming twelve months. From this point, Ernesto began to discuss the nature of testimony. The sermon was highly structured. Ernesto developed, in succession, the following four components he felt were the *sine qua non* of understanding testimony: *una experiencia de liberación* / an experience of liberation, *quienes deben dar testimonio* / who should give testimony, *donde se debe comenzar a testificar* / where one should begin to testify, and *el poder del testimonio* / the power of testimony.

Testimony was necessary, according to Ernesto, because introducing other people to Christ is the Christian's highest calling. This reflects, once again, the focus on personal salvation as the dominant element of my collaborators' preaching. Woven throughout his sermon was the theme of the importance of *conociendo a Cristo* / knowing Christ. This was certainly not surprising given the emphasis on this message throughout my collaborators' sermons, but the choice of phrase to describe personal salvation, *conociendo a Cristo* / knowing Christ, which was commonly used by a majority of the preachers involved in this study, is instructive. The Spanish language has two verbs, *saber* and *conocer*, which are both translated into English as "to know." The Spanish-Mexican philosopher Luís Villoro writes about the distinction between these two forms of knowing in his analysis of epistemology entitled *Creer, Saber, Conocer*. Villoro contends that the collapse of these two concepts in English into the single verb "to know" has contributed to a loss of clarity in discussions of epistemology.[24] The verb *saber* denotes having knowledge of something, while *conocer* implies a deeper level of understanding. Villoro elaborates:

Conocemos objetos o a personas, *sabemos* que algunos objetos tienen ciertas propiedades [. . .] pero no *sabemos* objetos ni *sabemos* personas. *Conozco* algo o a alguien, *sé* algo *acerca de* algo o *de* alguien. "Conozco la carretera a Guadalajara," pero "sé que la carretera a Guadalajara está en mal estado" o "sé llegar a Guadalajara por carretera."[25]	We know [*conocer*] objects or people, we know [*saber*] that some objects have certain properties [. . .] but we do not know [*saber*] objects nor do we know [*saber*] people. I know [*conocer*] something or someone, I know [*saber*] something about something or someone. "I know [*conocer*] the highway to Guadalajara," but "I know [*saber*] that the highway to Guadalajara is in bad condition" or "I know [*saber*] how to reach Guadalajara by highway."

Reading the English translation of Villoro's text quickly reveals the difficulty of separating these distinct concepts of knowing while using the same word. Although the verb *saber* is never used with objects or persons themselves, it is occasionally used to convey recognition of someone: "*Yo sé quien es ella.* / I know who she is." In typical usage, the English verb "to know" can reflect this limited sense of recognition or a much deeper relationship marked by mutual understanding. For one to say in English "I know him" is to open a wide space for interpretation spanning everything from limited knowledge to intimate relationship. The Spanish verb *conocer* solves much of this dilemma by separating knowledge in the form of information (*saber*) from knowing through experience (*conocer*).

Experiential knowledge, Villoro maintains, may also provide one with informational knowledge. Having met a person or having visited a city would also equip one with certain information based on his or her experience. Knowing details of a person or place, however, is not equivalent to *knowing* that person or place. Villoro offers the following example using the city of Río de Janeiro:

Puedo saber muchas cosas sobre Río y si me preguntan: "Bueno, pero ¿tú lo conoces?," confesar sin inmutarme: "No lo conozco, pero sé que es una ciudad extraordinaria." Conocer a Río es haber estado en esa ciudad, conocer una carretera es haberla transitado, conocer a Juan es tener una relación personal con él. Para conocer algo es preciso tener o haber tenido una experiencia personal y directa, haber estado en contacto, estar "familiarizado" con ello.²⁶	I can know [*saber*] many things about Río and if they ask me: "Alright, but do you know [*conocer*] it?," confess without contradicting myself: "I do not know [*conocer*] it, but I know [*saber*] that it is an extraordinary city." To know [*conocer*] Rio is to have been in that city, to know [*conocer*] a highway is to have traveled it, to know [*conocer*] Juan is to have a personal relationship with him. To know [*conocer*] something it is necessary to have or to have had a personal and direct experience, to have been in contact, to be "familiarized" with it.

When Ernesto preached of *conociendo a Cristo* / knowing Christ, he was of course following Spanish grammatical conventions in his verb choice, but he was also communicating a type of knowledge based on "personal and direct experience." To *know* Christ is not just to know *of* him but to have had an encounter with him in which one both comes to know the other and to be known by him or her. *Conociendo a Cristo* has as much to do with being known by Christ as it does with knowing Christ for oneself, making it resonate even more deeply with those immigrants like Ernesto and his congregants who had deeply felt the reality of being unknown.

Ernesto first grounds the theme of *conociendo a Cristo* / knowing (and being known by) Christ in the initial encounter between the demon-possessed man and Christ:

Le dijo al Señor Jesús cuando se encontró con él: "¿Que tengo que ver contigo, Jesús hijo del Dios Altísimo? Te imploro por Dios que no me atormentes." Más sin embargo después de haber tenido esa liberación que encontró él en Jesucristo y al haber conocido la salvación en Cristo Jesús, en el versículo dieciocho dice, "Al entrar él en la barca, él que había estado endemoniado le rogaba que le permitiera acompañarle."	He said to the Lord Jesus when he found himself with him: "What do I have to do with you, Jesus son of the most high God? I implore you by God not to torment me." But nevertheless after having received that liberation that he found in Jesus Christ and having known [*conocer*] salvation in Christ Jesus, in verse eighteen it says, "When he entered into the boat, he who had been demon-possessed begged him to let him accompany him."

Primero, no quería quedarse con Cristo—creía que Cristo le estaba atormentando. Mas sin embargo cuando él ha sido liberado de este sufrimiento y del temor, ahora él quiere quedarse con el Señor Jesús. ¡Qué maravilloso es cuando conocemos a Jesucristo! Primero no queremos saber quién es Jesús; primero no queremos tener un encuentro con Cristo Jesús. Más, sin embargo, cuando tenemos ese encuentro, queremos quedarnos con él. Queremos estar siempre con él. Queremos caminar con él.	First, he did not want to stay with Christ—he believed that Christ was tormenting him. But nevertheless, when he had been liberated from that suffering and from fear, now he wanted to stay with the Lord Jesus. How marvelous it is when we come to know [*conocer*] Jesus Christ! First, we do not want to know [*saber*] who Jesus is; first, we do not want to have an encounter with Christ Jesus. But, nevertheless, when we have that encounter, we want to stay with him. We want to be with him always. We want to walk with him.

When Ernesto spoke of knowing Christ, of wanting to be with him, he looked up from his notes and engaged much more fully with his hearers. There was a yearning in his voice that communicated the incomparable benefits of always being with Christ. Although Ernesto was a Baptist preacher, his message bore a strong resemblance to the Christology of Hispanic Pentecostals.[27]

As he elaborated upon his second point, Ernesto assured the congregation that their ability to serve as witnesses did not depend primarily on their personal qualities but on whether they had ever had a personal encounter with Jesus. Drawing on the experiences of David in the Old Testament, of Peter and John in the book of Acts, and of the writer of the epistle of 1 John, Ernesto highlighted the way in which powerful encounters with God undergirded and even compelled their testimony. In his third point, Ernesto returned to the story of the demon-possessed man, reflecting on the choice made by Jesus to reject this man's attempt to board the boat and join him. This was not simply a rejection by Jesus, according to Ernesto, but a commissioning of him as a disciple with a particular mission. Ernesto returned to the text to quote Jesus saying, "*Véte a tu casa, a los tuyos, y cuéntales cuan grandes cosas ha hecho el Señor por ti* / Go to your house, to your family, and tell them what great things the Lord has done for you." The place to begin testifying is in our own homes and among those familiar to us. Rather than interpreting this as an exclusive mission, Ernesto simply described it as a way to begin that left no excuse for any of his hearers—all of them had people who were most familiar to them with whom they could share the life-giving blessing of *conociendo a Cristo* / knowing Christ.

Finally, Ernesto spoke of the power of testimony being rooted in the power of Christ that had shown itself to be greater than the demonic power that had held the man in bondage. The power of Christ, however, was not only to be found in these pitched supernatural battles, but in the possibility of *conociendo a Cristo* / knowing Christ. Opening this doorway to knowing and being known was the true power of testimony. Ernesto exhorted his hearers to share their testimony in this way:

Digamos que en Cristo se encuentra descanso, se encuentra paz. Y es el mejor refugio en el cual podemos refugiarnos. Así como vemos a este hombre, ¿verdad? Después de estar sólo. Después de estar haciéndose daño él mismo, autodestruyéndose él mismo, ahora estaba vestido muy bien y estaba sentado al lado de Jesucristo como un discípulo. Cristo Jesús hace nuevo todas las cosas. Es lo que vemos en este hombre.	We say that in Christ one can find rest, one can find peace. And he is the best refuge in which we can take refuge. Like we see in this man, right? After having been alone. After having been doing harm to himself, destroying himself, now he was dressed well and he was sitting at Jesus' side like a disciple. Christ Jesus makes all things new. That is what we see in this man.
¡Y gloria al Señor porque Cristo puede hacer lo mismo para nosotros! Quizás algunos de los que estamos aquí también tuvimos una vida en la cual estábamos solos y nos estábamos autodestruyendo. Más, sin embargo, cuando Cristo vino a nuestras vidas, cuando tuvimos ese encuentro con él, nos ha cambiado y nos ha transformado. Somos personas diferentes porque conocemos a Cristo.	And glory to the Lord because Christ can do the same for us! Maybe some of us here have also had a life in which we were alone and were self-destructing. But, nevertheless, when Christ came into our lives, when we had that encounter with him, he changed us and he transformed us. We are different people because we know [*conocer*] (and are known by) Christ.

This conclusion to Ernesto's sermon draws the connection again between the condition of the demon-possessed man and that of Ernesto's hearers. They all know what it means to have been alone, separated from others by their status, unrecognized by those around them. The self-destruction comes not only from their own potentially negative choices, but also from the way in which their very selves are eroded by the isolation they endure. The encounter with Christ leads to change and transformation as it guides both the demon-possessed man and Ernesto's hearers out of self-destructive isolation. The possibility of knowing Christ as friend and companion and being known by him in the same manner is the great hope to which Ernesto urges his hearers to bear witness, as it is a hope that resonates deeply for his community.

GOD AS MIRACLE WORKER ON BEHALF OF THE MARGINALIZED

Another significant hope expressed in the preaching of many of my collaborators was the expectation that God would perform miracles on behalf of the marginalized. In *The Heart of Black Preaching*, Cleophus LaRue describes the primary *discrimen* of African American preaching as the identification of God as one who acts mightily on behalf of the oppressed: "From their initial embrace of the Christian religion to the present day, blacks tend to believe the scriptures demonstrate God's mighty actions on behalf of marginalized and powerless people."[28] LaRue asserts that this tendency is a "direct result of [African Americans'] struggle against oppression" and has guided black preachers toward specific narratives and other biblical passages bearing similar characteristics:

> The biblical stories and scriptural passages that have historically found their way into black preaching are those that have clearly demonstrated the mighty acts of God on behalf of people who were in situations of powerlessness consistent with, though not the same as, those of the forcibly displaced Africans in America.[29]

Although the Hispanic immigrant experience is not the same as the African American experience or the ancient Hebrew experience, the situation of powerlessness is consistent. Just as many of my collaborators shared God's miraculous work on their own behalf as part of their conversion and immigration stories, they also frequently employed texts in their preaching that highlighted God's mighty acts on behalf of the marginalized.

One particularly powerful example of this element within Hispanic Protestant preaching came from one of Ignacio's sermons entitled *La Fe que Maravilla a Jesús* / Faith that Amazes Jesus. Ignacio had chosen as his text Matthew 8:5-13, which tells the story of a Roman centurion who comes to Jesus seeking healing for one of his servants who is paralyzed and suffering terribly. As Ignacio began reading the text, I found myself leaning forward in anticipation of how this preacher, himself paralyzed, would interpret this particular passage. I looked around and saw that Ignacio had everyone's full attention. He preached from an iPad balanced precariously on one knee. In order to scroll down through his notes as he read the passage, he would drag the gnarled knuckle of his right index finger across the tablet's screen. Once he reached the end of verse 13, he looked up and said:

Esto es uno de los pasajes que me tocan en el corazón y me ayudan. Al principio, estos pasajes en la realidad fueron el alivio para mi situación porque veía esperanza en estos pasajes bíblicos. Veía el dolor en estas personas. Y veía como el Señor podía cambiar la vida de estas personas—sanar la vida de estas personas. Al principio—en realidad—estos pasajes me levantaron, diciéndome, "Sí mi parálisis se va a quitar. Sí, sí, Jesús va a tocar mi cuerpo y me voy a levantar." Pero con el tiempo entendí mejor lo que el pasaje decía.	This is one of the passages that touches me in the heart and helps me. In the beginning, these passages in reality were relief for my situation because I saw hope in these biblical passages. I saw the pain in these people. And I saw how the Lord could change the life of these people—heal the life of these people. In the beginning—in reality—these passages lifted me up, saying, "Yes, my paralysis is going to go away. Yes, yes, Jesus is going to touch my body and I will stand up." But with time I understood better what the passage was saying.

Ignacio both met and subverted the expectations of his hearers. He acknowledged that this was a passage that resonated deeply for him given his own physical condition. It was not just his presence in a mechanized wheelchair but also the movement of his body that underlined that connection for his hearers. Lacking full articulation of the fingers on either hand, Ignacio gestured throughout his sermon by flailing his balled-up fists out to the side or by extending one of them toward us. However, Ignacio had drawn a clear line of demarcation between his impending exegesis of this passage and his own personal hope of complete physical restoration. It left the question hanging in the air of what hope of the miraculous his congregation might therefore possess in light of this New Testament narrative.

Ignacio described this hope within the first point of his six-point sermon on *La Fe que Maravilla a Jesús* / Faith that Amazes Jesus:

Primero, encuentro que la fe que maravilla a Jesús es la fe que pide ayuda de él. Esa es la fe que maravilla a Jesús. Es la fe que puede sacar una sonrisa de Jesús. Y esa es la fe que puede a nosotros bendecir. Una fe que puede pedirle ayuda de Dios. Una fe que puede traer la necesidad a Dios. Una fe que puede traerle tus lágrimas a Dios.	First, I find that faith that amazes Jesus is faith that asks him for help. That is faith that amazes Jesus. It is the faith that brings a smile out of Jesus. And that is the faith that can bless us. A faith that can ask God for help. A faith that can bring need to God. A faith that can carry your tears to God.

Ignacio continually emphasized the importance of faith throughout his message. He encouraged his listeners first to take their needs and their tears to God because these actions underscored the kind of faith that God desired from them. What enabled them to approach God with this kind of faith, however, was the underlying reality of God's identity as the one who could work miracles on behalf of the marginalized. Ignacio continued, drawing parallels with the Roman centurion's motivation for seeking Jesus.

Dice el versículo, "se le acercó un capitán romano para pedirle ayuda a Jesús." Yo creo que este extranjero se dio cuenta que Jesús es esa fuente donde uno puede venir y decirle a Dios, "Ayúdame." "Tengo esta necesidad—socórreme." "Estoy pasando por esta situación—ayúdame."	The verse says, "a Roman captain drew near to ask Jesus for help." I believe that this foreigner realized that Jesus is that fountain where one can come and say to God, "Help me." "I have this need—rescue me." "I am going through this situation—help me."

The identification of Jesus as the fountain to which the needy can come for aid stayed in the background of this particular sermon until Ignacio arrived at his fourth point: "*la fe que maravilla a Jesús es la fe que entiende su autoridad* / faith that amazes Jesus is faith that understands his authority." Ignacio grounded this point in the assertion by the centurion that Jesus did not have to come to visit his servant in person but could simply give the word as someone with authority and the healing of the servant would be accomplished. The authority of Jesus to perform this miracle could be trusted by the centurion because of the miracles Jesus had previously performed on behalf of those who had come to him. Ignacio's conclusion to his sermon brought this point full circle: "*la fe que maravilla a Jesús es la fe que recibe sus milagros* / faith that amazes Jesus is faith that receives his miracles." He elaborated:

Una fe que maravilla a Jesús verá los resultados de la gracia de Dios en todos los aspectos de la vida. Miraremos en la realidad milagros más grandes.	A faith that amazes Jesus will look at all the results of God's grace in all aspects of life. We will see in reality greater miracles.

A faith that amazes Jesus, for Ignacio and for most of my collaborators, is a faith that has seen and will continue to see miracles in every aspect of life. These miracles are omnipresent because God is constantly performing them, especially for those whose need is compelling enough to drive them to ask for his help.

These possible miracles, as I heard them enumerated in many sermons, included the safe passage of loved ones during migration, provision of food and shelter for the poor, reconciliation within and between families, super-natural healing, and freedom from addiction. But in spite of Ignacio's own testimony that included a dramatic healing that restored partial mobility and his miraculous crossing of the border when he returned to the United States, he still named one miracle as being greater than all of the others:

El milagro más grande que sanar un cuerpo es el milagro de salvar un alma—es el milagro de transformar un corazón y una mente. Transformar una persona y convertirle en persona de fe y persona del reino.	The miracle greater than healing a body is the miracle of saving a soul—it is the miracle of transform-ing a heart and a mind. Transforming a person and converting him or her into a person of faith and a person of the kingdom.

It was a powerful moment in Ignacio's sermon. This man who had once looked to this particular passage primarily as an affirmation of the possibility that he might one day walk again now believed and proclaimed that the saving of a soul and transforming of a heart and mind were greater miracles still. Even as Ignacio's sermon focused on the wonder-working God so common in the preaching of my collaborators, it further underlined the more fundamental importance of individual conversion within Hispanic Protestant immigrant preaching. When Ignacio read over his sermon in a rough draft of this book, he offered the following simple but profound observation:

Muchos caminan por fuera pero están paralizados por dentro.	Many walk on the outside but are par-alyzed within.

Both Ignacio's sermon and his later reflection upon it shed a critical light on the idea of marginalization. Pablo Jiménez asserted that the lens of marginal-ization should be the Hispanic preacher's entry point into a text, but what kind of marginalization? Jiménez was referring to socioeconomic and racial/ethnic marginalization just as LaRue did in *The Heart of Black Preaching*, but Ignacio and many of the other preachers in this study more often focused on a kind of spiritual marginalization in which an individual is disconnected from God and the provision and purposes only God can provide. According to this par-adigm, the members of Hispanic immigrant congregations occupied a liminal space similar to the status of the early church. They might be despised by the world and materially marginalized, but they had also been chosen by Christ and were more than conquerors. The stories of God's miracle-working power on their behalf certainly provided relief from the dehumanizing forces arrayed against them, but they also—and perhaps even more importantly—underlined the ability of God to free them from the power of sin and the kind of marginalization that could paralyze them within.

GOD AS GATHERER OF A NEW PEOPLE

The Old Testament depicts God as one who gathers and regathers the Hebrew people. This theme first emerges in the flood narrative in Genesis prior to the actual origination of the Hebrew people. In the midst of what Scripture describes as great wickedness and corruption, God instructs Noah to build an ark of cypress wood and gather his family into it before the flood comes. This small group, consisting of Noah, his wife, his sons, and his sons' wives, represents a reconstituted people who will more closely adhere to God's vision for humanity. To help these chosen people more closely realize their identity, God provides them with moral parameters in the form of a covenant. The most famous part of this covenant is the rainbow that God places in the sky accompanied by his promise never to destroy the earth through flood again, but there are also moral imperatives given to Noah and his family. In the positive sense, they are to "be fruitful and multiply, abound on the earth and multiply in it."[30] But they are also to have a new respect for the "lifeblood" of all living things. When eating meat from animals they "shall not eat flesh with its life, that is, its blood."[31] They also must have a greater respect for one another's lives because God will now "require a reckoning for human life."[32]

These patterns repeat themselves in the story of Abraham. In the aftermath of the Tower of Babel narrative, in which humans are divided by their inability to communicate with one another and are scattered across the face of the earth, God begins the work of gathering a people once again through the call of Abram in the twelfth chapter of Genesis. God promises childless Abram a family that will grow into a great nation. This family will receive blessing from God and serve as an instrument of his blessing for others. Abram, like Noah, also receives a certain set of expectations as part of this calling. He is to act in faith and obedience, leaving behind "your country and your kindred and your father's house" in order to reach an unknown land.[33] He is also to adopt a new set of rituals, including most notably the practice of circumcision, which God describes as "a sign of the covenant between me and you."[34] Circumcision becomes a tangible sign of a gathered people, or at least of its male population.

In the story of Moses, the image of God as gatherer of a people takes on new significance. The people in this narrative are not exactly new, being described as descendants of Abraham who first journeyed into Egypt in the days of Joseph. They have, however, lost their sense of identity as God's people through many years of oppression and enslavement. Through the Exodus narrative, God's people are redeemed from slavery and reconstituted as a people once again worthy to receive God's blessing and to bless others. Through Moses' efforts and God's divine intervention, the people of Israel will eventually be reconnected with the promised land which forms such a large portion of their blessing and identity throughout the Old Testament. As the "family" being gathered is now much larger and more diverse than it was in Genesis, so the laws given to them as part of this new covenant are also far more numerous and wide-ranging. The moral imperatives extend beyond the prohibition of murder to the delineation of the Ten Commandments. In addition to the previously established rituals of sacrifice and circumcision, this regathered people will abide by expansive codes covering diet, attire, inheritance, and much more. These outward signs affirm their identity as those who have been gathered by God.

Another significant gathering occurs, at least prophetically, in the thirty-seventh chapter of the book of Ezekiel. The prophet Ezekiel describes being led by the spirit of the Lord into a valley full of dry bones. Then he records a conversation between God and himself:

> He said to me, "Mortal, can these bones live?" I answered, "O Lord GOD, you know." Then he said to me, "Prophesy to these bones, and say to them: O dry bones, hear the word of the LORD. Thus says the Lord GOD to these bones: I will cause breath to enter you, and you shall live. I will lay sinews on you, and will cause flesh to come upon you, and cover you with skin, and put breath in you, and you shall live; and you shall know that I am the LORD."[35]

Ezekiel does as the Lord commands, and the bones begin to join themselves together again. The processes of death and decomposition reverse themselves as sinews, then flesh, then skin reappear on the newly reassembled skeletons. God then commands Ezekiel to prophesy not just to the bones, but to the breath, and the four winds blow the breath of life back into the bodies so that they stand on their feet and live again. As Ezekiel completes the tasks set before him, the Lord speaks again:

> Then he said to me, "Mortal, these bones are the whole house of Israel. They say, 'Our bones are dried up, and our hope is lost; we are cut off completely.' Therefore prophesy, and say to them, Thus says the Lord GOD: I am going to open your graves, and bring you up from your graves, O my people; and I will bring you back to the land of Israel. And you shall know that I am the LORD, when I open your graves, and bring you up from your graves, O my people. I will put my spirit within you, and you shall live, and I will place you on your own soil; then you shall know that I, the LORD, have spoken and will act, says the LORD."[36]

The vision of the dry bones represents the resurrection and reconstitution of the people of Israel. Although there is no enumerated reminder or recapitulation of legal codes or moral expectations, the text implies the expectation of changed behavior in the recognition of God by the people. When their graves are opened, they will know that he is the Lord. They will also have his spirit within them, enabling them not only to live, but to live differently than before.

These Old Testament depictions of God as the one who gathers his people in the face of destruction, isolation, oppression, and death itself resonate deeply within Hispanic immigrant communities and connect with the experiences of my collaborators. One of them, an ordained United Methodist elder named Eduardo, preached a series of sermons in which he compared his congregation's relationship with God to the lived faith of the Hebrew people as experienced through its covenants. In one sermon in particular, entitled "*Bajo el Pacto de Dios* / Under God's Covenant," Eduardo draws on several Old Testament images of God gathering his people together through covenants. Although the principal text of the sermon comes from Exodus, Eduardo begins in the book of Genesis by describing the situation of rejection out of which God first needed to gather his people:

¿Cuál es la historia bíblica? Dios crea a Adán y Eva—los crea en su imagen y semejanza, pero Adán y Eva, no? Desobedecieron; cayeron en pecado. Entonces, ¿cuál era la sentencia? Fueron expulsados, perecieron y fueron expulsados de la presencia de Dios.	What is the biblical story? God creates Adam and Eve—he creates them in his image and likeness, but Adam and Eve, no? They disobeyed; they fell in sin. Then, what was the sentence? They were expelled—they perished and were expelled from the presence of God.

From this first explanation of humanity's alienation from God, Eduardo briefly highlights the need for a mediator to bring God and humanity together again. Knowing that he will return to this theme of reconciliation through Christ later on, Eduardo moves forward in his covenantal timeline:

Hasta ahí, la maldad del hombre había subido mucho. Si regreso un poquito al capítulo siete, la maldad, o sea, toda la maldad que Adán y Eva engendraron trajo como consecuencia que a Dios le dolió su corazón haber creado al hombre, y trajo diluvio, ¿recuerda? Y todo ser viviente de carne pereció. Entonces cuando Noé sale del arca en el capítulo 9, Dios se compromete *a su gente* . . . y hasta ahora lo ha cumplido, ¿cierto?

From that point, the evil of humanity had increased a lot. If I backtrack a little to chapter 7, the evil, that is, all the evil that Adam and Eve engendered, brought with it the consequence that God's heart hurt over having created humanity, and he brought the flood, you remember? And every living thing of flesh perished. Then, when Noah comes out of the ark in chapter 9, God commits himself *to his people* . . . and up till now he's kept his promise, right?[37]

On the surface, it appears as though Eduardo is just summing up previous sermons in his series, prior to connecting them into this particular Sunday's sermon, but this brief recapitulation of the flood narrative ends with Eduardo connecting the biblical story to the experiences of his congregants. Eduardo has a microphone on his lapel, allowing him to gesture with both hands as he leads his congregation along on this journey through God's unfolding covenants. When he arrives at the point in the excerpt above in which he speaks of God committing himself *a su gente* / to his people, he extends his left hand toward the congregation as if to indicate that they are these people with whom God is making this new covenant. The connection is further solidified when he asks them to corroborate God's ongoing faithfulness to this commitment by asking, "*¿cierto?* / right?"

As Eduardo segues into the story of Abraham and God's promise to him of multitudinous descendants, it is clear that this is not just an ancient genealogy, but an unfolding story in which the congregation also plays a part. Gradually, Eduardo arrives at the book of Exodus, where he lays out the situation of the Hebrew people in slavery:

Entonces, mira, por cuatrocientos años, ellos trabajan en servidumbre. Miren, eso es 2:23, lo tienen? Los hijos de Israel gemían a causa de la servidumbre y clamaron ¿y que pasó? Subió a Dios el clamor de ellos con motivo de su servidumbre.

Then, look, for four hundred years, they worked in servitude. Look, that is 2:23, do you have it? The children of Israel moaned because of their servitude and cried out, and what happened? Their cries regarding their servitude rose up before God.

¿Cuántas veces hemos clamado a Dios en momentos de dolor y de dificultad, de cosas imposibles, de enfermedad, de muerte, de traición, de peligro, de situaciones semejantes clamamos a Dios? ¿Usted cree que su clamor llega a Dios? ¡Dígame que su clamor llega a Dios! Amén, ¿verdad? Y aunque a usted no le haya respondido, su clamor llega a Dios. Porque Dios ha inclinado su rostro sobre nosotros. Y Dios atendió aquí el clamor de los Hebreos que por cuatrocientos años estaban sobre dura servidumbre.	How many times have we cried out to God in moments of pain and of difficulty, of impossible things, of sickness, of death, of betrayal, of danger, out of those kinds of situations we cry out to God. Do you think that your clamor reaches God? Tell me that your clamor reaches God! Amen, right? And even though he has not responded to you, your clamor reaches God. Because God has inclined his face upon us. And God attended to the clamor of the Hebrews who were under hard servitude for four hundred years.

Eduardo makes the connection between his congregation and the Hebrew people even more explicit in this passage. Just as the Hebrew people cried out in the midst of oppression and servitude, his people know what it means to cry out to God in moments of difficulty. Although Hispanic immigrant congregations are not unique in identifying themselves with the Old Testament nation of Israel, their experiences of immigration and denigration make them especially able to comprehend the situations of pain, difficulty, sickness, death, betrayal, danger, and impossible things out of which one might cry out to God. Recognizing the way in which God responded to the Hebrew people, in spite of those moments when they may have doubted whether their cries were even reaching him, gives Eduardo's congregation hope as well. They affirm through Eduardo's use of call and response that God is attending to their cries as well.

Continuing on in the book of Exodus, Eduardo again connects the identity of his congregation to the Hebrew people. Not only do they know what it means to suffer as the Israelites did, they also share a common destiny grounded in the concept of priesthood:

Y entonces Éxodo 19:5-6 dice . . . estas son las palabras . . . Éxodo 19. Dios empieza a preparar. Y le dice a Israel, escúchenme bien, que ellos fueron llamados, fueron liberados de esclavitud para ser una nación santa y un sacerdocio delante de Dios. ¿Amén?	And then Exodus 19:5-6 says . . . these are the words . . . Exodus 19. God begins to prepare. And he says to Israel, listen to me well, that they were called, were liberated from slavery in order to be a holy nation and a priesthood before God, Amen?

This rhetorical *Amén* provides an immediate segue into Eduardo's exploration of how his congregation, now clearly identified with the similarly long-

suffering Hebrew people, can live out their own identity as this holy nation and priesthood before God:

Su rol en la iglesia, su presencia en la iglesia, sea la edad que tenga, entienda o no, le guste o no—usted ha sido apartado por Dios para ser un sacerdocio delante del Señor. Y usted y yo somos responsables delante de Dios cómo manejamos ese sacerdocio. ¿Amén? Usted y yo tenemos que entender que Dios nos ha puesto aquí con un propósito dentro de nosotros. Jesús dice, "Vosotros sois luz del mundo" y "Vosotros sois sal de la tierra." No somos una casualidad.	Your role in the church, your presence in the church, whatever your age, whether you understand it or not, whether you like it or not—you have been set apart by God in order to be a priesthood before the Lord. And you and I are responsible before God for how we handle that priesthood. Amen? You and I must understand that God has put us here with a purpose inside of us. Jesus says, "You are the light of the world" and "You are the salt of the earth." We are not an accident.

No somos una casualidad / We are not an accident. These words resonate deeply with the members of the community. These community members have a purpose. They are not mere statistics in studies of human migration. They are not primarily a labor force to be used and then cast aside by any number of companies working within the fields of agriculture, construction, or hospitality. They are a chosen people. Living in a nation that chooses not to recognize their personhood and denies them the right to stay within its border to live, work, and raise a family, they instead cling to citizenship within a holy nation whose ruler sees them as valuable members of society.

This new identity as a royal priesthood and a holy nation transcends their migration status and even their country of origin.[38] Eduardo's congregation comprises members of several different nationalities. Eduardo himself is Peruvian, while the majority of his parishioners are from Mexico or Central America. While their cultural and linguistic differences owing to these disparate origins could serve as roadblocks to congregational unity, Eduardo uses the language of Exodus to provide an overarching framework for cohesion. Whatever their differences may be, God is the one who has gathered them together as he did the Hebrew people in the days of Noah, Abraham, and Moses. He has gathered them out of rejection and suffering. He has brought them together from individual isolation and anonymity. They are no longer solely Peruvian, Mexican, Guatemalan, Salvadoran, or Dominican—identities that are sometimes looked down upon in their new country of residence. They are a holy

people whom God has gathered to himself—a people with purpose. They are not an accident.

GOD AS LAWGIVER AND PROVIDER OF STRUCTURE IN THE MIDST OF CHAOS

Of course, God's role as gatherer of his people cannot be separated, either in Scripture or in the proclamation of the Hispanic immigrant church, from his identity as a lawgiver and provider of structure for his newly constituted people. God saves Noah's family from destruction but expects them to live up to their end of a new bargain. Abraham fulfills his portion of the covenant through faithful obedience and the ritual of circumcision. Moses delivers a vastly expanded enumeration of divine law to the Israelites on behalf of the God who has liberated them. Even Ezekiel suggests changed behavior from the newly resurrected nation of Israel through the gift of God's indwelling spirit. God both brings about and confirms the identity of the Israelites as God's people as they follow the moral code they have received. The same can be said of the Hispanic immigrants who find a new identity as a holy nation gathered by God. A close adherence to a new code of moral behavior both confirms the transforming work of God, which allows them to live by such a code, and helps to enact the transformation itself.

In the same sermon in which Pastor Eduardo identified his people with the various Old Testament covenants that God offered to the Hebrew people, he also laid out a case for changed moral behavior as a necessary human obligation in light of God's covenantal offer. Once again, he described the condition of his congregation as symmetrical to that of the Hebrew people:

Entonces, en este caso, los que salen de Egipto no están listos para cumplir ese sacerdocio y por lo tanto Dios los tiene que llevar en un tiempo de purificación. Era necesario. De la misma manera que usted y yo, no? Dios se toma su tiempo con nosotros para que nosotros seamos purificados, para que nosotros crezcamos en el entendimiento, para que nosotros discernamos su voluntad, sus propósitos.	Then, in this case, the ones who leave Egypt are not ready to fulfill that priesthood, and because of that God must take them through a time of purification. It was necessary. In the same way as for you and me, right? God takes his time with us so that we can be purified, so that we can grow in understanding, so that we can discern his will, his purposes.

Eduardo makes clear the connection between being purified and being able successfully to take on the identity of a new holy nation that God offers. The process to which he alludes that leads to greater understanding and discernment is neither short nor easy, as its Old Testament analogue is the forty years

of wandering in the wilderness experienced by the Israelites. But this was necessary then and remains necessary now "for you and me," according to Eduardo.

Living pure lives is not just a prerequisite for the Hispanic immigrant church to realize its identity as a royal priesthood and holy nation fully. It is also a mandatory condition for retaining the blessing of God. Eduardo elaborates:

¿Qué dice el verso 21? "Guárdate delante de él[40] y oye su voz y no le seas rebelde porque él no perdonará vuestra rebelión, porque mi nombre está en él." Dios es Espíritu y Dios es Santo, por eso es Espíritu Santo, ¿Amén? Entonces, ¿Qué es lo que le tocaba hacer a Israel? Oír la voz del ángel de Jehová; oír la voz y guardarse de no hacer nada rebelde.	What does verse 21 say?[39] "Guard yourself before him and listen to his voice and don't be rebellious toward him because he will not forgive your rebellion, because my name is in him." God is Spirit and God is Holy, that is why it is the Holy Spirit, Amen? Therefore, what did Israel have to do? Listen to the voice of the angel of Yahweh; listen to the voice and guard themselves against doing anything rebellious.
¿Qué le toca hacer a usted y a mí? ¿Qué le toca hacer a la iglesia si queremos estar dentro del pacto de Dios? ¡Ayúdame! ¿Qué le toca hacer a la iglesia? ¿Qué le toca hacer a usted y a mí para que nosotros estemos dentro de esta condición del pacto? El Espíritu de Dios está aquí. ¿Qué nos toca a nosotros? Obedecer, obedecer. No seas rebelde a su voz, dice, porque él no perdona la rebeldía. Queremos estar en el pacto de Dios, ¿verdad? Es asunto serio. Ser cristiano es cosa seria.	What do you and I have to do? What does the church have to do if we want to be within God's covenant? Help me! What does the church have to do? What do you and I have to do in order for us to be within this condition of the covenant? The spirit of God is here. What is our part? To obey, to obey. Do not be rebellious to his voice, because he does not pardon rebellion. We want to be in God's covenant, right? It is a serious matter. To be Christian is a serious thing.

"*Guárdate* / Guard yourself," is Eduardo's admonition. The offer of a covenant from God, according to his message, is a conditional one, hinging on the obedience of his people. This is just as true for Eduardo's congregation as it was for the Hebrew people listening to the words of Moses. Eduardo uses parallel constructions to underline this point: "*¿Qué es lo que le tocaba hacer a Israel?*" / "What did Israel have to do?" followed by "*¿Qué le toca hacer a la iglesia?*" / "What does the church have to do?" As if to emphasize the point that this is "*asunto serio*" / "a serious matter," Eduardo asks some version of that question directed *a la iglesia* / to the church, *a usted y a mí* / to you and me, or *a nosotros* / to us no less than five times. He then sums up the answer to all of those

questions in one word, which he repeats twice. What does the church need to do in order to remain with the covenant? *Obedecer* / Obey.

The homiletical emphasis on moral behavior in much Hispanic immigrant proclamation should be understood in light of the community's self-understanding as a people who have been newly gathered by God out of a situation of marginalization and rejection. Timothy L. Smith describes this moral focus as a common feature of immigrant religion. Ideas of "pilgrimage and expectations of personal and cultural change magnified concern for a basis of moral and religious authority that could provide a sense of permanence to those adapting themselves to shifting social realities."[41] In addition to whatever sociological role it may fulfill, however, the Hispanic Protestant church's adherence to a new code of moral behavior serves three primary ecclesial purposes. It is a covenantal obligation that ensures that God will continue to uphold his portion of the bargain. It serves as evidence of the reality of the faith community's status as God's people who have been empowered to live changed lives. Finally, adherence to this new moral code itself enacts the change within the community, transforming members of the church, often radically.

Over the course of my fieldwork, I often heard strongly moralistic preaching. One of my Pentecostal collaborators said that he and most of his colleagues had moved on from the intense *legalismo* / legalism that he remembered in the Pentecostal *concilios* / councils of his childhood. They no longer preached against women's use of makeup or wearing of pants. Indeed, the female members of his congregation were no longer distinguishable—except perhaps in the still-modest cut of their dresses—from any other nicely dressed women at a restaurant. There was still, however, a pervasive attempt within his congregation and those of my other collaborators to delineate the boundaries between the church's values and the surrounding culture. Preaching against the use of drugs or alcohol, which were seen nearly universally as ravaging the families and communities of my collaborators' congregations, was widespread. Other cultural flashpoints were also the focus of homiletical attention. On one particular Sunday at Iglesia Agua Viva when Esteban and Diana were absent, a layperson within the congregation preached a sermon giving an impassioned defense of family values in the face of what he saw as the rapidly advancing secularization of American culture. After having spent some time emphasizing the need for children to honor and obey their parents, he underlined his distrust of American society by pointing to the growing acceptance of homosexuality within the nation. He saw this as a sure sign of the coming apocalypse and the congregants' pressing need to align their lives more fully with scriptural guidelines as he understood them.

Sometimes the moralistic preaching of my collaborators had as much to do with avoiding materialism as it did with resisting secularism. This was the case in one of the more unusual sermons I heard during my fieldwork—a sermon indicting Santa Claus. The preacher in question, Marco, was a college-educated Baptist pastor from Costa Rica. With a background in psychology and clinical counseling, Marco had preached some particularly insightful and liberating messages focused on expanding the role of women in the church and valuing their agency in the home. His intent was to free women within his congregation from the cultural captivity of machismo. During the message in question, however, he was most concerned with his people falling into a new form of cultural captivity related to the suffocating materialism surrounding the celebration of Christmas in the United States. He titled his sermon *"Navidad contra Navidad* / Christmas versus Christmas" and explained in his introduction that there were in fact two Christmases engaged in a protracted conflict. Marco based his message on the text from the second chapter of the Gospel of Luke in which shepherds hear the tidings of the birth of Jesus from a heavenly host of angels and make their way into Bethlehem to see the baby wrapped in cloths and lying in a manger. He hails that moment as the *Monte Everest* / Mount Everest of the entire Bible, which he describes as being centered upon the incarnation of Christ from Genesis to Revelation. Marco talks about the way in which that angelically heralded birth in Bethlehem must be understood, and therefore honored, in its connection to the ministry, death, and resurrection of Christ and their subsequent impact on human salvation.

The birth of Christ was such a momentous event, according to Marco, that from the very beginning there were evil plans afoot to prevent it or blunt its impact:

Al igual que en el jardín de Edén, los demonios, Satanás, el mundo—llámelo quien quiera—había tratado y estuvo tratando de entorpecer el plan de Dios. Haciendo caer a Adán y Eva, el diablo o el mundo estaba tratando de entorpecer el nacimiento de este niño. Jesús era apenas un bebé. Era un bebé que María todavía tenía que alimentar de pecho.

Era un bebé inocente y ya tenía sobre él dos condenas de muerte de parte del mundo. La primera—por ley a María debieron apedrearla por haber quedado encinta fuera del matrimonio

In the same way as in the garden of Eden, the demons, Satan, the world—call it what you will—had tried and were trying to obstruct God's plan. Having caused Adam and Eve to fall, the devil and the world were trying to obstruct the birth of this child. Jesus was still just a baby. He was a baby that Mary still needed to feed from her breast.

He was an innocent baby, and he already had two death sentences on him from the world. The first—by law Mary should have been stoned for having been pregnant outside of marriage

y ni siquiera por el hombre con que ella estaba comprometida. La ley decía que María tenía que morir y con María tenía que morir el niño que tenía en su vientre—porque era fruto del pecado.

Eso era la primera condena de muerte y la segunda, el Rey Herodes—que podríamos representar hoy en día con los reyes, el orgullo de nosotros como seres humanos, nuestra soberbia, nuestro deseo de tener siempre más. En el Rey Herodes, vemos a un hombre que fue capaz, cuando le habían engañado, de mandar a matar a todos los niños varones de menos de dos años de esa región para callar a este niño.

and not even by the man with whom she was engaged. The law said that Mary had to die and with Mary the baby she had in her womb had to die—because he was the fruit of sin.

That was the first death sentence and the second, King Herod—whom we can represent today with the kings, with our pride as human beings, our arrogance, our desire always to have more. In King Herod, we see a man who was capable, when they tricked him, of ordering all the male children less than two years old to be killed.

Having equated the figure of Herod with contemporary humanity's pride and greed, Marco encourages the congregation to imagine what it must have been like for families whose homes were violently breached by soldiers who then murdered their little boys right in front of them. As the congregation struggles to process this disturbing image, Marco stresses that just as people back then went to great and terrible lengths to quiet Jesus, they are doing the same thing today. How does the world do this today? Marco offers an allegorical critique:

Imaginemos que acerca el cumpleaños de un amigo y queremos hacer una gran fiesta. Entonces vamos y alquilamos un salón de cinco estrellas y compramos comida—cantidades industriales de comida—y bebidas. Y contratamos un DJ con lo último en música y luces inteligentes y empieza la fiesta por el cumpleaños de nuestro amigo.

Toda la noche de fiesta, comemos, bebemos, bailamos, hacemos karaoke, nos divertimos, tomamos fotos y selfies. Queremos recordar todo porque esta es la fiesta del año. Todo fue excelente. El único detalle fue que nuestro amigo no vino porque nadie lo invitó.

Let us imagine that the birthday of a friend is drawing near and we want to put together a great party. So, we go and rent a five-star ballroom and buy food—industrial quantities of food—and drinks. And we hire a DJ with the latest in music and programmed lights, and the party starts for the birthday of our friend.

All through the night of the party, we eat, we drink, we dance, we sing karaoke, we have fun, we take pictures and selfies. We want to remember everything because this is the party of the year. Everything was excellent. The one detail was that our friend did not come because no one invited him.

Qué raro, ¿no? Pero eso es lo que está pasando con la navidad hoy en día. Es la fiesta más grande, la más hermosa, pero no estamos invitando a aquél que es el centro de esa fiesta.	How strange, right? But that is what is happening these days with Christmas. It is the biggest, most beautiful party, but we are not inviting the one who is the center of that party.

Marco then elaborates further on his allegory by supposing that instead of inviting our friend whose birthday should serve as the focus of this celebration, we instead bring out *Tontín* (the Spanish name of Dopey the dwarf from the classic Disney movie *Snow White*). He actually pulls out a plush two-foot tall figure of *Tontín* from behind the pulpit at this point and mimics the people at this imagined party embracing him and posing for selfies next to him. He describes the way people buy T-shirts with pictures of *Tontín* and come to the party wearing the same style cap that he wears. Everyone comes to our friend's party and celebrates *Tontín* instead. In case anyone has missed the context of his thinly veiled allegory, Marco presses forward:

¿Se oye? A mí me parece medio tonto eso, ¿verdad? Pero si vemos lo que están haciendo con la navidad hoy en día, no sólo están tratando de sacar al personaje principal de la navidad sino además están sustituyéndole por otro ser imaginario, que no existe, que es tan real como este muñeco. ¿Cómo se llama?	Did you catch that? To me it seems somewhat foolish, right? But if we look at what they are doing these days with Christmas, they are not only trying to remove the central character of Christmas but rather are also substituting him with another being, an imaginary one who doesn't exist, who is just as real as this doll. What is his name?

A voice in the sanctuary calls out "Santa Claus" in a Mexican accent. Although historically he has been known more commonly in Latin America as *San Nicolás* / Saint Nicholas or *Papá Noel* / Father Christmas, "Santa Claus" is the name he bears in the marketing campaigns that inundate the United States in the months leading up to Christmas. It is this secular marketing of Christmas as the sole domain of Santa Claus that Marco designates as the chief threat displacing Jesus in the present. The war on Christmas through his eyes has nothing to do with adherents of political correctness superimposing their "Happy Holidays" over the more traditional "Merry Christmas" and everything to do with North American Christians replacing their own Christ with a figure no more significant than Dopey the dwarf.

As Marco continues to describe the war between these two Christmases, he critiques parents who overspend on Christmas gifts while investing little time

and energy in the spiritual formation of their children. Functionally, according to Marco, his hearers become accomplices of the modern-day Herods who now silence the message of Jesus not through violence, but through a commercially minded game of bait-and-switch. There is no grey area in the invitation he offers—to celebrate one Christmas or another. But the stakes are, in fact, far higher than that. The choice before the congregation is to stay within the bounds established by God for their newly constituted identity as his people or to lose that identity within the *consumismo* / consumerism of American society. The preaching of my collaborators often harshly attacked the threats of hedonism, secularism, and materialism as forms of idolatry that threatened to erase the identity of their congregations by disrupting the moral codes binding them together.

GOD AS HEALER OF THE FAMILY

During my interviews, I asked each of my collaborators about the themes they most frequently addressed in their preaching. *La salvación* / salvation was their most common answer, one shared by nearly all of them. Their second most common answer, by far, was *la familia* / the family. Leo's response reflected that of many of my other collaborators as well. After talking about the need for preaching about salvation and instructing new believers in doctrine, he turned his attention to the needs of families within his congregation and gave his most extended and impassioned response:

> También hay que predicar sobre puntos familiares—el hogar, el matrimonio. A veces pienso que lo estoy empujando mucho. Tenemos que reconstruir nuestras relaciones, nuestras familias. Es un asunto muy importante por los Hispanos.

> Also, one must preach about points related to the family—the home, marriage. Sometimes I think that I am pushing it a lot. We must reconstruct our relationships, our families. It is a very important affair for Hispanics.

Just as my collaborators often preached about God's reconstitution of them as a people and a community within the church, they also proclaimed God's desire to reconstitute their individual families whose bonds had often been broken or strained by the stresses of migration and immigrant life. In chapter three, I discussed the frequency with which my collaborators experienced separation from their parents, but their familial difficulties certainly did not stop there. Sara, a Baptist associate pastor in a more established congregation, shared her story of just how desperate her family situation was prior to her conversion. She and her father had paid a coyote to bring them across the river

from Mexico in 1982, but after their eventual arrival in Florida, everything had gone wrong:

Yo tenía diecisiete años. Yo no tenía ropa, hermano. No tenía casa. A mi papá se lo llevó la migra a los ocho días de haber llegado. Y me quedé sola. Una niña de diecisiete años con una familia allí que no me hablaba. No tenía ropa. No conocía el dinero. No conocía a nadie. A mí me duele todavía. Yo les digo esto a mis hijos. Yo no puedo controlar mis lágrimas. Había una señora que me daba ropa. Ella me daba ropa y me dejaba usar sus vestidos. Conocí a mi esposo y dos meses más tarde, yo me fui con él. Salí con él para escapar de esa situación.	I was seventeen years old. I did not have clothes, brother. I did not have a house. Immigration took my dad away eight days after we arrived. And I was left alone. A seventeen-year-old girl with a family there that did not speak to me. I did not have clothes. I did not understand money. I did not know anyone. It still hurts me. I tell this to my children. I cannot control my tears. There was a lady who gave me clothes. She gave me clothes and she let me use her dresses. I met my [future] husband and two months later, I went away with him. I left with him to escape that situation.

In spite of Sara's hope that leaving with her future husband would bring her greater stability and prosperity, the first six years of her new domestic arrangement were chaotic and painful. She clearly attributed the familial discord of that period to the absence of Christianity in their lives.

No conocíamos a Cristo en aquel tiempo. En los primeros seis años con mi esposo, nosotros nos separamos dos veces. Porque yo en mi casa había visto violencia con mis padres. Mi papá abusaba de mi mamá, golpeándola, teniendo relaciones afuera. Y yo siempre dije, "Yo no quiero eso para mí." Mi mamá siempre me decía, "Es por Uds." Yo dije, "Aunque tenga hijos, no voy a soportar esto." Cuando mi esposo tomaba—ellos perdieron a su mamá cuando estaban pequeños, mi esposo tenía once años cuando perdieron a su mamá. A su papá no le importaba porque el mismo les daba de cerveza.	We did not know Christ at that time. In the first six years with my husband, we separated two times. Because I had seen violence in my house with my parents. My dad abused my mother, hitting her, having affairs outside of the home. And I always said, "I do not want that for myself." My mom always said to me, "It is for you all." I said, "Even if I have children, I will not put up with this." When my husband drank—they lost their mom when they were little, my husband was eleven years old when they lost their mom. Their dad did not care; he himself gave them beer.
En esos seis años no conociendo a Dios, no había nadie, hermano, quien nos diera consejo. No había quien nos	In those six years not knowing God, there was no one, brother, who could give us counsel. There was no one who

sentara y dijera, "Eso es así." Mis papás no estaban aquí conmigo. Estaban en México. El papá de él, nada hermano, era un descontrol. Yo dije a mi esposo, "Si tu no te compones, no puedo vivir así."	could sit us down and say, "It's like this." My parents were not here with me. They were in Mexico. His dad, nothing, brother, he was out of control. I said to my husband, "If you do not improve, I cannot live like this."

At that time, Sara and her husband were still migrating between North Carolina and Florida. They would spend six months in North Carolina during tobacco season and then six months in Florida working for tomato growers. This vocational transience, combined with the self-destructive and abusive behavior of Sara's husband, the low pay they received for their labor, and the needs of their now-expanding family, was pushing Sara to the breaking point:

No teníamos nada aquí. Alguien nos dio permiso de parquear el carro en su yarda. Mi casa era mi carro con mi niña de dos meses. Mi esposo no dejaba de tomar. Pero después de conocer a Cristo mi esposo dejó de tomar. Jamás tomó otra vez una cerveza. Y así fue como cambió nuestra vida. Empezamos a ir a la iglesia. No somos una familia perfecta, pero le echamos ganas para adelante.	We did not have anything here. Someone gave us permission to park the car in their yard. My house was my car with my two-month-old girl. My husband did not stop drinking. But after coming to know Christ, my husband stopped drinking. He never again drank a beer. And that is how our life changed. We started to go to church. We are not a perfect family, but we do our best to move forward.

It was stunning to me during our interview how quickly Sara moved from describing her family's dysfunction and poverty to its sudden transformation rooted in their conversion to Protestant Christianity. Indeed, in her recounting of the event, the most immediate effects of their spiritual awakening were experienced in their domestic life. Her husband's substance abuse ended both at once and permanently. As it had been the primary factor behind domestic abuse and infidelity, these issues also were curtailed. In Sara's experience, coming to know God through Christ had brought dramatic healing to her family. Her family had been so thoroughly transformed that her children only knew of the difficulties their parents once faced through Sara's occasional retellings of their preconversion troubles. These kinds of powerful experiences of familial transformation, whether personal or within their congregations, often underlie my collaborators' sermons dealing with marriage and family issues.

Even in sermons not directly dealing with family issues, the importance of family for my collaborators was still paramount. This was the case in one of Antonio's sermons dealing with the faith Abram exhibited in following God's direction to set out for an unknown land:

A Abram le dijo, "Vete de tu tierra, vete de tu parentela, de la casa de tu padre a la tierra que te mostraré." ¿Debía de irse de quién? Debía de irse de su propia tierra. Debía de irse de sus propios padres. Y quizás tú digas, "¿Cómo es posible que un Dios bueno sea capaz de alejarme de mis propios padres?"	To Abraham, he said, "Go away from your land, go away from your kin, from the house of your father to the land I will show you." From whom was he supposed to go away? He was supposed to go away from his own land. He was supposed to go away from his own parents. And perhaps you are saying, "How is it possible that a good God could be capable of taking me away from my own parents?"

The primary conundrum for Antonio in this passage was that a good God might disrupt the relationships of a family. In my interview with him, Antonio, a Baptist preacher who had already pastored several congregations, emphasized the importance of preaching about family issues. Perhaps some of this was the result of the separation from his own father he had experienced as a young man. In the previous chapter, Antonio also shared poignantly about the stress his own family had experienced as a result of his extensive secular work and ministry obligations. Having suffered strained and ruptured relationships as both a son and a father, Antonio paused in his exploration of Abram's faith to wrestle with the implications of God separating a family in the twelfth chapter of Genesis.

His primary argument to justify God's action came from Joshua 24:2, which describes Terah and the rest of Abram's ancestors as worshippers of idols. After having laid out this charge against Terah, Antonio continued:

Ahora podemos entender con más claridad porque Dios dijo a Abram, "Vete de tu tierra, vete de tu parentela, de la casa de tu padre."	Now we can understand with more clarity why God said to Abram, "Go away from your land, go away from your kin, from the house of your father."

From this point on, Antonio continued with his larger point that having faith means leaving behind the things that hinder us. First, however, it had been exceedingly important for him to make sure that his hearers understood that

God would not lightly involve himself in the disruption of a family. No less a sin than idol worship could justify such an action.

During one of his sermons at Iglesia Agua Viva, Esteban urged his hearers to understand the time committed to their families as part of the requirement for living a godly life. His text for the morning was Matthew 6:33, in which Jesus instructs his followers to *"buscad primeramente el reino de Dios y su justicia y todas estas cosas os serán añadidas*[42] / seek first the kingdom of God and his righteousness and all these things will be added to you." After reading the text, Esteban began to speak of how difficult it was to fulfill this command in a world that placed so many demands on his time and the times of his congregation:

Vivimos en un mundo que gira en torno de nuestros quehaceres y nuestras actividades diarias. Sabemos que en un día completo está distribuido lo que nosotros llamamos el día y la noche el cual está designado a sólo veinticuatro horas. El problema es que este tiempo no es suficiente para nosotros. Nos gustaría añadir algunas horas más a nuestro tiempo. Sabemos que nos fue otorgado una cantidad de horas por día para saber emplear nuestro tiempo. El problema es que, en lo práctico, lo invertimos mal y desperdiciamos este tiempo.	We live in a world that revolves around our chores and our daily activities. We know that in a complete day there is distributed what we call the day and the night, to which is designated only twenty-four hours. The problem is that this amount of time is not sufficient for us. We would like to add some more hours to our time. We know that we have been granted a quantity of hours each day in order to know how to employ our time. The problem is that, in practice, we invest it badly and waste this time.

Esteban began to speak about the difficulty of setting priorities in our lives so as to be able to seek first the kingdom of God and his righteousness. But within this discussion, he paused to remind his congregation that seeking God's kingdom was not to be done at the expense of spending time with one's family—not even for a pastor:

Hay algo muy importante que yo he tenido que aprender como ministro del Señor, como obrero del Señor, y es de apartar el tiempo necesario para dedicar a mi familia. Es tan difícil cuando tenemos que prepararnos en los mensajes, tenemos que visitar al hermano, tenemos que hacer tantas	There is something very important that I have had to learn as a minister of the Lord, as a worker for the Lord, and it is to take the time necessary to dedicate to my family. It is so difficult when we must prepare ourselves with our messages, we have to visit a brother, we have to do so many things. But

cosas. Pero al mismo tiempo, tengo unos hijos que necesitan jugar baloncesto conmigo, tengo una esposa que necesita un tiempo dedicado para hablar conmigo.

¿Cómo podemos distribuir este tiempo? Necesitamos buscar la dirección de Dios para saber dónde tienen que estar nuestras prioridades. Y las prioridades deben estar en su lugar correcto. Hay un orden que Dios emplea, que Dios manda—está Dios, la familia, y el ministerio. Y es necesario que, como pastor, tenga yo muy claro entender lo que es dedicarle para mis hijos, mi familia, mi esposa.

at the same time, I have children who need to play basketball with me, I have a spouse who needs some dedicated time to speak with me.

How can we distribute this time? We need to seek out God's direction in order to know where our priorities need to be. And the priorities should be in the correct place. There is an order that God employs, that God commands—there is God, the family, and the ministry. And it is necessary that, as a pastor, I have a very clear understanding of what it is to dedicate [time] for my children, my family, my wife.

As Esteban spoke of a God-ordained order for time management, he gestured with his hands, demonstrating the place of time spent with God as the highest of priorities, followed by the family, and then his ministry activities. Then he proceeded, offering himself as an example, to stress the importance of spending time with family over all forms of work, including working for the Lord:

El tiempo para familia es muy importante. Yo pudiera tener éxito como pastor. Pudiera ser el pastor más conocido del mundo entero, tener la congregación más grande que pueda tener en todos los estados unidos, pero ¿qué sería si mi familia fracasa? ¿Si mi matrimonio, si mi hogar fracasa porque yo no supe emplear mi tiempo correctamente?

Todo lo demás seguiría a la ruina. No tendría sentido yo estar pastoreando. No tendría sentido yo estar trabajando en el ministerio si yo no supiera darle lo que es el tiempo adecuado para mi familia. Si eso cae, si mi familia—mi hogar—se derrumba entonces hay un fracaso en mi vida. Como padre estaría arruinado. Como esposo sería un fracaso.

Family time is very important. I could have success as a pastor. I could be the best-known pastor in the entire world, have the biggest congregation that one could have in the United States, but what would I be if my family fails? If my marriage, if my home fails because I did not know how to employ my time correctly?

Everything else would go to ruin. It would not make sense for me to be pastoring. It would not make sense for me to be working in ministry if I do not know how to give adequate time to my family. If that falls apart, if my family—my home—collapses, then there has been a failure in my life. As a father, I would be ruined. As a husband, I would be a failure.

After hearing Esteban preach that day, I asked him why he had emphasized family issues so strongly during that particular message. He responded that he emphasized the family and the home as often as he could in every message. Then he shared with me a story he had included in another recent sermon that he found particularly moving:

Quizás tú has escuchado la historia del padre que siempre trabajaba largas horas. Un día, su hijo pequeño le preguntó, "¿Papa, cuánto dinero ganas al año?" El padre respondió, diciéndole, "Hijo, eso uno no se le pregunta a alguien." Pero el niño insistió, y finalmente, su padre le dijo. Entonces, el hijo le preguntó otra vez, "Y ¿cuánto ganas al mes?" Otra vez su padre le respondió. El niño continuó, "¿A la semana?" "Al día?" y su papá siguió contestándole. Finalmente, el niño preguntó, "¿Pues, cuánto dinero ganas por hora?" Su papá dijo. "Once dólares."

El niño fue a su cuarto y regresó en unos minutos con un puñado de monedas y algunos billetes arrugados y dijo, "Aquí están once dólares. Rompí mi cerdito para sacarlos. Quiero comprar una hora de tu tiempo para que la pases conmigo."

Maybe you have heard the story of the father who always worked long hours. One day, his young son asked him, "Daddy, how much money do you earn in a year?" The father responded, saying to him, "Son, you don't ask someone that." But the boy insisted, and finally, his father told him. Then the son asked again, "And how much do you make in a month?" Again, his father answered him. The boy continued, "In a week?" "In a day" and his dad continued to answer him. Finally, the boy asked, "Well, how much money do you make per hour?" His dad said, "Eleven dollars."

The boy went to his room and returned in a few minutes with a fistful of coins and few crumpled bills and said, "Here are eleven dollars. I broke my piggy bank to get them out. I want to buy an hour of your time so that you spend it with me."

Esteban had tears in his eyes as he came to the end of his story. He patted me on the shoulder and said, "Eso es tocante, hermano / That is touching, brother."[43] It was clear that Esteban felt deeply what he had preached to his congregation—that no amount of success outside of his home could make up for strained relationships within his own family. Like most of my collaborators, Esteban preached the value of family as second only to spiritual conversion itself.

CONCLUSION

In *Latino Protestants in America: Growing and Diverse*, Mark T. Mulder, Aida I. Ramos, and Gerardo Martí pose the question of "whether there is anything truly 'indigenous' to Latino Protestantism in the United States."[44] They take specific musical forms into consideration when evaluating that question, but my research indicates that the preaching of Hispanic Protestants, especially of first-generation immigrants, may also reveal an indigenous element. Whether consciously or not, the majority of Hispanic preachers with whom I worked read and interpreted scripture quite specifically in light of their overlapping immigration and conversion experiences. The God whom they encountered during migration is the one whom they proclaim. The gospel that resonated with them during their dislocation and marginalization is the one they share with their churches. This did not mean, however, that they approached the preaching task in the manner described by Justo González and Pablo Jiménez in *Manual de Homilética Hispana* and *Púlpito*. That style of preaching, oriented toward social and political liberation, was foreign to most of my collaborators, opening them up to González' critique that their preaching is somehow less contextually faithful to Hispanic immigrant reality.

The life experiences and proclamation of my collaborators prove that contextual faithfulness within Hispanic Protestant congregations may take on different forms. Far from engaging in disembodied forms of exegesis and preaching that had been imposed upon them by the dominant culture, the preachers participating in this study focused on themes with direct relevance to their lived experiences and what they perceived to be the needs of their immigrant congregations. My collaborators preached about the opportunity to have a personal relationship with Christ not only because of its emphasis within Anglo American Protestantism but because *conociendo a Cristo* / knowing Christ was a theme that resonated deeply for themselves and their congregations due to the isolation and loss of identity many of them suffered over the course of their journeys of migration. Their personal testimonies of God's miracle-working power at work in their own lives led them to preach hope to their parishioners who frequently faced seemingly insurmountable obstacles, which were often caused or exacerbated by their immigration status. My collaborators shared that the God who had brought them healing, deliverance, and restoration could do the same for their hearers as well. They looked to Old Testament passages in which they saw echoes of their own experience as a reconstituted people who had journeyed through the wilderness and found a new identity together as the church. This identity transcended their original nationalities and provided them with a sense of belonging despite the rejection they often faced. Inhabiting a very different cultural landscape, my collaborators found comfort and stability in the moral doctrine of scripture, which served as a bulwark against the eroding powers of the surrounding culture. Finally, they preached about the importance of family in order to help their congregants who were always in the process of reuniting with family members, renegotiating family connections, and trying to establish new traditions of family togetherness without the same presence of extended families that many of their hearers had enjoyed in their countries of origin.

Although the title of this chapter describes its intended focus as *la predicación misma* / the preaching itself, there can be no distillation of Hispanic immigrant preaching to that degree. The preaching of my collaborators was always integrally connected to their lived faith and their immigrant experiences. They proclaimed God as they had come to know him in the crucible of immigration, and their preaching resonated in the hearts of their hearers who had come, consciously or unconsciously, in search of just such a gospel.

5

Predicadoras / Female Preachers

I n the previous chapter, I explored the way in which the preaching I observed during my research was thoroughly grounded in the experiences of Hispanic immigrants, even if it did not adhere precisely to the model of authenticity advanced by Justo González and Pablo Jiménez in *Púlpito* and *Manual de Homilética Hispana*. I also highlighted the ways in which this preaching was both liberative and restorative in addressing the wounds of immigration that both the preachers and their audiences suffered. The liberation my collaborators imagined was, first and foremost, a spiritual liberation from sin. But it was also a personal and communal liberation from the anonymity, powerlessness, isolation, and instability attending their immigrant journeys. In these regards, the preaching of both the female and male preachers who collaborated in my research was remarkably similar. The female preachers, however, faced additional hurdles in their ministry that helped shape the content of their proclamation. In many ways their preaching, while still often being traditional, came closest to the ideal described by González and Jiménez. They preached a liberating word for women both in ministry and in their families and a restorative message for women whose immigrant experiences had also included abuse of various kinds. To begin this exploration of the unique experiences and messages of my female collaborators, I start with the woman whose preaching I heard most often—Pastora Diana of Iglesia Agua Viva (IAV).

I had already heard Pastor Esteban preach several messages before I heard his wife and *co-pastora* Diana preach for the first time. Esteban was always animated and dynamic in his sermon delivery, but in my conversations with the two of them, it was clear that Diana was an even more energetic communicator. She typically spoke with great intensity, leaning in and gesturing with her hands. In my early conversations with all of my collaborators, I tended to use humor as a way to move past initial awkwardness, and Diana always rewarded my attempts with a laugh so loud that it had the effect of drowning out any other conversations taking place in the same room. I was looking forward to seeing the way in which her personality came through in her proclamation as I walked into Agua Viva's sanctuary for one of their Thursday evening services and settled into the back row. One of the laywomen was leading the extemporaneous time of prayer that preceded all of IAV's services. Afterward, a worship team composed mainly of teenagers led the congregation through nearly twenty minutes of worship choruses, at the end of which Diana offered an impassioned prayer for the blessing of God and her own discernment for the word she was about to share. When I opened my eyes, I saw her standing to the side of the pulpit and resting her left hand upon it. This was Diana's most frequent position for preaching, possibly because if this diminutive woman were to stand behind the pulpit, it would almost entirely obscure her from the congregation's view.

Diana stands just over five feet tall and is quite petite. For church services, she usually pulled her voluminous curly dark hair back with a clip or into a bun. When she preached, she was more likely to wear a business suit than a dress, emphasizing her professionalism. Her messages were typically more structured than those of her husband, although she often improvised as she expounded the various points of the outline she was following. She referred to her notes only sparingly as she moved continually from one side of the pulpit to the other, occasionally descending the steps from the platform and approaching the congregation as a way of drawing them into her discourse. She gestured not only with her hands but with the full length of her body, crouching and leaning forward to convey the importance of a particular insight before straightening back up as a visual cue that she was about to transition to her next point.

The congregation followed her with their eyes from left to right, up and down, nodding their heads and speaking their assent through the occasional "¡Aleluya!" or "Amén." Their openness and verbal assent to her proclamation mirrored their response to Esteban's preaching. Indeed, in their ministry, Esteban and Diana appeared to function in a nearly interchangeable manner, reflecting the way they understood the calling they had received from God. Diana described their calling like this:

Tenemos un llamado especial. Siempre hemos trabajado juntos.	We have a special calling. We have always worked together.

In spite of this egalitarian description of their ministerial calling, Esteban was initially resistant to the idea of pastoral ministry. Esteban and Diana had worked together as volunteers, first in their church in an immigrant community in Brooklyn and then in a larger Pentecostal church in the suburbs of Raleigh about half an hour from their home. During this time, they noticed that there were very few congregations ministering to Hispanic immigrants in their own community. Diana was sure that God was calling them to plant a new congregation:

Cuando yo sentí el llamado de empezar una obra, Esteban no estaba listo. Pero yo lo sentí y cuando meditaba sobre ello, me venían las lágrimas.

La palabra dice que tiene que someterse al sacerdocio de la casa, quien es el hombre. Y por ejemplo en nuestra área hispana, cuando una mujer se levanta a responder al llamado a ser pastor, muchos usan el texto fuera del contexto. Hay que someternos, pero no a las cosas malas. Hay que someternos, pero a las cosas buenas y tratar de ponernos de acuerdo y llegar a un acuerdo para llevar acabo algo.

Oré al señor que él trabajara en mi esposo. Esteban todavía sentía un poco de temor, pero cuando Dios da un llamado, él respalda, y yo sentía una convicción que él iba a estar allí.

When I felt the call to begin a new work, Esteban was not ready. But I felt it and when I meditated upon it, I would cry.

The Word says that you have to submit yourself to the priesthood of the house, who is the man. And, for example, in our Hispanic context, when a woman rises up to respond to the calling to be pastor, many people use the text out of context. We do have to submit, but not to bad things. We do have to submit, but to good things and to try to agree and reach an accord to carry something out.

I prayed to the Lord that he would work in my husband. Esteban still felt a little fear, but when God gives you a call, he backs it up, and I felt a conviction that he was going to be there.

Diana's response highlighted the unique difficulties faced by my seven female collaborators as they entered the ministry. For many of them, an individual calling was not sufficient, even if their sense of the necessity of their calling was powerful enough to make them cry. In what Diana described as her "Hispanic context," the interpretation of particular passages of Scripture often raised difficulties for women who wanted to preach. Some of my collaborators were able to overcome these hurdles through liberative biblical interpretation at the congregational level or greater flexibility within their specific denominations that permitted women to engage in new forms of vocational ministry. Others benefited from the pneumatological emphasis of their churches or the power of their own testimonies. Still others were able to ease their way into ministry alongside a spouse, as Diana ultimately did. All of them, to one degree or another, affirmed the truth of what Diana said: when God gives you a call, he backs it up.

LIBERATIVE READINGS OF SCRIPTURE

In the fall of 2013, I was just beginning my participant-observation at Iglesia Agua Viva, and I was particularly interested in their practices of biblical interpretation. In addition to attending multiple worship services and Bible studies, I also conducted a series of focus group conversations with laypeople in the congregation. Pastor Esteban organized these groups for me according to gender,[1] so, for one of my conversations, I found myself with four men—Vicente, Osvaldo, Raimundo, and José—in a small classroom behind the sanctuary. At one point during this focus group, as we were discussing the resources these men employed to understand Scripture, one of them spoke of the significant interpretive guidance provided to them by both *el pastor y la pastora* / "the pastor and the pastor" in both masculine and feminine form. The other men around the table quickly voiced their agreement. When I asked them whether they accepted guidance from *el pastor* and *la pastora* in equal measure, they all answered affirmatively. All the men in this group had been born in Latin America and immigrated to the United States as adults. At the very least, they had brought with them to Iglesia Agua Viva some degree of *machismo* when it came to their understanding of gender roles and female leadership,[2] even if these attitudes existed only as "residuals."[3] In the case of Iglesia Agua Viva, these residuals related to gender roles were borne within the people themselves and had been carried, in some cases, for thousands of miles. Recent studies conducted by the Pew Research Center have shown that Hispanics in the United States are less likely than the overall population to accept traditional gender roles in marriage and family.[4] Protestant Hispanics, however, are more likely than Catholic Hispanics to hew toward traditionalism in this regard, with a majority of Hispanics who identify as evangelical agreeing with the statement that "a husband should have the final say in family matters."[5] Yet somehow, even in this ecclesial setting marked by a certain traditionalism, male congregants had connected with and developed respect for a female pastor. This occurred not in spite of their involvement with their congregation, but directly because of it. Their journey serves as a reminder that conservative traditionalism has its own resources to be liberative.

I wondered what connections might exist between the four men's practices of scriptural interpretation and their acceptance of Diana's pastoral ministry, so I asked, "*Cómo entienden Uds. el liderazgo de las mujeres en su iglesia al lado de las palabras de Pablo acerca de las mujeres en las primeras epístolas a Timoteo y a los corintios?* / How do you make sense of the leadership of women in your church alongside Paul's words concerning women in the first epistles to Timothy and to the Corinthians?"[6] The members of Iglesia Agua Viva were sufficiently acquainted with Scripture that I did not need to specify the passages to which I was referring. They knew them well, but I was interested to hear how these men, who up to that point in our conversation generally had favored a literal interpretation of all Scripture, would deal with the prohibitive nature of these texts. In response to my question, the conversation suddenly became more animated than it had been previously. Osvaldo immediately pointed to the distinction in 1 Timothy between what Paul characterizes as directives from God and what Paul himself permits. He then said this:

Tenemos que entender las palabras de Pablo en su contexto cultural. Estaba escribiendo a personas que tenían una baja opinión de las mujeres, y sus palabras podrían ser diferentes si estuviera escribiendo hoy.	We must understand Paul's words within their cultural context. He was writing to people who had a low opinion of women, and his words might be different if he were writing today.

Although these men all usually advocated for a plain-sense reading of Scripture, Osvaldo's words showed that they also understood the importance of contextual nuance. Their own shifting situations and locations have never afforded them the privilege of a stringent literalism tied to every letter of the text. Raimundo went a step further than Osvaldo, raising the possibility that these particular words might not be the product of divine inspiration but of Paul's potential chauvinism. Then he paused and asked, "*¿Por qué debemos tratar estas palabras de manera diferente al consejo de Pablo de no casarnos?* / Why should we treat these words any differently than Paul's advice not to marry?" He summed up his thoughts succinctly: "*Esto es comentario; no es ley.* / This is commentary; it is not law." The other men all nodded in agreement.

Then the conversation shifted to scriptural examples of women who had been used by God in unexpected ways. Osvaldo lifted up the example of the Samaritan woman by the well as the first evangelist in the gospel narratives. Raimundo spoke of Deborah's dual role as prophet and judge. Nearly interrupting him, José jumped in, affirming the calling of women because God had chosen women specifically as the first witnesses in the resurrection narratives. Osvaldo then recalled that there was an Old Testament passage in which a man died without sons and God directed Moses to distribute the man's inheritance to his two daughters just as it would have been given to sons.[7] Having sat silently up to this point, Vicente now spoke up and began to discuss a story he had seen on television recently about three women who had graduated from Marine infantry training. He offered this up as a story of how much things were changing in our own country, and how the difficulty that some people were having with this change was similar to the resistance toward women preaching or providing congregational leadership. This led him to make the following hermeneutical observation:

Es un mundo diferente. Si las mujeres hubieran trabajado fuera del hogar cuando Pablo estaba escribiendo, todos las habrían aceptado como predicadoras también.	It is a different world. If women had worked outside the home when Paul was writing, everyone would have accepted them as preachers too.

Once again, the men were in agreement about this contextualized interpretation of Pauline prohibitions. Raimundo, however, wanted to make sure that I understood that their acceptance of Diana was not simply based on their social location. What had occurred at Iglesia Agua Viva was not merely a change of opinion but a recognition of divine prerogative:

Al final, es el espíritu que confirma a las personas.	Ultimately, it is the spirit that confirms people.

THE HOLY SPIRIT AND CHANGING DENOMINATIONAL ATTITUDES

Raimundo's recognition of the Holy Spirit's role in opening doors for women in ministry is not unusual in Protestant churches, especially those that are part of Pentecostal movements or denominations. Three of my seven female collaborators were from Pentecostal churches. Linda and her husband, Álvaro, pastored two separate congregations affiliated with the Assemblies of God. Ana was the founding pastor of a church within the Iglesia de Dios Pentecostal Movimiento Internacional. Diana had been a member and volunteer within several Pentecostal denominations, but the church that she and Esteban copastored was nondenominational. In spite of this status, they still participated in a loose alliance with multiple other Hispanic Pentecostal congregations including those led by Linda and Ana. Of the other four women, all currently attending and preaching in United Methodist and Baptist churches, three had close ties to Pentecostalism as well. One had converted to Protestantism in a Pentecostal congregation in Mexico. The other two, both Baptists, served alongside male pastors who had been Pentecostal before later identifying as Baptist. All of these women found at least part of their legitimation in their church's or denomination's views of the Holy Spirit. Loida Martell-Otero emphasizes the importance of the Holy Spirit for Latina Protestants who, in general, believe that "the Spirit is the One who not only empowers women but also legitimizes their calling—an important role for those whose voices are often suppressed within patriarchal and racist social and ecclesial structures."[8] For my female collaborators, both the three who pastored specifically Pentecostal congregations and the others who, along with many of their parishioners, had been deeply influenced by Pentecostalism along their journeys of faith,[9] Pentecostal pneumatology contributed to this liberative view of the Holy Spirit. Leah Payne points to Pentecostalism's understanding of the Holy Spirit's role as creating space for women. This understanding was grounded in their interpretation of biblical passages such as Joel 2:28-29:

> Then afterward
> I will pour out my spirit on all flesh;
> your sons and your daughters shall prophesy,
> your old men shall dream dreams,
> and your young men shall see visions.
> Even on the male and female slaves,
> in those days, I will pour out my spirit.

Carrie Judd Montgomery and Alma White, both early Pentecostal preachers, argued explicitly that they "were the prophetic daughters of Joel 2."[10] Both women and men in Pentecostal movements also confirm their identity as recipients of the baptism of the Holy Spirit through displays of the Spirit's power, including *glossolalia*, or speaking in tongues.[11] At an institutional level, the Assemblies of God offered this affirmation of women in ministry through its *Weekly Evangel* in 1916:

> If a woman gave birth to our Lord, why not her daughters take part in His great work? Men have hypocritically objected to women making themselves conspicuous in pulpit work, but, thank God, this conspicuousness is of God Himself. They did not push themselves to the front, God *pulled* them there.[12]

With its liberative understanding of the Holy Spirit's role from both Scripture and praxis, Pentecostalism, in its earliest days, provided many more opportunities than other contemporary Protestant denominations for women to preach and pastor congregations.[13] During the early part of the twentieth century, nationally known Pentecostal preachers such as Maria Woodworth-Etter and Aimee Semple McPherson rose to prominence as they employed "revivalist methods infused with popular notions of womanhood, and combined with Pentecostal biblical and theological tropes and sensibilities."[14] In positions and places offering far less visibility, many other pioneering female Pentecostal preachers similarly broke new ground. Unfortunately for those women pursuing the call to ministry, this era of expanded opportunity did not last very long. Charles H. Barfoot and Gerald T. Sheppard point to Max Weber's analysis that religious organizations "react against pneumatic manifestations of charisma by women as they become more regimented and routinized."[15] This process of routinization led to an annual decrease after 1920 in the percentage of female ordained clergy within Pentecostal churches.[16]

The sudden diminishing of opportunities for twentieth-century female Pentecostal preachers is a continuation of a long-established pattern for female ministers in the United States,[17] but not all female Pentecostal ministers experienced this constriction in the same way. Gastón Espinosa claims that the situation for Latina Pentecostal ministers has not changed as dramatically or as negatively. As part of an analysis focusing primarily on records from the Assemblies of God denomination, Espinosa writes that there has been "no great reversal in the accumulation of power or the right to ordination for women in the Latino AG . . . as there was for Euro-American AG women."[18] The road to ordination and acceptance for Latina Pentecostal ministers, however, has not been without its fair share of obstacles. Rather than experiencing an explosion of opportunity followed by a rapid decline, Latina Pentecostals have instead engaged in what Espinosa characterizes as a long "uphill struggle against gender discrimination and the right to full ordination."[19]

Several of my female collaborators spoke of being beneficiaries of this determination of previous generations of female ministers. Ana's journey to ordination within the Iglesia de Dios Pentecostal M.I. benefited tremendously from the uphill struggle of her predecessors. When she first sensed a calling to preach and pastor a congregation, she was not sure whether she would ever be able to respond to it affirmatively:

No estaban abiertos en ese tiempo a tener mujeres como pastoras. Era parcial. No era para lo que llaman el "completo ministerio." Fue hasta los 90. Yo nunca pensaba que la mujer podía liderar. Si pude servir, pero no liderar.

Pero Dios me habló directamente en mi intimidad. Me dijo, "Tu eres pastora." Me dio un llamado a pastorear. Entonces oré, diciendo, "O me saca de aquí o cambia las leyes." Y yo pensaba que era algo imposible por M.I. porque el nivel más alto para las mujeres era misionera, pero no liderar.

They were not open at that time to having women as pastors. It was partial. It was not for what they call the "full ministry." That was until the '90s. I never thought that the woman could lead. I could serve, but not lead.

But God spoke to me directly in my quiet time.[20] He said to me, "You are a pastor." He gave me a call to pastor. Then I prayed, saying, "Either get me out of here or change the rules." And I thought that it was something impossible for M.I.[21] because the highest level for women was missionary, but they could not lead.

Ana truly believed that her ultimatum to God would result in her leaving the Iglesia de Dios Pentecostal M.I. for another denomination. Her intimate conversation with God had taken place while she was away on a vacation. When she returned, she discovered that she would neither have to leave nor fight for recognition:

Cuando regresé tuve un "voicemail" en mi máquina de la oficina regional de mi concilio que en la próxima convención me iban a ungir al completo ministerio porque en la bienal habían pasado la ley que las mujeres ahora podían participar en el completo ministerio. Con todo eso me quedé callada. Dios había abierto las puertas como él me había dicho a través de la biblia.	When I returned, I had a voicemail on my machine from the regional office of my council that in the next convention they were going to anoint me for full ministry because in the biennial they had passed the rule that women could now participate in full ministry. With all of that, I remained silent. God had opened the doors like he had told me he would through the Bible.

Ana believed God to have "opened the doors" for her in response to a promise made to her during her quiet time. More broadly speaking, this may have been a response to promises perceived by many aspiring female Pentecostal pastors who were part of the long uphill struggle before her. My other female collaborators who had been influenced by Pentecostal churches and ministered to congregants who had their own experiences of Pentecostalism were beneficiaries of that persistence as well.

The Baptist collaborators in this study shared that women had only recently gained access to the pulpit. Somewhat surprisingly, this openness toward female preaching had begun while the churches of my Hispanic collaborators were all still affiliated with the Baptist State Convention of North Carolina, a branch of the Southern Baptist Convention. Even though Southern Baptists specifically began prohibiting women from pastoral ministry in 2000,[22] the network of Hispanic Baptist churches established in North Carolina through Ignacio's ministry began opening doors for women around this same time. According to Ignacio, he had begun pushing for these changes long ago, prompted by his experience and education:

De 1990 hasta 2006, nosotros trabajábamos con la convención bautistas del sur, pero aun yo trabajando con la convención bautistas del sur, yo llegué a esta conclusión. En la iglesia que yo	From 1990 until 2006, we worked with the Southern Baptist Convention, but even with me working with the Southern Baptist Convention, I arrived at this conclusion. In the church that I

pastoreaba y en las iglesias donde me invitaban a predicar, yo veía a más mujeres involucradas en el trabajo de la iglesia que a hombres. Y a mí siempre me llamó la atención eso.

Y luego allá cuando fui a BUA,[23] aprendí de la historia del trabajo de la mujer en la iglesia. Antes en la iglesia siempre ha habido mujeres que enseñaban, que predicaban. Aunque siempre me ponían el ojo porque decían "Es que eso no es bíblico. No debes de dejar que suben al púlpito. Si quieren hablar, deben hacerlo, pero abajo. No dejes que suban arriba." Pero yo dije, "Las mujeres van a subir a predicar de allá."

Vi que tanto el hombre como la mujer puede enseñar, puede predicar. Yo empujé mucho que la iglesia abriera camino para eso. Tal vez empujé demasiado. Al punto de que yo tengo una mujer ordenada en la iglesia. Una mujer ordenada que predica, casa, y cuando yo no estoy, ella es la que se encarga de toda la iglesia. Puedo irme un mes si quiero. Ella brinca y ella predica. Y la iglesia está abierta y ha visto que las mujeres tienen dones súper-extraordinarios para servir a Dios.

pastored and in the churches where they invited me to preach, I saw more women than men involved in the work of the church. And that always caught my attention.

And then when I went to BUA, I learned the history of the work of women in the church. Before in the church there have always been women who taught, who preached. Even though they always looked at me because they said, "That is not biblical. You should not let them rise to the pulpit. If they want to talk, they should do it, but from below. Do not let them go up." But I said, "The women are going to go up to preach from there."

I saw that men and women can preach just the same. I pushed a lot for the church to open a way for that. Maybe I pushed too much. To the point that I have an ordained woman in my church. An ordained woman who preaches, marries, and when I am not there, she is the one in charge of the whole church. I can go away for a month if I want. She jumps up and preaches. And the church is open and has seen that women have super-extraordinary gifts for serving God.

THE POWER OF TESTIMONY

My female collaborators benefited greatly from certain contemporary interpretations of Scripture and from the pneumatology of their churches and denominations, but their own personal narratives also contributed in significant ways to the authorization of their ministry. These narratives, as shared within their faith communities, are both understood and shared as testimonies. Throughout this book, I have already noted the particular power of testimony for my collaborators. Not only does it provide the connecting link between stories of migration and narratives of calling, but it also serves as the foundation of their ministries. More than any particular theology, the lived experience of my collaborators and the recollection of that experience in the form of testimony validates them and their preaching ministry within their communities of faith.

Anna Carter Florence, a professor of preaching at Columbia Theological Seminary, asserts that "many historical women preachers" in the United States have "described their preaching as *testimony*,"[24] and postulates that they employed this terminology for two reasons. First, they did so to recognize that their more personal proclamation differed from the sermons, centered on biblical exegesis, delivered by their male contemporaries. Second, they used the word testimony (instead of preaching) to deflect criticism aimed at them as women entering a male-dominated space. This dissimulation was never quite successful, as their testimonies were almost always viewed, "by supporters and opponents alike, as *preaching*, no matter what the women themselves called it."[25] The testimonies that my collaborators most often shared focused on experiences of divine calling and faithful service.

Within my collaborators' congregations, clergy and laity alike frequently shared conversion narratives. The element of testimony serving as the primary distinction between these two groups was the story of their "calling."[26] Stories of calling are usually shared with a congregation as first-person "call-to-preach narratives," which are received as "sacred stories," given the importance of testimony.[27] These narratives have played an especially significant role in validating the preaching ministries of women.[28] Elizabeth Conde-Frazier asserts that for the Latino community, these recollections of "call," echoing biblical narratives and imbued with the presence of the divine, are "a place that the Latino community recognizes as being replete with the voice of God through the Holy Spirit and therefore a source of authority for the community's theological considerations."[29]

I have already shared the call narrative of Ana, who heard God speak to her directly during a quiet time of prayer, saying *"Tú eres pastora /* You are a pastor." When my collaborators, male or female, shared stories of calling with this kind of clear divine message, other Hispanic believers generally nodded their approbation. Divine messages are not to be ignored—not by those who are called into ministry nor by those to whom they minister. The community's affirmation of this very literal understanding of calling fosters bonds of mutual trust and respect between the pastor and congregation. The organic nature of calling and affirmation undergirds democratic and liberative dynamics within the congregation.

Not all of my female collaborators, however, had received this kind of direct word from God to authorize their ministry. Others first heard words of calling from the mouths of other pastors or church members. Eva, currently serving as an ordained elder in the United Methodist Church, came to understand her own calling only after both Catholic and Pentecostal congregations in Mexico recognized her for her leadership potential.

Cuando estaba en la preparatoria organicé una peregrinación de la escuela a la iglesia. Tenía dieciséis años. Era para el día de la Virgen de Guadalupe. Y fue algo curioso porque la escuela en México y la religión son separadas, se supone. Pero, organicé a todos con la ayuda de un profesor. Era una escuela pública, pero organizamos a todos los salones e hicimos una competencia construyendo carros para el evento.

Cuando la iglesia vió que organicé todo esto, me pusieron como líder de los jóvenes. Ellos querían que yo llevara jóvenes a la iglesia.

When I was in high school, I organized a pilgrimage from the school to the church. I was sixteen years old. It was for the day of the Virgin of Guadalupe. And it was strange because in Mexico school and religion are separate, one supposes. But I organized everyone with the help of a teacher. It was a public school, but we organized all the classes and made a competition building carts for the event.[30]

When the church saw that I organized all of this, they made me a youth leader. They wanted me to bring young people to the church.

Eva's efforts to honor the Virgin of Guadalupe resulted in her rising into a position of lay leadership within the youth ministry of her local Catholic church. The congregation had, once again, played a significant role in affirming the calling of God, this time as they had discerned its embodiment in Eva's actions. Initially enthusiastic about her new role, Eva eventually grew frustrated by what she described as a lack of training and support. During her college years, Eva and her boyfriend were invited to attend an Assemblies of God church in Monterrey, Mexico. Once again, she began to provide leadership within the youth ministry, but during one of the church's Sunday morning worship services, she also received a new calling, which the pastor affirmed as a specific call to ministry.

El llamado a predicar fue desde que tenía diecinueve años. Fue en mi iglesia local de Asambleas de Dios. Un día el pastor predicó sobre Isaías 6:8 de "Heme aquí Señor, envíame a mí." Entonces, yo pasé enfrente orando y diciendo eso a Dios. Yo estaba trabajando como una ingeniera industrial con una empresa grande. Lo estaba disfrutando mucho, era un buen trabajo, pero también estaba siempre encerrada y quería hacer más porque también era líder de jóvenes y no podía hacer lo que quería hacer con los jóvenes porque el trabajo era de las siete de la mañana hasta las cinco de la tarde.

The call to preach came from when I was nineteen years old. It was in my local Assemblies of God church. One day the pastor preached on Isaiah 6:8 on "Here am I, send me." So I went forward praying and saying that to God. I was working as an industrial engineer in a large company. I enjoyed it a lot, it was a good job, but I also was always inside and I wanted to do more because I was also a youth leader and I could not do what I wanted to do with the youth because my job lasted from seven in the morning until five in the afternoon.

Entonces yo estaba discerniendo, orando, pidiéndole a Dios que me diera la oportunidad de servirle más. En ese momento el pastor vino al altar y me habló en el oído diciendo, "Párate porque vas a predicar." Nunca había predicado en mi vida, pero me honró mucho que él me dijera eso, porque realmente él era un hombre que buscaba el llamado del espíritu santo. Y si él dijo eso pensaba que era lo que el espíritu santo estaba diciendo.

So I was discerning, praying, asking God to give me the opportunity to serve him more. In that moment, the pastor came to the altar and spoke into my ear saying, "Get up because you are going to preach." I had never preached before in my life, but I was very honored that he would say that to me, because he really was a man who looked for the calling of the Holy Spirit. And if he said that, I thought it was what the Holy Spirit was saying.

Eva did not immediately enter the ministry, but instead held this story close to her heart for many years. When ministry opportunities did arise, it was her husband who was first recognized for his pastoral potential, but gradually Eva too began to serve. Eventually, she began serving on her own as an associate pastor in a United Methodist Church. Her ordination followed soon after. In both her first sermon for her new congregation and throughout her ordination process, she shared her story of divine calling. The Pentecostal paradigm for understanding vocational discernment had opened up a space in which the male pastor of an Assemblies of God church in Mexico had mediated and confirmed Eva's calling. But Eva herself had carried this calling forward within her, beyond the borders of both her country of origin and her former denomination. An identity which began with a traditionalist pattern of male acknowledgment had been carried forward through female embodiment.

Not all testimonies shared by my collaborators focused on their calling. Some focused on the faithfulness and/or success of their ministerial service. These secondary narratives verified and undergirded their testimonies of calling. Elizabeth Conde-Frazier shares a personal testimony of this kind in *Latina Evangélicas*. She faced significant opposition at one point in her ministerial journey when she began serving in a community that had never before had a female pastor in any of its congregations. This resulted, Conde-Frazier recounts, in "many purportedly prophetic messages [being] uttered about my being out of order."[31] The rumblings of discontent within her broader community prompted Conde-Frazier to face the matter head on:

I invited the people from the different congregations to a gathering of discernment, and as they listened to my spiritual story of calling, they discussed the matter publicly. After sitting through much deliberation and a barrage of Bible verses, a female elder exclaimed, "You shall know them by the fruit they bear."[32]

The female elder's interjection cut through the noise of the gathering and led those assembled there to decide on a three-year trial period for Conde-Frazier, after which she reassembled the community leaders who then, having borne witness to the quality of her pastoral "fruit," unanimously acknowledged the legitimacy of her calling. Conde-Frazier's anecdote is instructive as an example of the way in which many female pastors surmount doctrinal obstacles through faithful service. Additionally, in the way she wields her story rhetorically, she presents herself as one who has already overcome whatever doctrinal concerns a community might have regarding the validity of her calling. According to her testimony, she has already been recognized as a true prophet and a true *pastora*.

Ana, the beneficiary of changing attitudes toward female pastors in the Iglesia de Dios Pentecostal M.I., began her vocational ministry in New York and New Jersey, but sensed a calling to come to the Raleigh-Durham area to begin a new mission. Many missionaries within her denomination begin their work with financial support, but Ana chose a different path.

Llegué aquí en Raleigh sin apoyo financiero. La iglesia M.I. puede darlo, pero yo no lo solicité. Ellos te dan una cuota, pero es para un tiempo ya fijo. Entonces si la obra no crece, tú tienes que buscar otros medios. Yo no quise tener esa presión. Me tomó dos años conociendo a la comunidad antes de empezar la obra.	I arrived here in Raleigh without financial support. The M.I. church can provide it, but I did not ask for it. They give you a certain portion, but it is for a predetermined amount of time. Then, if the work does not grow, you must look for other means. I did not want to have that pressure. It took me two years of getting to know the community before beginning the work.

As part of the first wave of female pastors in the M.I. church, Ana was eligible for financial support, but she was also very cognizant of the fact that this support could be revoked if her new church plant was not "growing." The degree of growth necessary at various intervals was based on somewhat subjective determinations by denominational officials, and Ana had to wonder, "Would she receive the same benefit of the doubt as male ministers overseeing new churches?" If her church failed to meet certain growth standards, would this negatively impact her future possibilities within a denomination that had only just recognized the validity of her calling? What effect might it have on other aspiring female ministers within the broader denomination, and how might it affect the view of women in pastoral ministry in the new M.I. mission field of North Carolina? All of these questions factored into her decision to forgo any financial support, but this decision, in her opinion, allowed God to further validate her calling. Needing to help provide financially for her family during these two years of scouting, Ana interviewed for a job as an ELL teacher's aide in the local school system.[33] Due to the explosive growth in Raleigh area schools, teacher hiring increased exponentially during the 1990s. This was especially true in the area of ELL, as Hispanic immigration and high fertility rates led to a dramatic demographic increase in Wake and Durham County Public Schools. Ana was hired by a school that had been built for four hundred students but was currently serving nine hundred. Her adjustment to this new job was immediately upended by unforeseen circumstances:

Ese año cuando yo llegué, el maestro de ELL renunció. No pudo soportar más. Yo estaba de asistente y me pusieron para dirigir el programa como maestra. Fue Dios. Esto sólo comparto con personas que conocen a Dios y entienden como obra Dios porque yo no tenía la preparación para ese tipo de trabajo.	That year when I arrived, the ELL teacher resigned. He could not handle it anymore. I was the assistant, and they had me direct the program as a teacher. It was God. I only share this with people who know God and understand how God works because I did not have the preparation for that type of work.

Ana's story regarding the beginning of her career as an ELL teacher in the Raleigh area was not a mere biographical detail to her; it was a story of divine providence confirming her calling and her choice to forgo denominational support. God himself, through the circumstances that unfolded around her secular employment, was providing her with ample income to be able to support her family as she researched her community and began the work of planting her church. This employment also brought her into close contact with many newly arrived Hispanic families, some of whom would form the nucleus of her ministry. She admitted that she did not always share this particular story with non-Christians due to their skepticism. But for those "who know God and understand how God works," this story was unmistakable proof of God's blessing on Ana's ministry and pastoral authority.

Ignacio also spoke of the way that the testimony of his wife's faithfulness opened the door for expanded ministry for her and other women in their network of churches. I have already spoken of the way his Pentecostal background, combined with his education and experience working among women, changed his own viewpoint about women in ministry. But Ignacio himself said that much of his congregation's acceptance of female pastors came from the faithful service of his wife, Perla.

Mucho se debe también a que Perla nunca pero nunca me dejó solo. Yo creo que este camino que se abrió aquí se debe a que Perla nunca dijo, "Ah no, él es el pastor" o "Yo no me meto allí porque él es el pastor." A causa de mi condición, si yo lo hacía, ella lo hacía también.

Eso[34] le dijo a la iglesia, "Pero siempre ha habido una mujer aquí haciendo cosas. Siempre ha habido una mujer aquí enfrente. Siempre ha habido una mujer enfrente de él, atrás de él, por todos lados de él. Si el predique es porque una mujer lo trae."

Es como si abrió los ojos a la iglesia para que estuvieran abiertas. Si Perla predica, la iglesia aplaude. O si otra predica, está feliz la iglesia. En los veintiún años desde que nosotros nos casamos, Perla ha dejado un legado muy bueno en la iglesia en el área de la mujer.

Much is due also to Perla never—and I mean never—leaving me alone. I believe that this pathway that opened here is due to Perla who never said, "Oh no, he is the pastor" or "I am not going to get involved there because he is the pastor." Because of my condition, if I did something, she did it too.

That said to the church, "But there has always been a woman here doing things. There has always been a woman here in front. There has always been a woman in front of him, behind him, on all sides of him. If he preaches, it is because a woman brings him."

It is as if she opened the eyes of the church so that they would be open. If Perla preaches, the church applauds. Or if another [woman] preaches, the church is happy. In the twenty-one years since we were married, Perla has left a very good legacy in the church in the area of women.

The example of Perla and many other women discussed in this chapter reveals that the opportunity to be heard and recognized as a preacher opens for many Hispanic women not necessarily through the presence of an overtly liberationist movement in their denominations but through the power of their own testimonies and lived faith.

SHARED SPOUSAL MINISTRY

Like Elizabeth Conde-Frazier, my female collaborators found space for themselves at the pulpit due to liberative readings of Scripture, Pentecostal understandings of the authorizing power of the Spirit, powerful testimonies, and fruitful ministries. Sometimes they wielded these weapons for themselves, and sometimes they were the beneficiaries of both women and men who had wielded them in prior generations. Like Perla, some of them also benefited from the presence of their spouses serving alongside them. Barfoot and Sheppard, chronicling the decline in opportunities for female Pentecostal ministers after the early twentieth century, theorize that "shared spousal ministry" may now present "the closest approximation to equal status for most women."[35]

This negative view of shared spousal ministry overshadows the positive opportunities it presents. It was through shared spousal ministry, in fact, that Hispanic women first received notice in the media coverage of the Azusa Street revival. Although the name of the woman in question did not appear in the article, there was a reference made to her as the wife of "a Spanish preacher" who joined him as they preached the gospel together.[36] This woman, whom other sources identify as Rosa López, seemed to have been able to preach due to the identity of her husband, Abundio, as a real "Spanish preacher." This pattern would appear over and over again in the early days of the Latino Asambleas de Dios as many of the earliest officially recognized female preachers were married to men who were also active in ministry. In the early twentieth century, it was considerably less common for the Assemblies of God to credential the ministry of single women who would not be ministering alongside a spouse.

Arlene Sánchez Walsh highlights the way in which Hispanic women, especially those who sensed a call to ministry, attended the Assemblies of God's Latin American Bible Institute in order "to meet like-minded, 'saved' men and to find a suitable marriage partner" with whom they might engage in ministry.[37] She also offers the example of Demetrio and Nellie Bazán, which reveals some of the nuance of shared spousal ministry. The couple was ordained together in 1920, and in 1932 Demetrio became the first Hispanic elected to a position of prominent leadership in the Assemblies of God. His ascension within the hierarchy certainly opened doors for Nellie's ministry, but his rise was also aided by Nellie's testimony. The Bazáns originally came to Pentecostal faith through Nellie's experience of dramatic healing after having been pronounced dead. Nellie's testimony served as the foundational story of her husband's calling to faith and ministry. Their ministry was not only shared but symbiotic.[38] A 2012 study by Otto Maduro of female Hispanic Pentecostal ministers in Newark, N.J., also sheds light on the importance of shared spousal ministry as a gateway to the recognition of female ministers.[39] A majority of Maduro's interviewees shared that they first occupied supporting roles in ministries that were primarily directed by their husbands. Only through their faithfulness in this arrangement did they eventually earn legitimacy as *pastoras* in the eyes of their congregants.

All seven of my female collaborators were currently participating in shared spousal ministries or had done so previously. The balance of power and preaching authority enjoyed by these women, however, differed dramatically from one situation to another. At one end of the spectrum were several of my collaborators who saw their primary ministry as supporting their husbands and engaging in areas of ministry most often carried out by women, namely, ministries to women and children. Linda, the wife of an Assemblies of God pastor, told me that "*las Asambleas de Dios reconocen que ambos somos pastores /* the Assemblies of God recognizes that both of us are pastors." When I asked her questions related to her preaching style, she interrupted me to offer some clarification:

Mayormente me desempeño en la enseñanza. Es un tipo de predicación, pero la enseñanza es para mí. Trabajo con niños y familias y con mujeres.	Mainly, I perform the teaching. It is a type of preaching, but teaching is for me. I work with children and families and with women.

Although I had not asked her anything related to ministering to specific populations within their congregations, Linda had connected her own seemingly self-imposed limitations in preaching with her ministerial niche of working with women and children. Although she did not believe that all women had to stay within this particular pastoral lane, it was the one in which she felt most comfortable operating.

Ignacio's wife Perla had clearly entered shared spousal ministry with a primary ambition of supporting her husband, whose physical condition required significant assistance. This support gradually changed perceptions among multiple Baptist churches of the role that women could play in ministry, but Perla also engaged in ministry beyond simply assisting Ignacio. Perla had first converted to Protestant Christianity as a young adult when she and her family began attending Ignacio's church. After serving in the church in the areas of youth and children's ministries for several years, Perla also began to develop personal feelings toward Ignacio, which he reciprocated. Perla's family was resistant to their growing relationship and worried about what Perla's life would look like having to care for a paraplegic husband, but Perla and Ignacio moved forward with marriage anyway, which also ushered in a new stage of Perla's ministry:

Nos casamos, y ya sentí el llamado y la pasión por servirle [a Dios] en cualquier área de la iglesia. Quería desarrollar las habilidades que tuve dentro del ministerio. Y más que nada apoyando el ministerio también de Ignacio en la obra aquí en nuestra iglesia. Nosotros nos casamos en 1996 y comenzamos a servir los dos juntos. Él no podía escribir, entonces yo escribí sus sermones en la computadora, los "powerpoint," los boletines.

We married, and I already felt the call and the passion to serve [God] in whatever area of the church. I wanted to develop the abilities that I had within ministry. And more than anything supporting the ministry as well of Ignacio in the work here in our church. We were married in 1996 and began to serve together. He could not write, so I wrote his sermons on the computer, the PowerPoints, the bulletins.

Much of the way that Perla initially described her shared spousal ministry involved work that she did to help Ignacio overcome difficulties caused by his disability. Ignacio's preaching ministry depended heavily on Perla's assistance in the areas of sermon preparation and transportation. When I pushed her to speak about her own preaching ministry, however, Perla immediately demurred:

Yo siempre he dicho a Ignacio, "No tengo el don de predicar, pero si doy estudios [bíblicos] a las mujeres y a los niños. Y he predicado en otras iglesias."

I have always said to Ignacio, "I do not have the gift of preaching, but I do give [Bible] studies to the women and the children. And I have preached in other churches."

Perla had, in fact, preached in her own church and other churches on multiple occasions. She had also spoken at many conferences hosted by Baptist churches that had been established by church planters sent out from Ignacio and Perla's church. Before she could elaborate further during that particular conversation regarding her perception of her lack of giftedness for preaching, Ignacio interrupted her. He had furrowed his brow as he heard his wife speak, concerned about the way she had spoken of not having the gift of preaching:

Yo no sé porque ella dice eso. Si tiene miedo que le voy a dar más trabajo acerca de la predicación. O si está tratando de mostrar la humildad. Pero ella siempre me ha dicho, "No tengo el don de predicar."

I do not know why she says that. Maybe she is afraid that I am going to give her more work when it comes to preaching. Or maybe she is trying to show humility. But she has always told me, "I do not have the gift of preaching."

Pero las veces que ha predicado, lo ha hecho bien. La han llamado a dar conferencias. Ella dice, "No estoy predicando—estoy dando una conferencia." Pero es predicar. Le dan una hora y media y no hay quien la pare—y está predicando.	But the times she has preached, she has done it well. They have invited her to give conferences. She says, "I am not preaching—I am giving a conference." But it is preaching. They give her an hour and a half, and no one can stop her—and she is preaching.[40]

In spite of Ignacio's defense of his wife's preaching, their situation, like Linda's, still fell into the kind of shared spousal ministry in which the husband was the primary minister whose wife worked in more of a supporting role. Among my collaborators, Esteban and Diana had the most balanced shared ministry, in which they identified themselves as copastors of the congregation and truly functioned accordingly. My other four female collaborators participated in shared spousal ministries in which they eventually became or always were the primary ministers. Eva, who had her call confirmed by her pastor during the invitation at a Pentecostal church in Mexico, had originally served alongside her husband in the United Methodist church. He was the one who first began teaching Bible studies and preaching in United Methodist churches around the Raleigh area. Because Eva's husband was the recipient of an R-1 visa to do religious work on behalf of the United Methodist Church, Eva actually was not permitted to have a paying job outside the church, in spite of her college education and previous work as an engineer. Denied any other possibilities and still sensing her own calling, Eva threw herself into the work of the church. She watched as her husband was ordained and began seminary training, but Eva eventually navigated all of those pathways as well. When her husband accepted a job in an academic setting, Eva became the associate pastor at one of the largest Hispanic churches in the North Carolina Annual Conference of the United Methodist Church. A shared spousal ministry in which she originally worked behind the scenes had paved the way for her own ministry in which she stood alone.

Ana, Sara, and Teresa (from M.I., Baptist, and United Methodist churches, respectively) also were the primary ministers in their marriages. Ana's husband's name appears on the church's sign next to her in the category of "*Pastores* / Pastors," but Ana's name comes first, and her husband's name appears on the following line. Ana had always been the primary pastor of the congregation, and when the church decided to elevate another laywoman into a ministerial role, she was given the title of "*co-pastora* / female copastor." Although this woman occupied a role a step below Ana's husband in the church's official hierarchy, she was still his functional equivalent or even his superior. Sara and her husband worked together to manage a small car lot, but when it came to pastoral vocation, she was clearly the minister, and her husband provided moral support. Teresa and her husband had served together as laypeople in a local United Methodist congregation before she became an associate pastor and eventually the senior pastor. Her husband was still very active within the leadership of the church, often teaching Bible studies and occasionally preaching as well, but it was clear that he was fulfilling these duties in support of her and as part of their shared commitment in marriage and ministry.

In some ways, these women were enacting a reverse shared spousal ministry in which their husbands were actually viewed as ministers through their wives' efforts and calling. Even in these situations, these women, and all my collaborators more broadly, were subject to expectations of what Gastón Espinosa identifies as "a kind of paradoxical domesticity."[41] Espinosa describes this as a phenomenon in which Hispanic female ministers "are exhorted to be both End-Times prophetesses and evangelists in the public sphere and devoted mothers and good wives in the private sphere."[42] There is a long history of female ministers in the United States using these expectations to help validate their ministries.

Leah Payne writes that women serving as ministers in the early twentieth century argued that "their status as ideal women—as educated mothers and/ or companionate wives" also validated their ministry.[43] In the early twenty-first century, several of my collaborators echoed the assertions of the pioneering female ministers described by Payne "that as long as they were dutiful wives with happy husbands and home lives, they were entitled to minister: their responsibilities to the men in their lives were fulfilled, and their free time could be invested in a pastorate."[44] They felt that the experiences of marriage and motherhood enhanced their ministry. Again, like their Pentecostal forebears, they described themselves "as mothers of congregations" who therefore "had authority to oversee the mental, spiritual, and physical needs of their spiritual children."[45]

Ana used the language of mothering to describe her work with the Evangelical Immigration Table, speaking of the need to be better informed about ongoing immigration issues so that she could "*criar y guiar a su gente* / nurture and guide her people." Teresa ran her church's domestic cleaning agency as a way to support the mission of the church financially, but also to provide income for several single mothers in the congregation. Her consequent close relationship with these women resulted in a kind of mothering mentorship. The fact that she often brought her two young children with her to church services and activities highlighted her identity as a mother in those moments.

In spite of the attempts of my female collaborators to fulfill the expectations of paradoxical domesticity, there were times when its incongruous demands led to inevitable conflict. In my second year of participant-observation at Iglesia Agua Viva, a dispute arose between several members of the lay leadership and the copastors, Esteban and Diana. The particular lay leaders in question had led the worship team, playing the keyboard and providing lead vocals, since the church's inception. Aside from Esteban and Diana, they were the most visible leaders of the congregation. Their original complaints had to do with how Esteban and Diana communicated and how they scheduled events, but as Esteban and Diana attempted to work through these issues with them, it became clear that the lay leaders had grown resentful of Esteban and Diana themselves. More particularly, they felt that Diana was too *mandona* / bossy. This term is most often used to describe a woman who "commands" or "runs the show" in her family, thus subverting the expectations of male domestic leadership. This would certainly run afoul of the expectations of paradoxical domesticity in which women are expected to be submissive within their own family structures. The lay leaders, however, were specifically complaining about Diana's leadership *in the church*, criticizing everything from the loudness of her voice to the vigor with which she expressed her opinions. These attributes were clearly in keeping with the idea of Diana being a fiery "End-Times prophetess," but in a moment of conflict, the contradictory expectations of paradoxical domesticity were conflated in such a way as to make Diana's fulfillment of them impossible.

The lay leaders ultimately left the church, taking several families with them and leaving Diana unsure as to how she should best embody her pastoral leadership. In our conversation about this difficult period, Diana alternated between attributing these incidents to petty jealousy on the part of her detractors and questioning aloud whether her own actions as a church leader had been somehow displeasing to God. She and Esteban both remarked that being a female pastor was "*muy duro* / very hard."

THE PULPIT AS PLATFORM

During my time of participant observation, I was able to witness sermons by many of my female collaborators and other Hispanic female ministers. The majority of these sermons were markedly similar to the sermons of their male counterparts in both focus and emphasis. They, too, reflect the intersection of traditionalist interpretation rooted in and shaped by the migrant experience and a deep connection to the lived reality of their congregations. My female collaborators were somewhat more likely to include references to marriage and family issues within their sermons, but the male Hispanic ministers in this study also did so with great frequency. One notable difference in the proclamation of my female collaborators was the regularity with which they incorporated personal testimony in their preaching. These narratives could come from their own life experiences or from stories that had been shared with them by others, but they almost always bore some personal connection.[46]

One sermon in particular, among the many that I observed by Hispanic female preachers, embodied the idea of interweaving testimony and contextualizing Bible passages in the light of women's experiences. Eva preached it in the Hispanic United Methodist church in which she served as an associate pastor. Her text for the day, one of the Sundays in Advent, was Luke 1:46-55, more commonly known as the Magnificat. The passage represents Mary's poetic response to the news, delivered by the angel Gabriel and confirmed by her cousin Elizabeth, that she would conceive and give birth to "the Son of the Most High."[47] Eva began by reading the full text very expressively. She particularly emphasized Mary's identification of herself as God's "*humilde sierva* / humble servant" and the way in which God's redemptive work "*ha exaltado a los humildes* / has exalted the humble" and "*a los hambrientes los colmó de bienes* / filled the hungry with good things." She closed her reading by recognizing that this was "*la palabra de Dios para nosotros, el pueblo de Dios* / the word of God for us, the people of God." Then she began reflecting on her experience as part of "*el pueblo de Dios*":

El mes pasado estaba recordando—mi esposo y yo estábamos recordando—que ya cumplimos doce años de llegar a este país, de llegar a los Estados Unidos. Doce años de vivir en Carolina del Norte, y doce años de servir aquí en la comunidad hispana, en la comunidad latina. En esos doce años, he vivido muchas cosas—hemos vivido muchas cosas. Y yo estaba meditando en las personas que he conocido durante esos doce años—en las personas con las que he tenido la bendición de caminar en esta jornada de la fe. Personas que han vivido diferentes experiencias de vidas.

Last month I was remembering—my husband and I were remembering—that we have now completed twelve years since arriving in this country, since arriving in the United States. Twelve years of living in North Carolina, and twelve years of serving in the Hispanic community, the Latino community. In those twelve years, I have lived through many things—we have lived through many things. And I was meditating over the people I have known during those twelve years—the people with whom I have had the blessing to walk on this journey of faith. People who have lived different experiences in life.

Interestingly, Eva included references to her husband (who was also a minister) twice during her introduction. It was they who remembered together and they who had lived through many things. This nod toward shared spousal ministry was made almost reflexively in the context of the people Eva had come to know through ministry in the Hispanic community. But her emphasis would not be primarily on all the people with whom she had served but a specific subset of the "*nosotros* / us" toward whom she believed this particular text was directed:

A todas las recuerdo, de todas he aprendido mucho, pero las que más han marcado mi vida son aquellas personas, especialmente mujeres con quienes he tenido la oportunidad de caminar en su jornada de fe y de sanidad emocional y espiritual. Mujeres que han sufrido violencia doméstica, física, y emocional. Mujeres que todavía están sufriendo por las heridas que dejaron en su alma y en su cuerpo y el trauma que sufrieron cuando eran niñas o adolescentes. Mujeres que todavía tienen pesadillas sobre el tiempo que vivieron siendo víctimas de tráfico humano.	I remember all of them, I have learned so much from all of them, but the ones who have marked my life most are the ones with whom I have had the opportunity to walk in their journey of faith and emotional and spiritual healing. Women who have suffered domestic, physical, and emotional violence. Women who are still suffering from the wounds left in their souls and in their bodies and the trauma they suffered when they were girls or adolescents. Women who still have nightmares about the time when they lived as victims of human trafficking.

The effect of these words on the hearers was twofold and immediately apparent. This was an unusual direction to take with a traditional advent text and some of the hearers reacted with puzzlement, turning their heads slightly to one side as if pondering where Eva was going with her reflection on abuse and human trafficking. Others, especially the women, began nodding their heads in assent as they recognized themselves or their friends and family members among this litany of women who had suffered. Some had tears shining in their eyes. Eva pressed on in pursuit of the common denominator that would connect the lived reality of these women to the words of the Magnificat:

Todas estas mujeres tienen algo en común. Han sido rechazadas por la sociedad y han sido relegadas por la iglesia. Yo he caminado con ellas y he podido ver como la sociedad las ve. Y he podido ver lo poco valoradas que son por la iglesia—que no las valora por lo que realmente son—amadas y valiosas hijas de Dios.

Pero tal vez no debería sorprendernos. La misma iglesia que es conocida por no valorar a la mujer. La misma María, la madre de Dios, no ha sido valorada por lo que realmente es—un ser humano esencial para el plan de salvación de Dios. María, la humilde sierva, la humilde sierva que Dios escogió para formar en su vientre a Dios encarnado. No ha sido valorada por la iglesia como tal.

All of these women have something in common. They have been rejected by society and relegated by the church. I have walked with them and been able to see how society sees them. I've been able to see how undervalued they are by the church—which doesn't value them for who they really are—beloved and valuable daughters of God.

But maybe that shouldn't surprise us. The same church which is known for not valuing women. Mary herself, the mother of God, has not been valued for who she really is—an essential human being for God's plan of salvation. Mary, the humble servant, the humble servant whom God chose to form in her womb the incarnate God. She has not been valued by the church as such.

All the suffering women catalogued by Eva had been victimized yet again by both society and the church. As she spoke of the church relegating these women, she motioned downward with both hands. A moment later, she raised her hands back up to emphasize the true identity of these women as "beloved and valuable daughters of God." In this sense, they have much in common with one another and with the one to whom the words of the Magnificat are attributed. Mary—valuable and essential in God's plan of redemption—historically has also been undervalued by the Protestant church.

At this point, I saw several furrowed brows among both the men and women in Eva's audience. Most of the adults had either converted to Protestantism from Roman Catholicism or had lived as *evangélicos* / Protestants for some time in majority–Roman Catholic parts of Central or South America. For many of them, these experiences had left them deeply skeptical and/or critical of the Catholic church's veneration of the Virgin Mary, a practice they described as misplaced worship at best and a form of idolatry at worst. For those with Pentecostal influences in their faith journey, this suspicion and animosity tended to be even greater. Some of those who had been ready to hear a hopeful word for women who had suffered were far less open to hearing

Mary discussed in such a positive light. But for Eva—who as a Catholic teen-ager had once organized a procession in honor of the Virgin of Guadalupe before identifying first as a Pentecostal and then as a United Methodist—this was an opportunity to weave together the testimonies of women, both ancient and contemporary, in a way that would be mutually beneficial for their place within the church's understanding. She began with Mary, casting her accep-tance of Gabriel's message as the heroic action that countered the events of the fall as recorded in Genesis:

A María se le conoce como "la nue-va Eva." La vieja Eva—por medio de la desobediencia de la vieja Eva, el pecado y el sufrimiento y la maldad entraron al mundo. Pero por medio de la obediencia de María, de la humil-de sierva, es que el plan de redención de Dios fue posible.

Eva escuchó a la serpiente que le decía, "Come del fruto prohibido, come de ese fruto del árbol del bien y el mal—de ese fruto de que Dios te dijo que no comieras." María escuchó al án-gel cuando le dijo que en su vientre iba a ser creciendo el hijo de Dios.

Eva obedeció a la serpiente, desobe-deciendo a Dios y comió de ese fruto. María respondió al ángel en obediencia a Dios diciéndole, "Ve aquí tu humilde sierva, que se haga conmigo como Dios ha dicho."

Mary is known as "the new Eve." The old Eve—through the disobedience of the old Eve, sin and suffering and evil entered into the world. But through the obedience of Mary, the humble servant, that's how God's plan of re-demption was possible.

Eve listened to the serpent who said to her, "Eat of the forbidden fruit, eat of that fruit of the tree of good and evil—that fruit that God told you not to eat." Mary listened to the angel when he told her that in her womb would begin to grow the son of God.

Eve obeyed the serpent, disobey-ing God, and ate of that fruit. Mary responded to the angel in obedience to God, saying to him, "See here your humble servant, that it may be done with me as God has said."

In Eva's exegesis of passages from both Genesis and the Gospel of Luke, "God's plan of redemption" is possible only because Mary's courageous obedience balances the scales with Eve's original disobedience. To provide a visual corol-lary for this juxtaposition, Eva paced back and forth on the platform, deliver-ing her remarks about Eve from one side of the pulpit and her description of Mary's importance from the opposite side.

Having already cast Mary as Eve's redemptive foil, Eva then stressed the importance of Mary's humanity and the closeness of her relationship with God as essential elements within God's larger plan:

Esa es María, esa humilde sierva, la que proveyó el material humano para la encarnación de Dios para que la encarnación de Dios mismo fuera posible. Del cuerpo de María es que el hijo de Dios se alimentó y se nutrió. En los brazos de María, el lloró cuando era bebé. Por medio de sus cuidados es que él pudo crecer y llegar hasta ese momento para el cual fue creado.

María es el ser humano que ha tenido una relación más íntima con Dios. No hay nadie en la creación de Dios, ningún humano en la creación de Dios, que ha tenido una relación tan íntima con Dios mismo. María es el ser humano, aparte de Jesús, mas importante para los planes de salvación de Dios.

That is Mary, that humble servant, the one who provided the human material for the incarnation of God so that the incarnation of God might be possible. From Mary's body, the son of God ate and was nourished. In the arms of Mary, he cried when he was a baby. Through her care he was able to grow and arrive at that moment for which he had been created.

Mary is the human being who has had the most intimate relationship with God. There is no one else in God's creation, no other human in God's creation, who has had such an intimate relationship with God himself. Mary is the most important human being, apart from Jesus, for God's plans of salvation.

Eva pantomimed cradling a baby in her arms as she imagined the nurture Mary provided to God incarnate. Only because of this level of closeness and care, according to her rhetoric, was Christ able to fulfill his destiny as savior. Mary is not to be thought of merely as a vessel, but as the most important character, next to her son, in "God's plans for salvation." She stepped forward, her palms facing upward, and nodded as she spoke these words as though she were inviting her hearers to accept the truth of her proposition. Then, having already presented Mary as Eve's superior in her obedience to the divine will, Eva began comparing Mary to Christ himself regarding the suffering they each experienced:

Pues, ella también sufrió para la salvación del mundo. ¿Qué dolor puede ser más grande que el dolor de una madre ver a su hijo siendo humillado, maltratado, torturado, crucificado y desangrado hasta la última gota de sangre? ¿Qué dolor puede ser más grande que ese? María también sufrió para la salvación del mundo.

No pudo haber en este mundo otro ser humano, aparte de Jesús, que haya sufrido más que María por el pecado de la humanidad, por la maldad de la humanidad y para cumplir el plan de redención de Dios.

Then, she also suffered for the salvation of the world. What pain could be greater than the pain of a mother seeing her son being humiliated, mistreated, tortured, crucified, and bled out to the very last drop of blood? What pain could be greater than that? Mary also suffered for the salvation of the world.

There could not have been in this world another human being, apart from Jesus, who has suffered more than Mary suffered for the sin of humanity, for the evil of humanity and to complete God's plan of redemption.

Rhetorically, this part of Eva's sermon connected the suffering of Mary to Christ's suffering while also echoing the suffering of the many *"amadas y valiosas hijas de Dios* / beloved and valuable daughters of God" to whose stories Eva had alluded at the beginning of her sermon. By elevating the value of Mary's suffering, Eva was calling for an increase in her esteem as well. This revaluation of the role of Mary was necessary because of the Hispanic Protestant church's misdirected focus and anti-Catholic sentiment in her regard:

Más, sin embargo, nos enfocamos más en pensar que si María murió siendo virgen o no, que si María tuvo más hijos aparte de Jesús o no. Muchas de nuestras denominaciones pierden tanto tiempo en esas cosas. Perdemos tanto tiempo en el afán de rechazar todo lo que suena católico romano que delegamos a María hasta el último lugar en los planes de salvación de Dios.	But, nevertheless, we focus more on thinking about whether Mary died as a virgin or not, whether Mary had other children apart from Jesus or not. Many of our denominations waste so much time on those things. We waste so much time in our eagerness to reject everything that sounds Roman Catholic that we delegate Mary to last place within God's plans of salvation.

With her full-throated defense of Mary now fully established, Eva returned to the present and to those suffering women with whom she had journeyed during twelve years of ministry in Hispanic churches:

Es por eso que no me sorprende que tantas mujeres en la sociedad y en nuestras iglesias han sido también delegadas hasta el último lugar en el orden jerárquico. Esa es la realidad en que vivimos. Es la realidad en el mundo, es la realidad en la sociedad. Es la realidad en nuestras iglesias. No hemos reconocido el valor de la mujer, así como no hemos reconocido el valor de esa humilde sierva—de esa humilde sierva.	That's why it doesn't surprise me that so many women in society and in our churches have also been delegated to last place in the hierarchical order. That is the reality in which we live. It's the reality in the world. It's the reality in society. It's the reality in our churches. We haven't recognized the value of women just as we haven't recognized the value of that humble servant—of that humble servant.

Of course, churches (and more broadly speaking, a society) that failed to recognize the worth of Mary—despite her courageous obedience, her essential nurture, and her atoning sacrifice—must also bear the blame for having delegated women to "last place" within their hierarchies. The worth of women—as of Mary—is self-evident, and the church has failed to recognize the gift God has given it yet again in the form of each and every *"humilde sierva* / humble servant." But just as so many of Eva's friends and female parishioners had been rejected like Mary, she saw them as having been chosen by God for his healing and blessing in such a way that they too could now stand and sing a Magnificat of their own:

Pero por la gracia de Dios, por la inmensa gracia de Dios, es que las mujeres y el ser humano en general puede ser sanado. Es que esas mujeres con las que he caminado por esos doce años pueden decir ahora como María lo dijo, *"Mi alma glorifica al Señor, y mi espíritu se regocija en Dios mi Salvador."*	But by the grace of God, by the immense grace of God, women and human beings in general can be healed. Because of that, those women with whom I walked for those twelve years can now say like Mary said, *"My soul glorifies the Lord, and my spirit rejoices in God my Savior."*

Eva concluded her sermon by situating her own proclamation within the actions of women who help other women to leave the "low place" to which they are often relegated. In her closing words, she spoke of the power women have to accomplish what Mary did, bringing about redemption by courageously accepting their own worth in God's eyes and helping other women to do the same:

Por la gracia de Dios, muchas mujeres ahora ayudan a otras a salir de ese lugar tan bajo donde la sociedad y la iglesia las han mandado. Por la gracia de Dios muchas de esas mujeres ahora están ayudando a muchas a sanar esas heridas causadas por la maldad y por el ser humano que insiste en obedecer a la serpiente. Por la gracia de Dios yo hoy me glorifico por lo que Dios me ha permitido en mi vida por doce años al lado de esas mujeres valiosas, hermosas que hoy extienden su mano a otras para que juntas puedan decir, "Mi alma glorifica al Señor." Amén.	By the grace of God, many women now help others to leave that low place to which society and the church have sent them. By the grace of God, many of those women now are helping many others, healing those wounds caused by evil and by human beings who insist upon obeying the serpent. By the grace of God, I give glory for what God permitted in my life for twelve years alongside those valuable and beautiful women who now extend a hand to others so that they might say together, "My soul glorifies the Lord." Amen.

Eva's sermon, employing the pulpit as a platform for the theological revaluation of women within Hispanic Protestant congregations, provides yet another example among many of *predicadoras* who "have generally stayed the course and continue to quietly and skillfully negotiate their own space" while struggling against "gender bias and discrimination and an uphill calling."[48] Although Eva was most specifically addressing lay women with whom she had served, increased esteem for women within the life of Hispanic Protestant congregations can only lead to more opportunities for *predicadoras* to pursue their calling as well.

CONCLUSION

"When God gives you a call, he backs it up." Those were Diana's words reflecting back on her calling to ministry. She had overcome residual machismo, the hesitancy of her husband, and gender-based conflict within her own congregation in order to respond to her calling. Like my other female collaborators, she persisted in her uphill climb as a *predicadora*, always believing that each new obstacle was simply another opportunity for the God who had called her to this life to prove himself faithful once again. The women in this study saw and experienced the providence of God in more liberative interpretations of Scripture and in a pneumatology that had changed perspectives within their denominations. They had added to these the power of their own testimonies as they navigated the somewhat perilous landscape of shared spousal ministry with its expectations of paradoxical domesticity.

The *predicadoras* in this study still bore much in common with the male collaborators. Even though their preaching employed traditional interpretations of Scripture and focused on personal conversion, it still sprang from and spoke to the wounds of their immigrant community. Given their own unique experiences, the *predicadoras* in this study also reflected on the additional wounds of marginalization and exclusion that they and their female hearers had suffered. Their witness reveals the ways in which the context of the migrant experience allows for the organic development of contextually faithful and liberative articulations even for congregations that are rooted in traditionalist beliefs and readings of Scripture. Integral to this development is the work of the Holy Spirit, which creates space for new practices and faithful reformulations. In many ways, my female collaborators understood the Spirit to be achieving the kind of liberative work desired by González and Jiménez. Not having had the opportunity to study academic liberation theology, the majority of these *predicadoras* were moved in liberative directions in their interpretation of Scripture through their own personal and communal experiences of the Holy Spirit.

From the perspective of many academics, the fact that most of the *predicadoras* in this study still relied—at least to some degree—on shared spousal ministry to legitimize their ministries might seem stunted, regressive, or even inauthentic. But within their own contexts, these women wielded significant power and have made great strides. There are relative degrees of liberation. It does not look the same in all bodies, in all spaces, or at all times. The reality for these women was that they had inherited certain benefits from their *predicadora* forebears, and through their example and rhetoric, they were using the pulpit as a platform to create greater opportunities for themselves and for future generations. Moved by the Spirit, they were extending a hand to other women so that together they might respond to God's calling and in their gladness sing, "*Mi alma glorifica al Señor* / My soul glorifies the Lord."

6
Conclusion

Conclusions are difficult. According to Esteban, the pastor of Iglesia Agua Viva, his first sermon had been an unmitigated disaster. He was still a layperson at the time, but the female pastor of the Pentecostal church he was attending believed that he had potential as a preacher, so she gave him the opportunity to preach during one of their evening services. Esteban began well, sharing a humorous personal story that connected with the congregation. Then he segued into an explanation of why his topic was relevant for his hearers. He articulated a clear thesis, developed several coherent points (as I hope I have done), and closed with an exhortation that he planned to reinforce by quoting a particular passage of Scripture. Instead, things started to unravel:

Dije yo, "Porque la Biblia dice . . . la Biblia dice. . . ."	I said, "Because the Bible says . . . the Bible says. . . ."

Esteban reenacted the dreadful moment for me with dramatic flair. He spoke the words "because the Bible says" with ringing authority, fully anticipating his ability to deliver a definitive word on behalf of the divine. Then there was a pause. He bit his bottom lip, and his eyes shifted down and to the right. He delivered the second "the Bible says" in a quavering voice, no longer certain whether this particular authoritative word was still present in the quiver of his memory. The next pause was longer than the first, as Esteban demonstrated for me the desperation with which he looked back and forth across the congregation, as if hoping that one of them was holding a cue card for him that evening. Finally, his eyes landed on his *pastora*, and he gave up all pretense of navigating his difficulty alone:

. . . ¿qué es lo que dice la Biblia, Pastora?	. . . what is it that the Bible says, Pastor?

As Esteban learned that day, it can be difficult to finish a sermon well. Another collaborator who participated in this study described the conclusion of his sermons like attempting to land a plane: sometimes you circle the runway a few times before you figure out how to do it.

What is true of preaching is true of ethnography as well: conclusions are difficult. The two great temptations, in my opinion, are to proclaim the existence of a forest when there are only trees or to become so enamored by the details and character of the trees themselves that you miss the forest altogether. By this I mean that many ethnographers may, in their desire to build careers and shake up academic guilds, draw conclusions that extend far beyond the support of the evidence they have gathered and presented. I have found the methodology of collaborative ethnography to be especially useful in helping me to avoid this particular pitfall as I have remained in communication with my collaborators throughout the process of writing, running things by them, and soliciting their feedback. Indeed, even as my dissertation committee was reading much of the material that would eventually form this book, I was also meeting once again with all of my collaborators to hear what changes they thought I should make throughout this text. Where I point to a forest, it is not solely I who am pointing, but we.

THE VALUE OF THE TREES THEMSELVES

I confess that the temptation to which I am most prone is the second one—to care more about the individual trees than the forest they comprise. I find the trees in this case—the journeys, testimonies, and practices of the individuals who participated in this study—to be poignant and inspiring, and one of the primary purposes of this work is to give them a place to appear. Returning to a quotation that I included in the introduction, I share once again Mary McClintock Fulkerson's observation that her ethnographic portrayal of Good Samaritan United Methodist Church "can be seen as a form of testimony to that which indicates the reality of God."[1] This study also is a form of testimony, bearing witness to the experiences and preaching of the *predicadores* who participated in it. To the degree that I have been able to render in print the reality of these individuals, I hope that the reader encounters each of them not as a point of data, but as a "face," a concept first proposed by the philosopher Emmanuel Levinas and elaborated upon by the theologian Edward Farley. According to Farley, the concept of the face refers neither to "physiognomy (the place of sensibility) nor acts which emotionally feel the other."[2] Instead, the experience of another's face is "the 'infinitely strange' and mysterious presence of something which contests my projecting meanings of it, an unforeseeable depth . . . which cannot be cognitively or emotionally mastered."[3] The experience of the face is not the mere recognition that the other exists but a primordial summons to compassionate obligation. Levinas describes the summons of the face in his essay "Meaning and Sense" as a challenge to the sovereignty of the self, based upon the fragility of the other:

> The epiphany of the absolutely other is a face, in which the other calls on me and signifies an order to me through his nudity, his denuding. His presence is a summons to answer. The I does not only become aware of this necessity to answer, as though it were an obligation or a duty about which it would have to come to a decision; it is in its very position wholly a responsibility or a diacony, as it is put in Isaiah, chapter 53.[4]

In the presence of the face, one does not pause to make a choice whether to act ethically or compassionately. The self is either radically reoriented by the vulnerability of the other (like the Suffering Servant of Isaiah 53 to whom Levinas alludes) or it remains locked in its previous egocentric state.[5]

The presence of my collaborators in this work is a "summons to answer," a call to "compassionate obligation," not just because of their vulnerability but also in light of their inherent worth and inspiring faithfulness. As I reveal their "faces" to you, insofar as a study of this sort permits, I want to say, "Here they are! Encounter these people—see who they are, and hear what they have to say. Be moved by them if you have a heart to be moved, but at the very least do not ignore them."

TURNING TOWARD THE FOREST

Although I believe that giving my collaborators a place to appear is extremely worthwhile in and of itself, I also believe that I would be doing them and their stories a disservice not to consider the broader implications of their journeys and experiences. As a work of practical theology, this study bears a commitment not just to describe "how people live as people of faith in communities and society," but also to reflect on "how they might do so more fully both in and beyond this life and world."[6] Therefore I will now consider the significance of my research, especially as it relates to questions of what constitutes "authentic" Hispanic preaching.

In the fourth chapter of this book, I shared the description of authentic Hispanic preaching presented by Justo González and Pablo Jiménez in *Púlpito: An Introduction to Hispanic Preaching* and *Manual de Homilética Hispana: Teoría y Práctica desde la Diáspora*. Although I wholeheartedly agree with them regarding the need for contextually faithful preaching, the experiences and practices of my collaborators continually blurred the lines of division González and Jiménez imagined between "traditional" and "authentic" preaching. Many of them clearly connected the social location of their communities with the social location of Scripture while still preaching fairly traditional sermons. Others emphasized private religiosity or individual morality but did so in ways that addressed their hearers' wounds of migration. Very few of them approached the Bible with anything that could be described as hermeneutical suspicion. And yet they preached sermons intended to sustain their marginalized hearers by emphasizing the wonder-working power of God and the solidarity of their own communities of faith.

MAKING SENSE OF THE DIFFERENCES

González himself admits that the large majority of Hispanic Protestant preaching in the United States falls into the category of traditional (and thus, for González, less authentic preaching). His particular vision of authenticity seems to be based on the practices of a certain subsection of Hispanic preaching, particularly within mainline Protestant denominations, as well as on a liberative ideal.[7] That is not to say that his emphasis on non-innocent reading and social concerns is unimportant for the Hispanic church or for the church at large. Indeed, I found the description of Hispanic preaching offered by González and Jiménez to be particularly moving myself, and so I looked for evidence of its use throughout my fieldwork over the course of several years. What I found was that, of my collaborators, only five of them ever expressed any awareness of the concept of approaching Scripture in this way. These five collaborators also happened to be the five preachers in this study who had received the most graduate theological training in the United States. Four of them had earned master's degrees in divinity from a prominent, mostly Anglo American divinity school, while the other had attended a predominantly African American theological seminary. All five were ministers in the United Methodist Church. One of them in particular, a United Methodist minister named Isaac, shared a view of Hispanic preaching's prophetic role that had much in common with González' vision:

Creo que la predicación hispana tiene tanto potencial de revitalizar la vida de La Iglesia Metodista Unida. Entonces yo considero que en el futuro tenemos que crear espacios bien intencionales para proclamar la palabra desde la perspectiva hispano latina en la iglesia general.	I believe that Hispanic preaching has so much potential to revitalize the life of the United Methodist Church. So I think that in the future we must create very intentional spaces in order to proclaim the word from the Hispanic-Latino perspective within the church in general.

No porque seamos buenos predicadores—yo no pienso que soy uno de ellos—sino porque a la palabra traspasarnos y producir todo lo que tiene que producir la palabra, de esa experiencia proclamarla a la iglesia en general. Ese mensaje abre ojos, abre corazones, abre mentes. Así la palabra se humaniza. Se pone relevante a la realidad actual de este país. Yo soy idealista tal vez.

Not because we are good preachers—I do not think I am one of them—but rather because as the word passes through us and produces all that the word has to produce, from that experience proclaiming it to the church in general. That message opens eyes, opens hearts, opens minds. That is how the word becomes human. It becomes relevant to the actual reality in this country. Maybe I am an idealist.

Isaac paused for a moment at this point in our conversation, stroking his goatee as he pondered the effect that the proclaimed word, humanized through the lives and experiences of Hispanic preachers, might have on the United States. Then he offered an example of a text that might be preached differently after passing though the hermeneutic of Hispanic immigrant reality:

Al predicar un sermón sobre José, la iglesia anglosajona piensa atrás en Egipto y la historia. Al contextualizarlo a la situación actual de los hispanos en este país toma un sentido totalmente diferente. A José lo acusaron, y la mujer dijo, "El Hebreo—el inmigrante, el foráneo, no digno de confianza—él me violó." No dijo el sirviente. Dijo el extranjero.

Cuando Ud. oye en las noticias, "Atropellaron a una persona y por cierto iba borracho la persona manejando," puede Ud. pensar, "que tipo tan desafortunado." Pero al momento que Ud. escucha que el conductor no tenía documentos, Ud. se va a pensar, "Pero ¿cómo es posible que dejemos entrar a esa gente?"

La palabra está traspasando nuestras heridas como la palabra traspasó las heridas de Cristo.

Preaching a sermon on Joseph, the Anglo-Saxon church thinks back on Egypt and history. Contextualizing it to the actual situation of Hispanics in this country takes a totally different sense. They accused Joseph, and the woman said, "The Hebrew—the immigrant, the foreigner, not worthy of confidence—he raped me." She did not say the servant. She said the foreigner.

When you hear in the news, "They ran over a person and the person driving was definitely drunk," you can think, "what an unfortunate guy." But at the moment that you hear that the driver was undocumented, you are going to think, "But how is it possible that we let those people enter?"

The word is passing through our wounds like the word passed through the wounds of Christ.

Isaac's vision of the way in which Hispanic preaching can serve as a corrective lens for the broader church and society in the United States was powerful and bore strong resemblance to the vision that González and Jiménez elucidated. During our conversation, however, Isaac was not speaking about the kind of preaching in which he engaged on a regular basis within his own congregation. He was referring, rather, to a form of prophetic proclamation that Hispanic United Methodist preachers might direct toward the larger non-Hispanic constituency within their denomination. This kind of preaching was not the dominant paradigm at work among my collaborators, even for Isaac and the other four United Methodist ministers who shared some of his sensibilities.

González implies that it is the dominant, Anglo-Saxon Protestant culture that has carried out what he describes as the miseducation of Hispanic preachers, a kind of colonization that has caused them to abandon their own perspectives and interpretations in favor of those preferred by the dominant culture. My collaborators, however, did not feel as though they had been indoctrinated by Anglo American theology and hermeneutics. Most of them credited their conversion to Protestant Christianity to the influence of entirely Hispanic congregations, some in the United States and others in their countries of origin. In many cases, due to the inaccessibility of formal theological education in the United States, the same churches that had been sites for their conversion experiences had also provided much of their ministerial preparation. Thus, my collaborators identified their practices of preaching and scriptural interpretation to be truly "theirs," whether or not they aligned with certain visions of "authenticity."

During a second round of conversations I had with my collaborators, I asked them to join me in co-interpreting the seeming absence of traditional liberation preaching. Eva, a United Methodist minister well-versed in the writings of Justo González, offered a succinct analysis:

| Siempre predico a las necesidades del pueblo. | I always preach to the needs of the people. |

Whereas the needs of her congregation occasionally called for the kind of hermeneutics and preaching described by González—she recalled preaching in this way in an effort to reassure her church shortly after the election of Donald Trump—she found their most pressing needs to be spiritual conversion and addressing their wounds of migration. While González rightly pushes back against the dangers of colonization being imposed, subtly or overtly, upon Hispanic preachers, his work also suggests a series of hermeneutic principles that were mostly alien to the ministers who participated in this study. What he described as being "ours" was certainly not "theirs" in a native sense, but was only something to which a few of them had been introduced as "theirs" while in the process of attending predominantly non-Hispanic seminaries.

This observation calls for greater sensitivity in describing what is "ours" or what qualifies as authentic in relation to Hispanic homiletics in general. In the introduction I discussed the concerns voiced by Mulder, Ramos, and Martí related to the dangers of essentialization and generalization within sociological studies of Hispanic Protestantism.[8] But the danger is just as real for descriptions of Hispanic Protestant preaching, and it calls for greater breadth in our determinations of what qualifies as contextually faithful. Throughout this study, I have presented my research as depictive of the practices of first-generation Hispanic Protestant immigrant preachers, but it is almost certain that future works will discover more complexity within this population than what I observed and have portrayed—as they should.

In addition to its focus on the nature of Hispanic preaching, my research also touches on important topics related to the field of homiletics, the understanding of vocational discernment, the practice of collaborative ethnography, the evolution of theological education, and the future of the Hispanic Protestant church.

HOMILETICS

What Helmut Thielicke alluded to in his parable of the young theologian and what Henry Mitchell stated forcefully regarding black preaching, my collaborators proved through their everyday reality of living, working, and serving: namely, the incredible importance of understanding and being able to "work *within* the culture of the congregation."[9] The Hispanic immigrant pastors who collaborated with me in this study were completely immersed in the culture of their people, having also dealt with the realities of transnational identity, ongoing secular occupations, and bicultural environments at home. In addition, many of them were, at any given moment, helping their congregants through immigration issues or providing them with services that were difficult for them to access in any other way due to their documentation status or lack of English proficiency.

In a way, my collaborators experienced a liminality very similar to my own as a participant-observer among them and their congregations. They participated fully in the same life experiences as their parishioners, and yet were also the ones tasked with observing and reflecting theologically on the nature of God's presence and purposes in and for lives such as theirs. Each Sunday they interpreted Scripture for a community whose path they had intimately shared. Furthermore, their mere presence in the pulpit served as an embodiment of the grace of God in a new place. If the pastor could live a productive life in spite of his physical handicap, or remain at peace despite her undocumented status, or come and preach after laying bricks all day, then the congregation saw that there was hope for them as well. One area for future consideration would be to examine the way in which ministers representing other specific ethnicities/populations appeal to shared knowledge (as many Hispanics do with immigration) to foster faith formation.

But these insights also bear significant implications for churches and denominations in which the clergy has become more professionalized. How can a full-time pastor whose schedule is running over with committee meetings, community involvement, homiletical preparation, and pastoral care duties preach as an insider to his or her congregation? How can ministers bridge the cultural chasm separating them from their congregations if they are also separated by regional divides, socioeconomic circumstances, or urban vs. suburban vs. rural experiences? Certainly, one element of the gulf between preacher and congregation will always remain in these situations: a pastor who does not closely approximate the background of his or her hearers cannot serve as an embodiment of God's possibilities for members of that community to the same degree as my collaborators could.

Yet there still remains the possibility of preaching in a way that connects with the lived experiences of the hearers and "partakes of the power and lasting quality" of the surrounding culture.[10] Although this kind of preaching is certainly most attainable for insiders, I believe that it can also be learned to some extent by outsiders who are willing to engage in a process of faithful attentiveness. During my own time collaborating with Hispanic pastors and congregations, I also had the opportunity to preach several times at Iglesia Agua Viva and for other Hispanic audiences.[11] Incorporating the insights I had gleaned through my research, I gradually learned to preach in a way that resonated more deeply for these hearers. I believe that contextually faithful proclamation requires the preacher to be an ethnographer as well. The need to exegete the congregation has been part of homiletical wisdom since at least the early fifth century when Augustine, in his *First Catechetical Instruction*, advised teachers and preachers to consider the cultural context of their audience, taking into account whether they are "learned or unlearned," "townsfolk or countryfolk," or "a gathering in which all sorts and conditions of men are represented." These observations are necessary in Augustine's opinion because "it cannot fail to be the case that different persons should affect in different ways the one who intends to instruct orally and likewise the one who intends to give a formal discourse."[12]

Although many homileticians over the years have prescribed imagination or some degree of pastoral involvement as necessary tools for attaining this contextual knowledge, Leonora Tubbs Tisdale was the first to advocate specifically for the use of ethnography as a path toward more contextually faithful preaching.[13] Her book *Preaching as Local Theology and Folk Art*, first published in 1997, remains of great importance today. Most helpful are its applications of ethnographic methodology to the processes of getting to know a new or current congregation, selecting sermon themes/passages, and either affirming or challenging the existing practices or doctrinal positions of a local body of believers. The teaching of preaching could be improved by working ethnographic exercises into the curriculum so as to teach future pastors how to develop a deeper and more nuanced understanding of the congregations they will one day engage through preaching. A promising area for future research would be to undertake an anthropological study of currently serving pastors learning about and applying ethnographic methodology within their congregations as a pathway toward more contextually faithful preaching. Insights from those pastors and their congregations could further establish the merits of ethnography in the service of homiletics.

Finally, as it relates to homiletics, this study highlights the redemptive and prophetic possibilities of preaching for those congregations that bear the scars of migration or other pervasive wounds. All of my immigrant collaborators and their congregations came to the United States in some sense seeking a net gain for their lives. They believed that the difficulties of immigration would be offset by financial gain, or the escape from violence, or a brighter future for their children. When their hope was shaken by the reality of their journeys, wounds, and ongoing difficulties, it was preaching that not only engendered or restored their faith, but also renewed their immigrant hopes. Identifying with the Old Testament Hebrew people or the New Testament early church reinforced for them the possibilities that they also might experience a promised land and citizenship through their faith communities. Even though these hopes were construed spiritually, they still served to offset partially the disappointment felt by many congregants over the unattainability of these goods in a political sense. This kind of preaching did more than simply offer an escape from oppression; it gave people a vision of a brighter future that enabled them to endure the present and continue to move forward in hope.

VOCATIONAL DISCERNMENT

In the second chapter, I shared the way in which my collaborators' journeys of migration and vocational discernment usually intersected. Immigration often left my collaborators with a variety of wounds, ranging from actual physical wounds to a broad array of psychological wounds, including the losses of identity and community. They experienced their sense of calling in the healing (divine or communal) of these wounds and sometimes found their calling to be part of the healing itself, both for themselves and for others. The way in which their vocational discernment was informed by very specific immigrant experiences gave their ministries a definite trajectory. They entered into ministry and began to preach with a clear desire for others within the larger immigrant community to experience what they had—physical healing, a new-found identity through Christ, and a sense of belonging to a new community. This close connection between the context that helped shape my collaborators' sense of calling and the circumstances in which their parishioners lived made their preaching and overall ministry especially effective.

Several larger questions emerge from this observation. First, to what degree do the contexts for vocational discernment for ministers from different ethnicities and/or circumstances align with the lived experiences of their congregants? Is an Anglo American minister who experiences vocational discernment during a period of dissatisfaction with graduate school similarly shaped by the context of his or her calling to minister to the needs of future congregants?[14] Certainly more research would need to be done about the effect that the context of vocational discernment has on ministerial effectiveness, but this study suggests that understanding one's vocation in the light of circumstances not unlike those experienced by the congregation one serves has a positive effect on an individual's ministry. How then could churches lead people of all ages to consider the possibility of ministerial vocation within circumstances that are most common throughout their congregation? How could seminaries and divinity schools help future ministers to broaden their understanding of the context of their callings in order to minister more effectively?

A second line of thinking emerges from the way in which vocational discernment served as part of the cure for these preachers' wounds. Their understanding of discernment was, in many cases, both occasioned by an experience of the divine within a season of woundedness and heightened by their acute sense of divine presence in those difficult moments. I wonder to what extent this process might also bring healing for laity undergoing a process of vocational discernment for their roles both within and beyond the church? This kind of process is already taking place within many of the Hispanic congregations included in this study, not necessarily with the intent of providing healing for migration's wounds, but in an effort to train leaders for churches that do not have many because of their recent establishment and transient congregations. This study highlights the possible benefit of engaging in vocational discernment not just for congregational support but as a means of providing some measure of healing for parishioners' wounds. This application of vocational discernment would seem to be fruitful for churches with members of any ethnicity.

COLLABORATIVE ETHNOGRAPHY

The commitments of collaborative ethnography are intended to foster greater mutuality between researchers and those whose communities serve as the objects of that research. The dialogic approach I adopted in this study served as both a form of aggravation and of comfort throughout my work. As I conducted interviews and transcribed them, I would discuss my current ideas with my collaborators either informally or in the context of other interviews. To my dismay, they always introduced greater complexity into my developing reflections! This often led to a change in certain interview questions (and the need to reinterview collaborators whose first interviews I had already transcribed) and even the reshaping of entire chapters. This process, however, also gave me a greater sense of writing *with* the community rather than simply writing *about* them. The increased degree of honesty and accountability required of practitioners of collaborative ethnography helped me deal with my own personal questions as to whether someone such as myself (still a Hispanic immigrant, but one who had experienced migration, assimilation, and ministry very differently) was capable of (or even deserving of) portraying the lived faith of these collaborators. Ultimately, however, I found my collaborators eager to share their stories with me and to help me reflect theologically on their journeys and preaching in ways that helped me overcome my own inner doubts.

That is not to say that this work of collaborative ethnography transcends all ethical quandaries. Although "collaborators" is certainly a more inclusive word than "informants" or "sources" and reflects their value and contribution more fully than "consultants" or "interlocutors," there are still significant issues with the nature of our collaboration and even with how I have employed the term. Given my obligation to protect the identity of the women and men who participated in this work and the identities of the people they served, I employed pseudonyms for them and their churches and provided the vaguest of geographic information as to the locations where their congregations worshipped. The importance of this kind of anonymity only seemed to increase throughout 2017 as immigration crackdowns increased and a few of my Hispanic minister friends either entered sanctuary churches or dropped below the radar in order to avoid immediate deportation. Given the necessity of anonymity, the end result is a book in which the only real names that appear are mine and those of scholars whose works I have quoted. I have given my collaborators a place to appear—but only partially, having also stripped them of the names given to them by parents from whom the majority of them have also been separated.

Collaborative ethnography's commitment to clearer and more accessible writing was also difficult to uphold throughout this work. First, I have written the vast majority of this book in English. Only the actual words of the collaborators themselves appear in Spanish, meaning that while they can see whether they were quoted accurately, some of them could not read the surrounding paragraphs that reveal the context in which their words are being employed and the connections and conclusions I draw from them. When I met with them following the completion of my rough draft, I had to explain in Spanish the ways in which I had used their words, and they had to trust that I was accurately representing my work to them. The dynamic of this exchange was not ideal but was the best I could do given the circumstances. I also shared digital or printed copies of my rough draft with all of my collaborators, highlighting for them the areas in which their words and stories appeared. In spite of my desire to avoid theological, homiletical, or ethnographic jargon as much as possible, there were still several phrases and concepts that I had to decipher for certain collaborators, even though they read English well.

In addition, I am painfully aware that I have referred to the twenty-four *predicadores* included in this study as "my" collaborators more times than I can count. Try as I did, I could not find a similarly brief yet still equally accurate way to refer to them on most of these occasions. I do not mean to imply that they, or their stories, or their sermons belong either to me or to this study. Instead, I hope the reader will understand those many possessive adjectives in the same sense as if I were speaking of "my" friends or "my" family. They are the collaborators with whom I found myself many times over the last few years, and although they certainly do not belong to me, I feel as though I belong to them in the sense of being indebted to them for their friendship, hospitality, and openness. My ethical and moral responsibility to them continues in various forms as I advocate on behalf of undocumented immigrants and continue to work alongside these collaborators and other Hispanic pastor friends to help them gain access to the kinds of theological education and ministerial preparation that they desire for themselves.

THEOLOGICAL EDUCATION

In chapter 3, when discussing the *identidades multiples* inhabited by my collaborators, I shared the reflections of Agustín, who worried that professional-

ization might diminish or even corrupt the understanding of vocation among Hispanic clergy:

Lo que yo he experimentado aquí es que se profesionaliza tanto la labor del pastor y del predicador que se puede caer en eso. ¿Voy a asimilar a esta manera de trabajar o voy a preservar esta vocación—la manera en que los hispanos vean la vocación? No es una profesión si no un verdadero llamado de Dios.	What I have experienced here is that the work of the pastor and preacher is so professionalized that it can fall into that. Am I going to assimilate to this manner of work or am I going to preserve this vocation—the way in which Hispanics view the vocation? It is not a profession but rather a true call of God.

I will write more extensively about the future of the Hispanic Protestant church in the following section, but I believe Agustín's questions are also important for the endeavor of theological education. Without doubt, Hispanic pastors are not the only ones whose understanding and practice of vocation can be diminished through certain modes of theological education that are more focused on professionalization, credentialing, or even academic pontificating than they are on the real needs of local congregations.

Throughout my work, so many of my collaborators spoke of having received their first ministerial training within their local congregations. Rather than simply attending worship services and Bible studies geared toward their own individual spiritual growth, they were also mentored for ministerial tasks, often from the early days of their involvement in their churches. Some of their pastors taught small classes focused on scriptural exegesis or preaching. One congregation hosted a series of workshops to help people learn to share their testimony in public. They were motivated by pastors and others to lead Bible studies and preach and felt more comfortable doing so because it was a fairly regular practice within their congregations, thus making the idea more seriously imaginable for them.

All of these forms of training were tightly connected to the real need for these skills in an ecclesial setting. The end result of a class on biblical interpretation was not a student's rigidly formatted exegesis paper, but the opportunity to lead a weeknight Bible study. The fruit of a preaching seminar was not a theologically cutting-edge sermon shared under carefully controlled circumstances with one's seminary peers, but the opportunity to preach on a Sunday morning in front of people—one's own community—who had come not out of compulsion but because of desire and deep need, people whose response would be either joyously or maddeningly unpredictable, depending on one's point of view.

There were definitely limitations to these church-based forms of instruction and preparation, but I believe the tremendous value of them was in the close connection between content and context. Courses were offered based on the actual contemporaneous needs of the congregation, and the knowledge and skills cultivated within each course were tailored to those needs as well. Furthermore, once my collaborators had perceived a sense of divine calling, in many cases through these early forms of ministerial training and opportunity, they did not pause their ministerial endeavors in order to become full time students. The vast majority of them had neither the means nor the access to engage in theological education without also working full time in some other capacity, so they piecemealed their training between conferences, certificate programs, and *institutos bíblicos* / biblical institutes that they could squeeze in around ministry and secular work. Although there is certainly a downside to handling that kind of workload, as was seen in the family dynamics of at least one of my collaborators, I believe that continuing to rethink theological education to make it more concurrent with actual ministerial work would be beneficial for so many seminarians who often experience theological education as a disruption between their calling and service to the church. Seminary students who were actively engaged in ministry would be more likely to see points of connection between their coursework and its implementation and more likely to demand relevant class material in those cases in which it did not already exist. As seminaries and divinity schools ponder the future of theological education in an environment of dwindling denominational support and decreased enrollment, there is also hope that a change to less centralized modes of education that allowed for ministry and training to run in parallel could bring about a revitalization.

Also, just as researchers must be careful not to overwrite the practices of Hispanic Protestant immigrants with their own sociological theories, institutions offering theological education to this population must exercise similar caution. Hispanic Protestant communities of faith need content that connects with their context. The experiences of my collaborators point to the need for theological education that is closely connected to congregational life and ministry, and this is perhaps most true for the dynamic of Hispanic Protestants in a state like North Carolina where their history only stretches back a few decades. Their current theology and preaching are truly "theirs," shaped by the hardship of immigration as well as the practices of their local congregations. There was remarkable similarity across denominational lines regarding the aims of preaching, even

between preachers who engaged in radically different liturgical practices. In light of these circumstances, theological education offered for Hispanic populations,[15] whether guided by Anglo American or Hispanic leadership, must be exceedingly careful to impart knowledge without imposing it, thereby replacing a community's embodied wisdom with someone else's view of what is orthodox or even what is naturally "theirs." Such education must always impart content through context.

THE FUTURE OF THE HISPANIC CHURCH IN NORTH CAROLINA

North Carolina's Hispanic population has experienced incredibly rapid growth in the last few decades. According to census data included in the introduction, the number of individuals self-identified as Hispanic increased from 76,726 in 1990 to 913,895 in 2015. The vast majority of this population comprises first-generation immigrants and their children. One of my collaborators who had previously been part of the Assemblies of God in New York described the way in which Hispanic AG congregations there had typically been oriented either to first-generation immigrants or toward their more acculturated children and grandchildren. Several of my collaborators pointed toward the beginnings of this kind of stratification already taking place in their congregations as children and teenagers had difficulty reading and understanding Spanish. Leo, a Baptist pastor, believed that change was coming soon for Hispanic congregations like his:

Pienso que las congregaciones van a mantener su español pero también se van a disminuir, puede ser en cinco o diez años. Los muchachos van a tener sus propias congregaciones bilingües porque todos los muchachos que batallan con el español van a decir, "Necesitamos algo de lo nuestro."	I think that the congregations will retain their Spanish, but they are also going to decrease, maybe in five or ten years. The young people are going to have their own bilingual congregations because all the young people who struggle with Spanish are going to say, "We need something of our own."

Álvaro, an Assemblies of God pastor with two decades of ministerial experience in the Raleigh area, felt that first-generation churches would maintain steady membership due to continuous migration in spite of what he also foresaw as an exodus of second-generation members. For him, this meant that churches like his would retain not only their character, but also their challenges:

Nuestros hijos aquí hablan más ingles que español. Se convierte en su primer lenguaje. Entonces andamos siempre ganando y perdiendo porque ellos se van a la iglesia americana. Entonces seremos siempre la iglesia hispana, prácticamente vamos a decir de nuevas personas llegando. Los niños que van a la iglesia y que desarrollan su carrera más profesional ya no están con nosotros. Siempre estamos trabajando con la gente menos capacitada. Y eso es complicado. No tienen carro, licencia, casa. Siempre estamos en eso. Esa crema que se levanta se nos va.

Our children speak more English here than Spanish. It becomes their first language. Therefore, we continue always gaining and losing because they go to the American church. So we will always be the Hispanic church, practically we will say of new people coming. The children who go to the church and who develop more professional careers are no longer with us. We are always working with the least equipped people. And that is complicated. They do not have a car, a license, or a house. We are always [dealing with] that. The cream that rises up leaves us behind.

Leo and Álvaro's reflections certainly fit within previous observations of second-generation immigrants gradually leaving their "home" churches due to differences in language fluency and socioeconomic status between generational cohorts. My work with these *predicadores* points to an additional possibility: the decreased resonance of their preaching's immigration-related themes for younger generations. Not only do members of the second generation not fully identify with the preacher's actual experience of immigration; they actually inhabit a different semiotic world that has been shaped by very different pressures.

Much has been written on whether immigrant churches serve as sites of cultural assimilation or ethnic identity maintenance, but at least one of my collaborators, a younger Pentecostal pastor named Fernando, thought there was something more significant taking place within his congregation:

Nosotros tenemos una iglesia bilingüe. Yo pienso que estamos en un momento de avivamiento global. Y porque es global se trata de una unificación de culturas. En el principio, algunos de los hermanos levantaban las cejas—pensaban, "Por qué está traduciendo sus sermones el hermano si somos una iglesia hispana?" Querían saber si estábamos convirtiéndonos en

We have a bilingual church. I think we are in a moment of global revival. And because it is global it is about a unification of cultures. In the beginning, some of the brothers and sisters raised their eyebrows—they thought, "Why is the brother translating his sermons if we are a Hispanic church?" They wanted to know if we were converting into an American church. It is not that,

una iglesia americana. No es eso, sino que Dios está haciendo algo lindo. Es un avivamiento global.

El libro de Apocalipsis dice que enfrente del trono había gente de todas naciones y de todas lenguas, los grandes y los pequeños. Dios no le interesa mucho la cultura de cada región porque hay una cultura superior. Cuando hay contacto, no puede sobrevivir el racismo. Cuando hay contacto no te veo como salvadoreño, ni como mexicano, ni como guatemalteco, ni como gringo, sino como mi hermano. El futuro de la predicación es un futuro mezclado.

but rather that God is doing something beautiful. It is a global revival.

The book of Revelation says that before the throne there were people of all nations and all tongues, the great and the small. God is not very interested in the culture of each region because there is a superior culture. When there is contact, racism cannot survive. When there is contact, I do not see you as Salvadoran, nor as Mexican, nor as Guatemalan, nor as a gringo, but rather as my brother. The future of preaching is a blended future.

Fernando did not see himself as a passive character in an inevitable process that social scientists have long described. Instead, he was an active agent working in conjunction with an overarching divine purpose of global revival.[16] For him, the blending of cultures and languages in worship and preaching was not a concession to reality but a step toward coming victory. Although Fernando's rhetoric on this matter was stronger than that of the rest of my collaborators, many of the younger participants in this study shared his optimism for a blended future.

I had originally intended to write more extensively within this book of the way in which preaching in the Hispanic church contributed to either ethnic identity maintenance or cultural assimilation, but I quickly discovered that these were not the most pressing questions for my collaborators. They did not feel that either of these possibilities was a significant goal of their proclamation. The echoes of their journeys of migration within their preaching promoted more of a specific immigrant-identity maintenance rather than a broader maintenance of ethnic identity. Even taking this into consideration, they focused much more intently upon their congregants' need to find new identities in Christ and the culture of a heavenly kingdom. When their practices of preaching seemed to support theories of assimilation (such as in their blending of languages within sermons), their motive was not cultural assimilation but a desire to meet the spiritual needs of younger generations or to fulfill a larger vision of revival and reconciliation. Given my employment of collaborative ethnography and its commitment to co-interpretation, I necessarily changed my focus to be more in line with theirs. Engaging in detached reflection about whether what they were "actually" doing was proving one of two sociological theories would have marginalized my collaborators within their own narratives and practices of preaching.

CONCLUSION

During the same time period when I was finalizing the manuscript for this book, I happened to be eating lunch at a table with some of the teenagers from Iglesia Agua Viva. Some of them had still been young children, and others had not yet joined the church when I first began my participant-observation in their congregation more than six years earlier. None of them knew or remembered the autobiographical details I had shared with the congregation on the first Thursday night I had attended one of their services, so they began asking me questions: Where did you say you were born? How old were you when you came to the United States? Are you a citizen? Did you always speak Spanish at home? Are you teaching your children to speak Spanish?

Their questions reminded me once again of the unbelievable complexity present within the larger category of Hispanic identity and of the difficulty of labeling any one homiletical style or hermeneutical approach as being "authentic" for Hispanic preaching as a whole. Justo González and Pablo Jiménez describe as authentic a particular style of preaching that resonates within their own contexts even if its hermeneutical orientation seems to have arisen primarily from academic conversations surrounding Latin American liberation theology. Although this preaching may have been transmitted primarily through seminaries rather than individual churches, it has now taken root and manifests integrity within certain contexts just as the preaching of my collaborators does within their own.

This observation serves as a reminder that authenticity—to whatever degree that term remains useful—is not only variegated but also fluid. What is "authentic" today in one place or for one population may not be so tomorrow. The lived experience of Iglesia Agua Viva's teenagers who speak Spanish and English fluently will generate new and yet still contextually faithful expressions of faith—including preaching—that may bear little resemblance to either the kind of preaching called for by González and Jiménez or the preaching described in this book. Other academics will need to come along and listen for the ways in which new preaching voices reflect the lived experiences of both ministers and congregations in contextually faithful and life-giving ways.

Notes

1 INTRODUCTION

1   As I discuss later on, one of my primary commitments to my collaborators, some of whom were undocumented immigrants or pastors of congregations that included undocumented immigrants, was to protect their identities. Therefore, I employ pseudonyms for all the pastors, congregants, and congregations in this study.

2   I feel comfortable sharing this degree of detail for two reasons: 1) They provide some sense of the space of Iglesia Agua Viva (IAV) and its surrounding geography while remaining sufficiently vague so as to avoid identification; and 2) Since my first visits, IAV has moved from this location to a different rented space in another community.

3   I use this term throughout this book with the full awareness of its implications and limitations. In *Introducing Latino/a Theologies*, Miguel A. De La Torre and Edwin David Aponte argue that the term "Hispanic" is used nowhere else but in the United States, where it serves as a "governmental construction designed to lump everyone who comes from a Spanish-speaking culture together in one group" (Miguel A. De La Torre and Edwin David Aponte, *Introducing Latino/a Theologies* [Maryknoll, N.Y.: Orbis Books, 2001], 15). Because "Hispanic" is a language-based ethnic category, it also leaves out or marginalizes many Latin American immigrants whose primary language is Portuguese, Quechua, Quiché, Dutch, English, or any number of other languages spoken in Central America, South America, and the Caribbean.

Many Latin American scholars prefer to use some form of the traditional adjective "Latino" while reforming its preferentially gendered nature. Thus, neologisms such as "Latina/o" and "Latinx" appear frequently within academic writing. Although I certainly agree with the reasoning behind the use of these terms and have used them myself in previous publications, I have, unfortunately, found them to be much less well known among Latin American immigrants outside of academia.

Since this work uses collaborative ethnography (which I discuss in greater detail later in this chapter), my terminology must abide by the underlying commitments of that methodology, including commitments to "more accessible writing" and "co-interpretation" with collaborators. These commitments privilege the understanding of collaborators over and above that of the researcher. My collaborators speak of themselves as *pastores hispanos* / Hispanic pastors engaged in *el ministerio hispano* / Hispanic ministry, so, out of respect for their self-understanding, I will refer to them the same way.

4 Throughout this book, I will include English translations next to all words, phrases, or quotations in Spanish. I will also show the original Spanish for all the responses, sermons, or other contributions of my collaborators. I believe this is an important commitment when it comes to representing the voices and lived experiences of my collaborators: they should be able to appear in this study as themselves in their own *idioma de corazón* / heart language. Also, because every act of translation is also an act of interpretation, the positioning of my translation alongside their Spanish-language responses is a mechanism not only to privilege their original communication, but also to hold myself as the researcher accountable for faithfully interpreting that communication for another audience.

5 In writing of the impact of the ethnographic researcher's social location upon his or her work, Joanna Herbert and Richard Rodger assert that the "extent to which the researcher and respondent share the same cultural background and worldview has been noted as an important factor in gaining access to the respondents and also securing their trust" (Joanna Herbert and Richard Rodger, "Frameworks: Testimony, Representation and Interpretation," in *Testimonies of the City: Identity, Community, and Change in a Contemporary Urban World*, ed. Richard Rodger and Joanna Herbert [Burlington, Vt.: Ashgate, 2007], 8).

6 Antonio Flores, Gustavo López, and Jynnah Radford, "2015, Hispanic Population in the United States Statistical Report," *Hispanic Trends*, Pew Research Center, September 18, 2017, https://www.pewhispanic.org/2017/09/18/facts-on-u-s-latinos-trend-data/. These figures are based on the Census Bureau's 2015 American Community Survey (ACS) and the 2000 decennial census. I have calculated the following figures and percentages based on this data as it is presented by the Hispanic Trends Project of the Pew Research Center in their Statistical Portrait of Hispanics in the United States.

7 Laura López-Sanders, "Bible Belt Immigrants: Latino Religious Incorporation in New Immigrant Destinations," *Latino Studies* 10, nos. 1–2 (2012): 129.

8 Data and calculations are based on U.S. census data from 1990, 2000, and 2010, as well as 2015 estimates from the U.S. Census Bureau: "Quick Facts: North Carolina," United States Census Bureau, accessed January 21, 2017, http://www.census.gov/quickfacts/table/PST045216/37; "NC Census Lookup," Log Into North Carolina, accessed January 25, 2017, now online at https://linc.osbm.nc.gov/pages/home/.

9 Leo Grebler, Joan Moore, and Ralph Guzman, *The Mexican American People: The Nation's Second Largest Minority* (New York: Free Press, 1970), 487.

10 Pew Research Center, "Changing Faiths: Latinos and the Transformation of American Religion," *Hispanic Trends*, April 25, 2007, http://www.pewhispanic.org/2007/

04/25/ii-religion-and-demography/. The Hispanic Trends Project uses the terms Hispanic and Latino interchangeably.

11 Wendy Cadge and Elaine Howard Ecklund, "Immigration and Religion," *Annual Review of Sociology* 33 (2007): 359–79.

12 Gastón Espinosa, *Latino Pentecostals in America: Faith and Politics in Action* (Cambridge, Mass.: Harvard University Press, 2014). Espinosa's primary focus is the Latino constituency within the Assemblies of God.

13 Paul Barton, *Hispanic Methodists, Presbyterians, and Baptists in Texas* (Austin: University of Texas Press, 2006).

14 Luis G. Pedraja, "Guideposts along the Journey: Mapping North American Hispanic Theology," in *Protestantes/Protestants: Hispanic Christianity within Mainline Traditions*, ed. David Maldonado Jr. (Nashville: Abingdon, 1999), 123.

15 José D. Rodriguez, "Confessing the Faith from a Hispanic Perspective," in Maldonado, *Protestantes/Protestants*, 113.

16 Francisco García-Treto, "Reading the Hyphens: An Emerging Biblical Hermeneutics for Latino/Hispanic U.S. Protestants," in Maldonado, *Protestantes/Protestants*, 161.

17 Mark T. Mulder, Aida I. Ramos, and Gerardo Martí, *Latino Protestants in America: Growing and Diverse* (Lanham, Md.: Rowman & Littlefield, 2017), 139. Italics appear in the original text.

18 Mulder, Ramos, and Martí, *Latino Protestants in America*, 4–5.

19 Mulder, Ramos, and Martí, *Latino Protestants in America*, 140.

20 Clifford Geertz, *The Interpretation of Cultures* (New York: Basic Books, 1973), 5.

21 Geertz, *Interpretation of Cultures*, 10.

22 The insider/outsider debate is also often characterized as a discussion of the relative merits of an "emic" (insider) approach to research versus an "etic" (outsider) one. For more information, see Donald A. Messerschmidt, ed., *Anthropologists at Home in North America: Methods and Issues in the Study of One's Own Society* (Cambridge: Cambridge University Press, 1981); and Thomas N. Headland, Kenneth L. Pike, and Marvin Harris, eds., *Emics and Etics: The Insider/Outsider Debate* (Newbury Park, Calif.: Sage, 1990).

23 John L. Aguilar, "Insider Research: An Ethnography of a Debate," in Messerschmidt, *Anthropologists at Home in North America*, 23–24.

24 Mary Clark Moschella, "Ethnography," in *The Wiley Blackwell Companion to Practical Theology*, ed. Bonnie J. Miller-McLemore (Oxford: Wiley-Blackwell, 2012), 225.

25 Christian Scharen and Aana Marie Vigen, *Ethnography as Christian Theology and Ethics* (New York: Continuum, 2011), 16.

26 Mary McClintock Fulkerson, *Places of Redemption: Theology for a Worldly Church* (Oxford: Oxford University Press, 2007), 254.

27 Bonnie Miller-McLemore, "Practical Theology," in vol. 1 of *Encyclopedia of Religion in America*, ed. Charles H. Lippy and Peter W. Williams (Washington, D.C.: CQ Press, 2010), 1740.

28 Moschella, "Ethnography," 232.

29 Kate Bowler, *Blessed: A History of the American Prosperity Gospel* (Oxford: Oxford University Press, 2013).

30 James S. Bielo, *Words upon the Word: An Ethnography of Evangelical Group Bible Study* (New York: New York University Press, 2009).

31 Susan J. Dunlap, *Caring Cultures: How Congregations Respond to the Sick* (Waco, Tex.: Baylor University Press, 2009).

32 Luke Bretherton, *Resurrecting Democracy: Faith, Citizenship, and the Politics of a Common Life* (Cambridge: Cambridge University Press, 2015).

33 Pamela Moss and Isabel Dyck, *Women, Body, Illness: Space and Identity in the Everyday Lives of Women with Chronic Illness* (Oxford: Rowman & Littlefield, 2002), 70.

34 Michael Kammen, *People of Paradox* (New York: Vintage, 1973), 97. Building upon the idea of what W. E. B. DuBois calls a "felt twoness" within the African American experience, Michael Kammen writes of the concept of "biformation" as a critical component toward understanding the shaping of African American perspective. Even the descriptive term "African American" speaks of the duality that every member of a minority population experiences living a life that is privy to the realities of a unique minority culture as well as those of the dominant culture.

35 De La Torre and Aponte, *Introducing Latino/a Theologies*, 37.

36 Aguilar, "Insider Research," 16.

37 Aguilar, "Insider Research," 18.

38 Luke Eric Lassiter, *The Chicago Guide to Collaborative Ethnography* (Chicago: University of Chicago Press, 2005), x.

39 For a more detailed account of this exchange, see Lassiter, *Chicago Guide to Collaborative Ethnography*, 4–8.

40 Lassiter, *Chicago Guide to Collaborative Ethnography*, 79.

41 Beginning in 2015, North Carolina began issuing limited-privilege driving permits to undocumented immigrants if they came forward and proved their identity and state residency. Although this allowed for legal driving, many immigrants did not come forward out of fear that their self-identification would one day be used as part of a government crackdown and mass deportation effort. Therefore, the possession of one of these permits or the lack of a current driver's license could be used to detect undocumented immigrants at police checkpoints.

42 "Fiscal Year 2017 ICE Enforcement and Removal Operations Report," U.S. Immigration and Customs Enforcement, accessed January 18, 2018, https://www.ice.gov/removal-statistics/2017.

43 Elliot Spagat and Jill Colvin, "Detentions Spike, Border Arrests Fall in Trump's First Year," *AP News*, December 5, 2017, accessed January 18, 2018, https://www.apnews.com/3252d88390ed4ddea736b4a85a0b78a9.

44 These threats include the danger to previously secure populations of immigrants. In September of 2017, President Trump also suspended the Deferred Action for Childhood Arrivals program (DACA), which had allowed nearly 800,000 undocumented people in the United States who had been brought here as children to come out of the shadows and register for work permits. One of the preachers who collaborated in this study was a DACA recipient who spoke about how hard it was to have to worry once again about what might happen to her young children if she were to be deported.

45 Lassiter, *Chicago Guide to Collaborative Ethnography*, 132.

46 Carol A. B. Warren, "Qualitative Interviewing," in *Handbook of Interview Research: Context and Method*, ed. Jaber F. Gubrium and James A. Holstein (Thousand Oaks, Calif.: Sage, 2002), 98.

47 John D. Brewer, *Ethnography* (Buckingham: Open University Press, 2000), 59.

48 The exception was Rafael, a Pentecostal pastor, who immigrated from Puerto Rico to New York as a very young child.

49 See table 1.1 regarding Hispanic population growth in North Carolina.

50 It is reasonable to assume that some of the 76,726 Hispanic residents of North Carolina in 1990 moved out of the state or died between 1990 and 2015.

51 The term *evangélico* does not have the same ecclesial or political connotations as its English cognate form "evangelical" does in North America. Nor does the word *cristiano*, when used by many Hispanic Protestants, embrace all of the possible denominational identities that are usually included under the heading of "Christian." My collaborators typically used both *evangélico* and *cristiano* as umbrella terms to describe Protestant as opposed to Catholic identity.

Arlene Sánchez Walsh also documents this usage of *cristiano* in her interviews with Hispanic Pentecostal students at the Latin American Bible Institute. They saw themselves as having "converted to 'Christianity,' leaving the Catholic 'religion'" behind (Arlene M. Sánchez Walsh, *Latino Pentecostal Identity: Evangelical Faith, Self, and Society* [New York: Columbia University Press, 2003], 71).

2 VIAJES CONCURRENTES / OVERLAPPING JOURNEYS

1 McClintock Fulkerson, *Places of Redemption*, 13.

2 McClintock Fulkerson offers the examples of the wound of ecclesial idolatries in Germany that prompted Karl Barth to develop his theology of the Word and the wound of falsely universal white theologies that spurred James Cone to articulate black theology; McClintock Fulkerson, *Places of Redemption*, 13–14.

3 David T. Abalos, *Latinos in the United States: The Sacred and the Political* (Notre Dame: University of Notre Dame Press, 2007), 9.

4 Seth M. Holmes, *Fresh Fruit, Broken Bodies: Migrant Farmworkers in the United States* (Berkeley: University of California Press, 2013), 8.

5 Holmes, *Fresh Fruit, Broken Bodies*, 30.

6 Holmes, *Fresh Fruit, Broken Bodies*, 30.

7 Holmes, *Fresh Fruit, Broken Bodies*, 89.

8 In Spanish, this name is pronounced "Dah-'veed."

9 Oscar Handlin, *The Uprooted*, 2nd ed. (Toronto: Little, Brown, 1973), 94–95.

10 Timothy L. Smith describes "the guilt for imagined desertion of parents and other relatives, and the search for community and identity in a world of strangers" beginning the very moment that "the nearest range of hills shut out the view of the emigrant's native valley" (Timothy L. Smith, "Religion and Ethnicity in America," *American Historical Review* 83, no. 5 [December 1978]: 1174).

11 Handlin, *Uprooted*, 129–30.

12 Eduardo meant that many Hispanic workers worked overtime willingly and without additional overtime compensation.

13 Smith, "Religion and Ethnicity in America," 1181.

14 Daniel Ramírez, *Migrating Faith: Pentecostalism in the United States and Mexico in the Twentieth Century* (Chapel Hill: University of North Carolina Press, 2015), 8.

15 John Adam Kern, *The Way of the Preacher: An Interpretation of a Calling* (Nashville: Publishing House of the M. E. Church, South, 1902), 72.

16 James O. Chatham, *Is It I, Lord?* (Louisville: Westminster John Knox, 2002), 8–9.

17 *Hermana* / sister and *hermano* / brother are typical expressions within Hispanic Protestant communities to refer to fellow believers. Regardless of age or social status, all members of a congregation are *hermanas y hermanos* in Christ.

18 Until recently, Mexico City was officially known as *La Ciudad de Mexico, D.F.*, with D.F. standing for Distrito Federal. This designation is similar to the status of Washington, D.C., in the United States as part of the District of Columbia rather than belonging to one of the fifty states. In common parlance, Mexico City is often referred to as *el distrito federal* or *el D.F.*

19 In "Guideposts along the Journey: Mapping North American Hispanic Theology," Luis G. Pedraja discusses the important role of testimony for Hispanic Protestants:

> [The] way in which popular religion expresses itself in Protestant Hispanic communities is through the *testimonio*. In the *testimonio*, congregants are invited to speak during the service to give their testimony of how God is active in their lives. *Testimonios* provide a concrete dimension to the faith by articulating how God is active in the present. In this sense, *testimonios* provide a dual vehicle of empowerment. First, they empower ordinary members of the congregation to speak about their faith and life. In the *testimonios* it is not the clergy or the institution that speaks and teaches about God. Instead, they invite the people to interpret everyday circumstances and attest to God's power and presence in them. In this act, the hermeneutical prerogative is taken away from the institution and placed with the people. (Pedraja, "Guideposts along the Journey," 134)

All of Pedraja's insights are consistent with the experiences of my collaborators. Testimonies provide a concrete dimension to the faith, bridging the gap between lived faith and liturgical ritual. But they also bridge the gap between laity and clergy in a practical sense, as they not only provide a platform for ordinary members of the congregations to speak but also a pathway for them to become preachers.

20 Writing of the growth of Pentecostalism in the borderlands, Daniel Ramírez recounts the following episode: "In 1919, Nava and Ramón Ocampo, a young convert from Zacatecas, Mexico, left Riverside to evangelize in Yuma, Arizona, where Nava's sister lived. Her reported healing from cancer brought several families from the Mexican Methodist and Baptist churches into the apostolic fold in early 1920, including Baptist elders Bernardo Hernández and Jesús Torres" (Ramírez, *Migrating Faith*, 39).

21 Kathleen Sullivan, "Iglesia de Dios: An Extended Family," in *Religion and the New Immigrants: Continuities and Adaptations in Immigrant Congregations*, ed. Helen Rose Ebaugh and Janet Saltzman Chafetz (Walnut Creek, Calif.: AltaMira, 2000), 143.

22 *Aleluya* is a mocking term for a Protestant Christian in Mexico. Daniel Ramírez writes that "the expression 'aleluya' (heard emanating from the noisy temples and houses where the Pentecostals worshipped) served detractors as a common epithet to hurl at this particularly troublesome brand of *evangélico*" (Ramírez, *Migrating Faith*, 72–73).

23 It was obvious during our conversation that this was a story Ignacio had told on more than one occasion. His pauses and facial expressions had been tuned for greatest effect through repetition. Also, when he began to share this testimonial set piece, his wife sat back and began to smile, knowing beat-for-beat what was coming but appreciatively anticipating the impact of the story and my ensuing reaction.

24 Daniel Ramírez shares a similar testimony of two undocumented Pentecostal women attempting to enter the United States near San Diego. Their coyote (smuggler), noticing they are Christians, encourages them to pray for rain because the agents at the San Onofre border station are unlikely to inspect their vehicle in a downpour. The women begin to pray and eventually cross the border unscrutinized in the midst of a rainstorm (Daniel Ramírez, "Public Lives in American Hispanic Churches: Expanding the Paradigm," in *Latino Religions and Civic Activism in the United States*, ed. Gastón Espinosa, Virgilio Elizondo, and Jesse Miranda [Oxford: Oxford University Press, 2005], 186).

25 The sixteenth chapter of the book of Acts tells the story of the imprisonment and miraculous release of the missionaries Paul and Silas from a jail in the city of Philippi. Set free from their captivity by an earthquake they attribute to divine action, Paul and Silas successfully employ the story of their deliverance as part of their evangelistic efforts.

26 Christian Lalive d'Epinay, *El Refugio de las Masas—Estudio Sociológico del Protestantismo Chileno* (Santiago: Editorial del Pacífico, S.A., 1968), 79.

27 Just as González worries whether the training of many Hispanic pastors has in fact been an act of hermeneutical assimilation, other scholars question whether conversion to Protestantism is an act of cultural assimilation by Hispanic immigrants. In the case of the collaborators who contributed to this book, fourteen of the twenty-four already identified as Protestants prior to their arrival in the United States. Several had been raised from birth in Protestant faith traditions, as Methodists in Mexico or Peru, or in Pentecostal denominations in the Dominican Republic or Puerto Rico. The other ten collaborators did convert to Protestantism in the United States, but all of them did so within the context of entirely Hispanic-led congregations.

  Growing Protestant populations throughout Central and South America have continually increased the likelihood of Hispanic Protestant immigration to the United States. Gastón Espinosa asserts that "Protestants make up 29 percent (50 million) of all Brazilians, 27 percent (4 million) of all Chileans, 25 percent

(2.8 million) of all Guatemalans, 22 percent (1.4 million) of all El Salvadorians, 22 percent of all Puerto Ricans (867,000), 20 percent (7 million) of all US Latinos, 19 percent (950,000) of all Nicaraguans, and 18 percent of all Hondurans (1.1 million) and all Panamanians (520,000)" (Gastón Espinosa, "The Pentecostalization of Latin American and U.S. Latino Christianity," *Pneuma* 26, no. 2 [2004]: 268–69).

3 *IDENTIDADES MULTIPLES* / MULTIPLE IDENTITIES

1 Helmut Thielicke, *Little Exercise for Young Theologians* (Grand Rapids: Eerdmans, 1962), 8.

2 Thielicke, *Little Exercise for Young Theologians*, 4–5.

3 Henry H. Mitchell, *Black Preaching: The Recovery of a Powerful Art* (Nashville: Abingdon, 1990), 14. Italicization of "within" is original to Mitchell's work but also coincides with an underlying message of this chapter.

4 Mitchell, *Black Preaching*, 15.

5 Mitchell, *Black Preaching*, 16.

6 Cecilio Arrastía, *Teoría y Práctica de la Predicación* (Miami: Editorial Caribe, 1978), 15.

7 Arrastía, *Teoría y Práctica de la Predicación*, 15.

8 *Coraje* usually means courage, while another word like "*rencor*" would more commonly be used to describe the kind of anger of which Antonio spoke. In context, however, it was clear that Antonio was describing a long-simmering anger or bitterness, and I took his usage of *coraje* to be colloquial.

9 Pablo A. Jiménez and Justo L. González, *Manual de Homilética Hispana: Teoría y Práctica desde la Diáspora* (Barcelona: Editorial CLIE, 2006), 54.

10 Jiménez and González, *Manual de Homilética Hispana*, 54.

11 Jiménez and González, *Manual de Homilética Hispana*, 55.

12 Jiménez and González, *Manual de Homilética Hispana*, 33.

13 Espinosa, *Latino Pentecostals in America*, 113.

14 Espinosa, *Latino Pentecostals in America*, 126.

15 Espinosa, *Latino Pentecostals in America*, 208.

16 Barton, *Hispanic Methodists, Presbyterians, and Baptists in Texas*, 71.

17 Barton, *Hispanic Methodists, Presbyterians, and Baptists in Texas*, 76.

18 Annual conferences of the United Methodist Church hold the deeds to all of their congregations' church buildings and facilities, not just those connected with Hispanic congregations.

19 Ana's involvement with La Iglesia de Dios Pentecostal Movimiento Internacional had begun in New York prior to her coming to North Carolina as a missionary. The first Iglesia de Dios Pentecostal M.I. missionary to the United States arrived in New York in 1929. Ana's arrival in North Carolina represented an expansion of the movement.

20 The Cooperative Baptist Fellowship, hereafter CBF, is a more moderate offshoot, both theologically and politically, of the Southern Baptist Convention, hereafter SBC. The CBF was originally established in 1991 during a time of great upheaval in Southern Baptist life that paralleled the rise of the Religious Right in the political

sphere. At stake were such issues as the leadership of SBC seminaries and commit-tees, the ordination and role of women in the convention, and beliefs regarding the nature of Scripture's inspiration. The CBF describes itself on its website as a network of 1,800 churches operating in eighteen different states. They have a par-ticularly strong presence in North Carolina.

21 The United Methodist Church includes a lay missionary initiative within its National Plan for Hispanic Ministries. Manuel's program was a local embodiment of that initiative, but one that he felt would not have begun or continued without his ongoing efforts.

22 Carlos B. Córdova, "The Social, Cultural, and Religious Realities of Central Amer-ican Immigrants in the United States," in *Dialogue Rejoined: Theology and Ministry in the United States Hispanic Reality*, ed. Ana María Pineda and Robert Schreiter (Collegeville, Minn.: Liturgical Press, 1995), 30.

23 Rafael was the most fully bilingual of all of my collaborators. We began to converse in Spanish before he asked me whether I would prefer to conduct our interview in English or Spanish. I deferred to him, and he ultimately chose English for the open-ended interview from which this response came.

24 During this last sentence, Rafael gestured outside of the building for "out there," then directed both hands back toward his chest for "in here." The implication, in line with his previous words, was that a healthy and prosperous integration in soci-ety was essential for the spiritual well-being of both his congregants and the His-panic community at large.

4 *LA PREDICACIÓN MISMA* / THE PREACHING ITSELF

1 Justo L. González and Pablo A. Jiménez, *Púlpito: An Introduction to Hispanic Preaching* (Nashville: Abingdon, 2005), x.

2 Jiménez and González, *Manual de Homilética Hispana*, 33.

3 Jiménez and González, *Manual de Homilética Hispana*, 35.

4 González and Jiménez, *Púlpito*, 18.

5 González and Jiménez, *Púlpito*, 19.

6 Jiménez and González, *Manual de Homilética Hispana*, 36.

7 González and Jiménez, *Púlpito*, 22.

8 González and Jiménez, *Púlpito*, 44.

9 As an aside, I have used some of Pablo Jiménez' homiletical materials in Spanish-language classes I have taught in the United States, Guatemala, El Salvador, and Peru. As for Justo González, I am one of many Hispanic scholars who has bene-fited tremendously from the ecology of programs he has created and the example he has set.

10 In various sermons I heard during my fieldwork, individual preachers called for immigration reform, greater respect for women, and more compassionate outreach to those living in poverty.

11 Ramírez, *Migrating Faith*, 64.

12 Deborah Root, *Cannibal Culture: Art, Appropriation and the Commodification of Difference* (Boulder, Colo.: Westview, 1996), 79.

13 Root, *Cannibal Culture*, 79.

14 Root, *Cannibal Culture*, 80.

15 Jonathan E. Calvillo and Stanley R. Bailey, "Latino Religious Affiliation and Ethnic Identity," *Journal for the Scientific Study of Religion* 54, no. 1 (2015): 74.

16 Pablo A. Jiménez, *Principios de Predicación* (Nashville: Abingdon, 2003), 13.

17 Jiménez, *Principios de Predicación*, 23.

18 Jiménez, *Principios de Predicación*, 23.

19 Jiménez, *Principios de Predicación*, 25.

20 Rodriguez, "Confessing the Faith from a Hispanic Perspective," 111.

21 As will be shown in this chapter, even the language most often used for experiences of conversion resonates in specific and powerful ways for first-generation Hispanic immigrants.

22 Barton, *Hispanic Methodists, Presbyterians, and Baptists in Texas*, 45.

23 Smith, "Religion and Ethnicity in America," 1178.

24 Luís Villoro, *Creer, Saber, Conocer* (Mexico City: Siglo Ventiuno Editores, 1996), 197.

25 Villoro, *Creer, Saber, Conocer*, 197. Italics are original to Villoro's text and indicate his emphasis. To avoid confusion in my English translation, I have placed the appropriate Spanish infinitive in brackets after each occurrence of the verb "to know."

26 Villoro, *Creer, Saber, Conocer*, 197–98.

27 Sammy Alfaro writes of Hispanic immigrant communities who "view Jesus as *El Divino Compañero*—their Divine Companion—the One who walks with them in midst of pain and struggle, and makes provision for their needs through his Spirit" (Sammy Alfaro, *Divino Compañero: Toward a Hispanic Pentecostal Christology* [Eugene, Ore.: Pickwick, 2010], 134). Alfaro borrows the language of the Divine Companion from a *corito* (a Spanish-language praise chorus) written by a Mexican Pentecostal, which includes these lyrics, translated by Alfaro into English:

> Divine Companion of the way
> Your presence I feel as I walk
> Christ has dissipated all shadow
> I now have light, the divine light of his love
> Stay, Lord, it's getting late
> I offer you my heart to inhabit.

28 Cleophus J. LaRue, *The Heart of Black Preaching* (Louisville: Westminster John Knox, 2000), 15. LaRue borrows *discrimen* terminology from David Kelsey's *Proving Doctrine* and uses it to describe a prevailing hermeneutical orientation to Scripture and to the task of preaching.

29 LaRue, *Heart of Black Preaching*, 14, 15.

30 Genesis 9:7.

31 Genesis 9:4.

32 Genesis 9:5.

33 Genesis 12:1.

34 Genesis 17:11.

35 Ezekiel 37:3-6.

36 Ezekiel 37:11-14.

37 Emphasis original.

38 Mark T. Mulder, Aida I. Ramos, and Gerardo Martí find that "religious identity tends to supersede racial/ethnic identity" in just this way among Hispanic Protestants (Mulder, Ramos, and Martí, *Latino Protestants in America*, 12).

39 Eduardo is paraphrasing Exodus 23:21.

40 This *él* / "him" is the angel God promises to send (in the previous verse) to protect and guide his people.

41 Smith, "Religion and Ethnicity in America," 1179.

42 Reina-Valera, 1995.

43 Esteban's usage of *tocante* was colloquial in this case, and I translated it as such.

44 Mulder, Ramos, and Martí, *Latino Protestants in America*, 140.

5 *PREDICADORAS* / FEMALE PREACHERS

1 Esteban's reasoning for segregating groups by gender was so that the women would feel greater freedom to share their views.

2 Machismo is often defined as exaggerated masculinity or hegemonic masculinity that is harmful and disempowering to women. Omar Castañeda warns that the concept of machismo "is complex and multifaceted and too often, in Anglo-American interpretations, reduced to self-aggrandizing male bravado that flirts with physical harm to be sexual, like some rutting for the rights to pass on genes" (Omar S. Castañeda, "Guatemalan Macho Oratory," in *Muy Macho: Latino Men Confront Their Manhood*, ed. Ray González [New York: Anchor, 1996], 37). In this context, I am simply highlighting the obstacle that machismo potentially presents to female leadership within churches. Karin Kleinke describes the "male machismo ethic" as "one of the most far-reaching and visible, yet the most difficult to overcome, of the barriers to women's leadership" in Latin American culture (Karin Kleinke, *Women and Leadership: A Contextual Perspective* [New York: Springer, 1996], 233).

3 Mary McClintock Fulkerson uses the concept of residuals to describe "elements of previous places and times" that persist even within a "new synchronic formation" of place (McClintock Fulkerson, *Places of Redemption*, 34).

4 Pew Research Center, "The Shifting Religious Identity of Latinos in the United States," *Religion and Public Life*, May 7, 2014, http://www.pewforum.org/2014/05/07/the-shifting-religious-identity-of-latinos-in-the-united-states/.

5 Pew Research Center, "Shifting Religious Identity."

6 Specific passages within these two Pauline epistles are among the scriptures most frequently cited as injunctions against the pastoral leadership of women in the church. In 1 Timothy 2:11-14, Paul writes, "Let a woman learn in silence with full submission. I permit no woman to teach or to have authority over a man; she is to keep silent. For Adam was formed first, then Eve; and Adam was not deceived, but the woman was deceived and became a transgressor." The text of 1 Corinthians 14:34-35 words this prohibition perhaps even more strongly, asserting that "women

should be silent in the churches. For they are not permitted to speak, but should be subordinate, as the law also says. If there is anything they desire to know, let them ask their husbands at home. For it is shameful for a woman to speak in church."

7 The story of Zelophehad's two daughters is found in Numbers 27:1-11.

8 Loida I. Martell-Otero, Zaida Maldonado Pérez, and Elizabeth Conde-Frazier, *Latina Evangélicas: A Theological Survey from the Margins* (Eugene, Ore.: Cascade Books, 2013), 9.

9 For a more in-depth analysis of my collaborators' indebtedness to Pentecostalism, see chapter 3.

10 Leah Payne, *Gender and Pentecostal Revivalism: Making a Female Ministry in the Early Twentieth Century* (New York: Palgrave Macmillan, 2015), 41.

11 Jane E. Soothill, *Gender, Social Change and Spiritual Power: Charismatic Christianity in Ghana* (Leiden: Brill, 2007), 54.

12 "The Apostolate of Women," *Weekly Evangel* (St. Louis, Mo.), March 18, 1916, 6. Emphasis original.

13 Charles H. Barfoot and Gerald T. Sheppard, "Prophetic vs. Priestly Religion: The Changing Role of Women Clergy in Classical Pentecostal Churches," *Review of Religious Research* 22, no. 1 (1980): 4. Barfoot and Sheppard characterize the period from 1901 to 1920 as a period of "Prophetic Pentecostalism" during which church and denominational practices had not yet been routinized. Without rigid hierarchies in place, local bodies of believers were free to make their own decisions regarding who would preach from their pulpits or lead their churches.

14 Payne, *Gender and Pentecostal Revivalism*, 131.

15 Max Weber, *The Sociology of Religion*, trans. Ephraim Fischoff (Boston: Beacon, 1963), 104.

16 Barfoot and Sheppard, "Prophetic vs. Priestly Religion," 16. These findings were based upon evidence reviewed in 1980.

17 In *Strangers and Pilgrims: Female Preaching in America, 1740-1845*, Harvard history of religion professor Catherine A. Brekus traces the rise and fall of opportunities for female preachers based on the relative routinization of their particular denominations. During the rapid growth of Separate Baptists in North Carolina in the mid-1700s, for example, Martha Stearns Marshall became known for her ability to bring "a whole concourse to tears by her prayers and exhortation" (Robert B. Semple, *A History of the Rise and Progress of the Baptists in Virginia* [Richmond, Va.: John O'Lynch, 1810], 374. Quoted in Catherine A. Brekus, *Strangers and Pilgrims: Female Preaching in America, 1740-1845* [Chapel Hill: University of North Carolina Press, 1998], 62). Although Separate Baptists were greatly disparaged for their openness to female exhorting, they maintained the practice up until a confluence of routinizing events took place in the latter part of the eighteenth century, after which they "followed the example of their northern counterparts" and "forbade women to exhort or preach in public" (Brekus, *Strangers and Pilgrims*, 65–66).

The story of Jarena Lee and her work as a pioneering preacher within the African Methodist Episcopal denomination fits this mold as well. The AME founder, Bishop Richard Allen, had mentored Lee and, in 1819, helped launch her itinerant ministry that saw her preaching as many as seven hundred sermons a year. After Allen's death, however, the next generation of church leadership pushed for a more educated and more male clergy (Anna Carter Florence, *Preaching as Testimony* [Louisville: Westminster John Knox, 2007], 39). Thirty-three years after Lee had officially embarked on her vocation as a preacher, her denomination voted to bar women from preaching, "and Jarena Lee herself disappeared from the historical record" (Florence, *Preaching as Testimony*, 40).

18 Espinosa, *Latino Pentecostals in America*, 283–84.

19 Gastón Espinosa, "'Third-Class Soldiers': A History of Hispanic Pentecostal Clergywomen in the Assemblies of God," in *Philip's Daughters: Women in Pentecostal-Charismatic Leadership*, ed. Estrella Alexander and Amos Yong (Eugene, Ore.: Pickwick, 2009), 96.

20 Several of my collaborators referred to their "quiet time" (a typically solitary time spent in Bible reading, prayer, and reflection) as "*mi intimidad* / my intimacy."

21 "M.I." was the abbreviation Ana used most often for her denomination, La Iglesia de Dios Pentecostal Movimiento Internacional.

22 Although a large segment of the Southern Baptist Convention has historically been opposed to female pastoral leadership, the more conservative segment of the SBC that rose to power beginning with the 1979 election of Adrian Rogers as SBC president officially codified this position within the Baptist Faith & Message, the SBC's doctrinal statement, in 2000. The language added in pertaining to female pastors is unambiguous: "While both men and women are gifted for service in the church, the office of pastor is limited to men as qualified by Scripture." "Comparison of 1925, 1963 and 2000 Baptist Faith and Message," Southern Baptist Convention, accessed January 20, 2018, now available online at https://bfm.sbc.net/comparison-chart/.

23 The Baptist University of the Americas (BUA), located in San Antonio, Texas, was originally established in 1947 by the Baptist General Convention of Texas as the Mexican Baptist Training School. It continues to offer ministerial training and theological education in both Spanish and English. Ignacio and his wife attended several summer units of study there over the years.

24 Florence, *Preaching as Testimony*, xix.

25 Florence, *Preaching as Testimony*, xx.

26 Barfoot and Sheppard see this distinction as part of the legacy of Pentecostalism that now exists within many Protestant denominations (Barfoot and Sheppard, "Prophetic vs. Priestly Religion," 2).

27 Elaine Lawless writes of the credentialing power of these "call-to-preach narratives" within Pentecostalism. It was certainly true for all of my collaborators, whether they were serving in specifically Pentecostal congregations or in churches influenced by Pentecostalism. Elaine J. Lawless, "Not So Different a Story After All," in *Women's Leadership in Marginal Religions: Explorations outside the Mainstream*, ed. Catherine Wessinger (Urbana: University of Illinois Press, 1993), 44.

28 The prominent early-twentieth-century Pentecostal evangelist Aimee Semple McPherson used her call narrative to dispel any doubts about her authority to preach. Her story incorporates elements of both the disciple John leaning against

Jesus during the last supper (in John 13:23) and Simon Peter being recommissioned into ministry by the shores of the Sea of Tiberias (in John 21). McPherson recounts:

> Then I drew closer yet. He said I might lay my head upon His bosom and I might rest awhile. It is when we draw close to Him there that our own hearts catch the throbbing of His heart and we say, "Lord, I will never leave you. I am going to stay right here with you."
>
> He then asked, "Do you love me?"
>
> "Yes, Lord, you know I love you."
>
> "Then feed my sheep. Feed my lambs." (Aimee Semple McPherson, "The Temple of the Word: Dome of Revelations," *The Bridal Call Foursquare* 11, no. 3 [1927]: 11. Quoted in Payne, *Gender and Pentecostal Revivalism*, 55)

McPherson's story of call, recapitulating elements from the lives and callings of the disciples Peter and John, was one that her audience received as a sacred story that undergirded her ministry. In *Strangers and Pilgrims*, Brekus demonstrates that Aimee Semple McPherson is part of a long line of female preachers who "modeled their spiritual narratives on the stories of biblical prophets such as Jonah, Deborah, Jeremiah, and Huldah" (Brekus, *Strangers and Pilgrims*, 172). Women's call narratives also, as in the example above, often reflected an unmediated experience of the divine. Brekus elaborates on this element within the testimonies of eighteenth- and nineteenth-century female preachers:

> All female preachers, whether black or white, described their calls to preach as immediate, irrefutable, and most of all, beyond their control. Even more than men, they declared that they never would have dared to speak publicly if not for the immediate revelation of the Holy Spirit. Defending themselves against their critics, they maintained that the decision to preach had been not their own, but God's. (Brekus, *Strangers and Pilgrims*, 185)

29 Martell-Otero, Maldonado Pérez, and Conde-Frazier, *Latina Evangélicas*, 96.
30 These carts are analogous to the floats often used in parades in the United States. They might have images of the Virgin or other sacred symbols mounted on top and are pulled by hand or by livestock.
31 Martell-Otero, Maldonado Pérez, Conde-Frazier, *Latina Evangélicas*, 24.
32 Martell-Otero, Maldonado Pérez, Conde-Frazier, *Latina Evangélicas*, 24. Conde-Frazier explains in a footnote to this passage that the female elder's exclamation was a paraphrase of Matthew 7:16, which presents the quality of a prophet's "fruit" as the key criterion for identifying whether a particular prophet is true or false.
33 The acronym ELL refers to the English Language Learners program, known elsewhere as ESL, or English as a Second Language.
34 *Eso* = her actions.
35 Barfoot and Sheppard, "Prophetic vs. Priestly Religion," 17.
36 Espinosa, *Latino Pentecostals in America*, 285.
37 Sánchez Walsh, *Latino Pentecostal Identity*, 77.
38 Sánchez Walsh, *Latino Pentecostal Identity*, 42–44.

39 Otto Maduro, "Becoming Pastora: Latina Pentecostal Women's Stories from Newark, New Jersey," in *Global Pentecostal Movements: Migration, Mission, and Public Religion*, ed. Michael Wilkinson (Leiden: Brill, 2012), 195–210.

40 Catherine Brekus relates the testimonies of early female preachers in the eighteenth and nineteenth centuries who similarly attempted to avoid the label of preaching by characterizing their ministry as one of public prayer, bearing personal witness, or leading Bible study. Perla was one in a long line of women who, due to outright hostility, their own internal conflict, or what they perceived to be the expectations of those around them, have cast themselves as something other than "preachers."

41 Espinosa, *Latino Pentecostals in America*, 284.

42 Espinosa, *Latino Pentecostals in America*, 284.

43 Payne, *Gender and Pentecostal Revivalism*, 34.

44 Payne, *Gender and Pentecostal Revivalism*, 34.

45 Payne, *Gender and Pentecostal Revivalism*, 34.

46 Loida Martell-Otero affirms the importance of personal testimony for Hispanic Protestant women who explore the truth of biblical narratives by "interweaving them with *testimonios* of their encounters with God." Martell-Otero, Maldonado Pérez, and Conde-Frazier, *Latina Evangélicas*, 40.

   Anna Carter Florence writes more broadly of women across American history and today, asserting that they "read and interpret the Bible differently from the men of their day; they hear in Scripture a different and liberating Word about women; they place this Word in the context of their own experience as women." Florence, *Preaching as Testimony*, xix.

47 These words are attributed to the angel Gabriel in Luke 1:32.

48 Espinosa, "'Third-Class Soldiers,'" 110.

6 CONCLUSION

1 McClintock Fulkerson, *Places of Redemption*, 254.

2 Edward Farley, *Good and Evil: Interpreting a Human Condition* (Minneapolis: Fortress, 1990), 39.

3 Farley, *Good and Evil*, 39.

4 Emmanuel Levinas, "Meaning and Sense," in *Collected Philosophical Papers*, trans. Alphonso Lingis (Dordrecht: Martinus Nijhoff, 1987), 97.

5 In spite of being despised, the figure of the Suffering Servant in Isaiah 53 still bears the infirmities and carries the diseases of those who reject him, even going so far as to be wounded for their transgressions and crushed for their iniquities.

6 Miller-McLemore, "Practical Theology," 1740.

7 In some ways, González' vision of "authentic" Hispanic preaching can be traced back to the publication of *Liberation Preaching: The Pulpit and the Oppressed* (coauthored with Catherine González) in 1980. In this homiletical guide, the authors foreground their indebtedness to Latin American liberation theology as a resource for the kind of preaching they advocate. They also point to liberationist positions adopted by "North American blacks and women who have known the pain of the limitations set on them by the surrounding culture" (Justo L. González and

Catherine G. González, *Liberation Preaching: The Pulpit and the Oppressed* [Nashville: Abingdon, 1980], 109). The book argues for "ideological suspicion" as a necessity for any theologian or preacher who would promote liberation, but it does not describe it as a significant factor among North American Hispanic preachers.

Many of the ideas present in *Liberation Preaching* take on a more fully realized form in González' later work, particularly in *Mañana: Christian Theology from a Hispanic Perspective* (Nashville: Abingdon, 1990), perhaps the most influential theological book written to date by a Hispanic Protestant theologian in the United States. There, González begins his exploration of Hispanic theology by rooting it in the perspective of a marginalized people. This orientation presents the possibility of Hispanic theology operating with a critical lens and a prophetic voice vis à vis the dominant culture in which it exists. González argues that for Hispanics to find the voice needed for themselves and the church at large, they need to "read the Bible in Spanish." For González, this entails reading with the kind of ideological suspicion he advocated in *Liberation Preaching* and asking not only questions about the spiritual possibilities presented in a particular text but also about the political realities it presents in its own time and illuminates in ours (González and González, *Liberation Preaching*, 109.).

Púlpito and *Manual de Homilética Hispana*, arriving fifteen years after the publication of *Mañana* and twenty-five years after *Liberation Preaching*, build on aspects of these earlier works to construct a vision of "authentic" Hispanic preaching grounded in a communal experience of marginalization. This entry point calls for "reading the Bible in Spanish," in order to produce a "reading of resistance." Such an approach foregrounds political and social concerns through a liberative eschatological lens.

In sum, the description of authentic Hispanic preaching offered by González and Jiménez seems to have evolved from an emphasis in *Liberation Preaching* borrowed from Latin American liberation theology to a description in *Mañana* of a unique Hispanic theological orientation, and from there to a portrayal of what González and Jiménez consider to be the preferred orientation within Hispanic homiletics.

8 Mulder, Ramos, and Martí, *Latino Protestants in America*, 139.

9 Mitchell, *Black Preaching*, 14.

10 Mitchell, *Black Preaching*, 16.

11 Especially after the departure of some key leaders from IAV (which I discussed in chapter 5), Pastor Esteban and Diana did not have as many laypeople with the confidence and experience to preach. In order to be able to speak at another church, attend a conference, visit family, or take the rare vacation, they occasionally asked me to fill in for them. Given our friendship and my commitment to mutuality as part of my practice of collaborative ethnography, I agreed whenever possible.

12 Augustine, *The First Catechetical Instruction (De Catechizandis Rudibus)*, trans. Joseph P. Christopher, Ancient Christian Writers 2 (Westminster, Md.: Newman, 1946), 50.

13 Leonora Tubbs Tisdale, *Preaching as Local Theology and Folk Art* (Minneapolis: Fortress, 1997).

14 I shared the autobiographical recollections of just such a minister in chapter 2.

15 Many programs of theological education are offered specifically to Hispanic populations due not only to the language barrier, but also to the bivocational schedules of many Hispanic ministers.

16 Fernando's understanding of his role in this revival was consistent with Jonathan E. Calvillo and Stanley R. Bailey's assertion that within some multiethnic congregations, "ethnicity may be purposefully downplayed and wane as religious identity flourished somewhat disconnected from ethnic particularism" (Calvillo and Bailey, "Latino Religious Affiliation and Ethnic Identity," 59). Fernando understood his congregation to be multiethnic and multicultural rather than simply Hispanic due to his congregants' many different countries of origin.

Bibliography

Abalos, David T. *Latinos in the United States: The Sacred and the Political.* Notre Dame: University of Notre Dame Press, 2007.

Aguilar, John L. "Insider Research: An Ethnography of a Debate." In Messerschmidt, *Anthropologists at Home in North America*, 15–26.

Alfaro, Sammy. *Divino Compañero: Toward a Hispanic Pentecostal Christology.* Eugene, Ore.: Pickwick, 2010.

"The Apostolate of Women." *Weekly Evangel* (St. Louis, Mo.), March 18, 1916.

Arrastía, Cecilio. *Teoría y Práctica de la Predicación.* Miami: Editorial Caribe, 1978.

Augustine. *The First Catechetical Instruction (De Catechizandis Rudibus).* Translated by Joseph P. Christopher. Ancient Christian Writers 2. Westminster, Md.: Newman, 1946.

Barfoot, Charles H., and Gerald T. Sheppard. "Prophetic vs. Priestly Religion: The Changing Role of Women Clergy in Classical Pentecostal Churches." *Review of Religious Research* 22, no. 1 (1978): 2–17.

Barton, Paul. *Hispanic Methodists, Presbyterians, and Baptists in Texas.* Austin: University of Texas Press, 2006.

Bielo, James S. *Words upon the Word: An Ethnography of Evangelical Group Bible Study.* New York: New York University Press, 2009.

Bowler, Kate. *Blessed: A History of the American Prosperity Gospel.* Oxford: Oxford University Press, 2013.

Brekus, Catherine A. *Strangers and Pilgrims: Female Preaching in America, 1740–1845.* Chapel Hill: University of North Carolina Press, 1998.

Bretherton, Luke. *Resurrecting Democracy: Faith, Citizenship, and the Politics of a Common Life.* Cambridge: Cambridge University Press, 2015.

Brewer, John D. *Ethnography.* Buckingham: Open University Press, 2000.

Cadge, Wendy, and Elaine Howard Ecklund. "Immigration and Religion." *Annual Review of Sociology* 33 (2007): 359–79.

Calvillo, Jonathan E., and Stanley R. Bailey. "Latino Religious Affiliation and Ethnic Identity." *Journal for the Scientific Study of Religion* 54, no. 1 (2015): 57–78.

Castañeda, Omar S. "Guatemalan Macho Oratory." In *Muy Macho: Latino Men Confront Their Manhood*, edited by Ray González, 37–56. New York: Anchor, 1996.

Chatham, James O. *Is It I, Lord?* Louisville: Westminster John Knox, 2002.

"Comparison of 1925, 1963 and 2000 Baptist Faith and Message." Southern Baptist Convention, accessed January 20, 2018, now available at https://bfm.sbc.net/comparison -chart/.

Córdova, Carlos B. "The Social, Cultural, and Religious Realities of Central American Immigrants in the United States." In *Dialogue Rejoined: Theology and Ministry in the United States Hispanic Reality*, edited by Ana María Pineda and Robert Schreiter, 23–42. Collegeville, Minn.: Liturgical Press, 1995.

De La Torre, Miguel A., and Edwin David Aponte. *Introducing Latino/a Theologies*. Maryknoll, N.Y.: Orbis Books, 2001.

Dunlap, Susan J. *Caring Cultures: How Congregations Respond to the Sick*. Waco, Tex.: Baylor University Press, 2009.

Espinosa, Gastón. *Latino Pentecostals in America: Faith and Politics in Action*. Cambridge, Mass.: Harvard University Press, 2014.

——. "The Pentecostalization of Latin American and U.S. Latino Christianity." *Pneuma* 26, no. 2 (2004): 262–92.

——. "'Third-Class Soldiers': A History of Hispanic Pentecostal Clergywomen in the Assemblies of God." In *Philip's Daughters: Women in Pentecostal-Charismatic Leadership*, edited by Estrella Alexander and Amos Yong, 95–111. Eugene, Ore.: Pickwick, 2009.

Farley, Edward. *Good and Evil: Interpreting a Human Condition*. Minneapolis: Fortress, 1990.

"Fiscal Year 2017 ICE Enforcement and Removal Operations Report." U.S. Immigration and Customs Enforcement, accessed January 18, 2018, https://www.ice.gov/ removal-statistics/2017.

Florence, Anna Carter. *Preaching as Testimony*. Louisville: Westminster John Knox, 2007.

Flores, Antonio, Gustavo López, and Jynnah Radford. "2015, Hispanic Population in the United States Statistical Report." *Hispanic Trends*, Pew Research Center. September 18, 2017. https://www.pewhispanic.org/2017/09/18/facts-on-u-s-latinos -trend-data/.

García-Treto, Francisco. "Reading the Hyphens: An Emerging Biblical Hermeneutics for Latino/Hispanic U.S. Protestants." In Maldonado, *Protestantes/Protestants*, 160–73.

Geertz, Clifford. *The Interpretation of Cultures*. New York: Basic Books, 1973.

González, Justo L. *Mañana: Christian Theology from a Hispanic Perspective*. Nashville: Abingdon, 1990.

González, Justo L., and Catherine G. González. *Liberation Preaching: The Pulpit and the Oppressed*. Nashville: Abingdon, 1980.

González, Justo L., and Pablo A. Jiménez. *Púlpito: An Introduction to Hispanic Preaching*. Nashville: Abingdon, 2005.

Grebler, Leo, Joan Moore, and Ralph Guzman. *The Mexican American People: The Nation's Second Largest Minority*. New York: Free Press, 1970.

Handlin, Oscar. *The Uprooted*. 2nd ed. Toronto: Little, Brown, 1973.

Headland, Thomas N., Kenneth L. Pike, and Marvin Harris, eds. *Emics and Etics: The Insider/Outsider Debate*. Newbury Park, Calif.: Sage, 1990.

Herbert, Joanna, and Richard Rodger. "Frameworks: Testimony, Representation and Interpretation." In *Testimonies of the City: Identity, Community, and Change in a Contemporary Urban World*, edited by Richard Rodger and Joanna Herbert, 1–23. Burlington, Vt.: Ashgate, 2007.

Holmes, Seth M. *Fresh Fruit, Broken Bodies: Migrant Farmworkers in the United States*. Berkeley: University of California Press, 2013.

Jiménez, Pablo A. *Principios de Predicación*. Nashville: Abingdon, 2003.

Jiménez, Pablo A., and Justo L. González. *Manual de Homilética Hispana: Teoría y Práctica desde la Diaspora*. Barcelona: Editorial CLIE, 2006.

Kammen, Michael. *People of Paradox*. New York: Vintage, 1973.

Kern, John Adam. *The Way of the Preacher: An Interpretation of a Calling*. Nashville: Publishing House of the M. E. Church, South, 1902.

Kleinke, Karin. *Women and Leadership: A Contextual Perspective*. New York: Springer, 1996.

Lalive d'Epinay, Christian. *El Refugio de las Masas—Estudio Sociológico del Protestantismo Chileno*. Santiago: Editorial del Pacifico, S.A., 1968.

LaRue, Cleophus J. *The Heart of Black Preaching*. Louisville: Westminster John Knox, 2000.

Lassiter, Luke Eric. *The Chicago Guide to Collaborative Ethnography*. Chicago: University of Chicago Press, 2005.

Lawless, Elaine J. "Not So Different a Story After All." In *Women's Leadership in Marginal Religions: Explorations outside the Mainstream*, edited by Catherine Wessinger, 41–54. Urbana: University of Illinois Press, 1993.

Levinas, Emmanuel. *Collected Philosophical Papers*. Translated by Alphonso Lingis. Dordrecht: Martinus Nijhoff, 1987.

López-Sanders, Laura. "Bible Belt Immigrants: Latino Religious Incorporation in New Immigrant Destinations." *Latino Studies* 10, nos. 1–2 (2012): 129–54.

Maduro, Otto. "Becoming Pastora: Latina Pentecostal Women's Stories from Newark, New Jersey." In *Global Pentecostal Movements: Migration, Mission, and Public Religion*, edited by Michael Wilkinson, 195–210. Leiden: Brill, 2012.

Maldonado, David, Jr. *Protestantes/Protestants: Hispanic Christianity within Mainline Traditions*. Nashville: Abingdon, 1999.

Martell-Otero, Loida I., Zaida Maldonado Pérez, and Elizabeth Conde-Frazier. *Latina Evangélicas: A Theological Survey from the Margins*. Eugene, Ore.: Cascade Books, 2013.

McClintock Fulkerson, Mary. *Places of Redemption: Theology for a Worldly Church*. Oxford: Oxford University Press, 2007.

McPherson, Aimee Semple. "The Temple of the Word: Dome of Revelations." *The Bridal Call Foursquare* 11, no. 3 (1927): 11.

Messerschmidt, Donald A., ed. *Anthropologists at Home in North America: Methods and Issues in the Study of One's Own Society*. Cambridge: Cambridge University Press, 1981.

Miller-McLemore, Bonnie. "Practical Theology." In *Encyclopedia of Religion in America*, edited by Charles H. Lippy and Peter W. Williams, 1:1739–43. Washington, D.C.: CQ Press, 2010.

Mitchell, Henry H. *Black Preaching: The Recovery of a Powerful Art*. Nashville: Abingdon, 1990.

Moschella, Mary Clark. "Ethnography." In *The Wiley Blackwell Companion to Practical Theology*, edited by Bonnie J. Miller-McLemore, 224–33. Oxford: Wiley-Blackwell, 2012.

Moss, Pamela, and Isabel Dyck. *Women, Body, Illness: Space and Identity in the Everyday Lives of Women with Chronic Illness*. Oxford: Rowman & Littlefield, 2002.

Mulder, Mark T., Aida I. Ramos, and Gerardo Martí. *Latino Protestants in America: Growing and Diverse*. Lanham, Md.: Rowman & Littlefield, 2017.

Payne, Leah. *Gender and Pentecostal Revivalism: Making a Female Ministry in the Early Twentieth Century*. New York: Palgrave Macmillan, 2015.

Pedraja, Luis G. "Guideposts along the Journey: Mapping North American Hispanic Theology." In Maldonado, *Protestantes/Protestants*, 123–29.

Pew Research Center. "Changing Faiths: Latinos and the Transformation of American Religion." *Hispanic Trends*. April 25, 2007. http://www.pewhispanic.org/2007/04/25/ii-religion-and-demography/.

———. "The Shifting Religious Identity of Latinos in the United States." *Religion and Public Life*. May 7, 2014. http://www.pewforum.org/2014/05/07/the-shifting-religious-identity-of-latinos-in-the-united-states/.

Ramírez, Daniel. "Public Lives in American Hispanic Churches: Expanding the Paradigm." In *Latino Religions and Civic Activism in the United States*, edited by Gastón Espinosa, Virgilio Elizondo, and Jesse Miranda, 177–97. Oxford: Oxford University Press, 2005.

———. *Migrating Faith: Pentecostalism in the United States and Mexico in the Twentieth Century*. Chapel Hill: University of North Carolina Press, 2015.

Rodriguez, José D. "Confessing the Faith from a Hispanic Perspective." In Maldonado, *Protestantes/Protestants*, 107–22.

Root, Deborah. *Cannibal Culture: Art, Appropriation and the Commodification of Difference*. Boulder, Colo.: Westview, 1996.

Sánchez Walsh, Arlene M. *Latino Pentecostal Identity: Evangelical Faith, Self, and Society*. New York: Columbia University Press, 2003.

Scharen, Christian, and Aana Marie Vigen. *Ethnography as Christian Theology and Ethics*. New York: Continuum, 2011.

Semple, Robert B. *A History of the Rise and Progress of the Baptists in Virginia*. Richmond, Va.: John O'Lynch, 1810.

Smith, Timothy L. "Religion and Ethnicity in America." *American Historical Review* 83, no. 5 (1978): 1155–85.

Soothill, Jane E. *Gender, Social Change and Spiritual Power: Charismatic Christianity in Ghana*. Leiden: Brill, 2007.

Spagat, Elliot, and Jill Colvin. "Detentions Spike, Border Arrests Fall in Trump's First Year." *AP News*, December 5, 2017, accessed January 18, 2018, https://www.apnews .com/3252d88390ed4ddea736b4a85a0b78a9.

Sullivan, Kathleen. "Iglesia de Dios: An Extended Family." In *Religion and the New Immigrants: Continuities and Adaptations in Immigrant Congregations*, edited by Helen Rose Ebaugh and Janet Saltzman Chafetz, 141–51. Walnut Creek, Calif.: AltaMira, 2000.

Thielicke, Helmut. *A Little Exercise for Young Theologians*. Grand Rapids: Eerdmans, 1962.

Tisdale, Leonora Tubbs. *Preaching as Local Theology and Folk Art*. Minneapolis: Fortress, 1997.

Villoro, Luís. *Creer, Saber, Conocer*. Mexico City: Siglo Ventiuno Editores, 1996.

Warren, Carol A. B. "Qualitative Interviewing." In *Handbook of Interview Research: Context and Method*, edited by Jaber F. Gubrium and James A. Holstein, 83–102. Thousand Oaks, Calif.: Sage, 2002.

Weber, Max. *The Sociology of Religion*. Translated by Ephraim Fischoff. Boston: Beacon, 1963.

$\mathcal{I}ndex$

Abalos, David T., 22
Agustín, 40–42, 50–51, 156–57
Álvaro, 39, 76–77, 118, 159–60
Ana, 59, 118, 120–21, 123, 126–27, 132–33, 175n21
Antonio, 47–49, 107, 170n8
Aponte, Edwin David, 9, 163n3
Arrastía, Cecilio, 45
Assemblies of God, 14, 31, 41, 56–57, 118–20, 124–25, 129–30, 159
assimilation, 5–6, 12, 55, 155, 160–61, 169n27

Bailey, Stanley R., 78, 179n16
Baptist, 14–15, 17, 24–25, 35, 39, 41–42, 52, 54, 57–62, 64, 86, 101, 104, 107, 118, 121, 130–32, 159, 168n20, 170n20, 174n17, 175n22, 175n23
Barfoot, Charles H., 120, 128, 174n13, 174n16, 175n26
Barton, Paul, 57–58, 81
bicultural, 15, 44, 46, 51–52, 55, 71, 151n9

bilingual, 15, 51–53, 55, 67, 159–60, 171n23
bivocational, 15, 41, 44, 46–51, 55, 71, 80, 179n15

calling, 2, 15, 17, 20–22, 26–28, 31, 33, 38, 42, 50, 55, 57, 70, 84, 92, 96, 114–15, 117–20, 122–27, 129, 131–33, 142–43, 147, 154, 157–58, 175n27, 176n28
Calvillo, Jonathan E., 78, 179n16
Catholic, 5, 8, 40, 81, 116, 123–24, 137–38, 140, 167n51
CLADIC, 56
Conde-Frazier, Elizabeth, 123, 125–26, 128
conversion, 14–15, 39, 75–78, 81, 88, 91, 104, 106, 110–11, 118, 123, 130, 137, 142, 150, 167n51, 169n27, 172n21
Córdova, Carlos B., 69

David, 22–23, 47
De La Torre, Miguel, 9, 163n3
deportation, 10–11, 25, 33, 35–37, 59, 155, 166n41

d'Epinay, Christian Lalive, 38, 42
Diana, 31–33, 47, 49, 52–53, 59,
    100, 113–16, 118, 132, 134, 142,
    178n11

Eduardo, 24–26, 94–99, 168n12,
    173n39
education, 14, 27, 38, 54, 69; theo-
    logical, 16, 43–44, 57–58, 121,
    127, 150–51, 156–59, 175n23,
    179n15
Ernesto, 39–40, 42, 54–55, 77,
    81–88
Espinosa, Gastón, 56–58, 120, 133,
    165n12, 170n27
Esteban, 2–3, 31–33, 36–37, 46–47,
    49–50, 52–53, 59, 100, 108–10,
    113–16, 118, 132, 134, 145–46,
    173n43, 178n11
ethnic identity maintenance, 5, 12,
    160–61
Eva, 53–54, 123–25, 132–33,
    135–42, 150
evangélico, 14, 57, 167n51, 169n22

Farley, Edward, 146
Fernando, 160–61, 179n16
Florence, Anna Carter, 123,
    175n17, 177n46
Fulkerson, Mary McClintock, 8, 21,
    26, 146, 173n3

García-Treto, Francisco, 6
González, Justo, 16, 51, 54–56,
    73–75, 111, 113, 142, 147–48,
    150, 162, 169n27, 177n7

Handlin, Oscar, 23, 25
healing, physical, 29–30, 33, 37, 78,
    88–91, 129, 154, 168n20; from
    wounds of migration, 15, 26–27,

31, 41–42, 80, 104, 106, 111, 136,
    141, 154–55
Holmes, Seth, 22
Holy Spirit, 53, 93–94, 98–99,
    125; and pastoral authoriza-
    tion, 118–19, 123, 128, 142–43,
    172n27, 176n28

Iglesia Agua Viva, 1–5, 13, 33, 35,
    46, 52, 59, 68, 100, 108, 113–14,
    116, 118, 134, 145, 152, 162,
    163n2
Iglesia de Dios Pentecostal Mov-
    imiento Internacional, 15, 57,
    59, 118, 120–21, 126, 170n19,
    175n21
Ignacio, 17–22, 27, 33–35, 49,
    60–62, 82, 88–91, 121, 127,
    130–32, 169n23, 175n23
Isaac, 28–30, 37–38, 66–68, 148–50

Jiménez, Pablo, 16, 73, 75, 78–80,
    91, 111, 113, 142, 147–48, 150,
    162, 178n7
Juan, 35–38

LaRue, Cleophus, 88, 91, 172n28
Lassiter, Luke Eric, 10–12
Leo, 41–42, 52–53, 104, 159–60
Levinas, Emmanuel, 146–47
liminality, 7, 26, 45, 83, 91, 151
Linda, 39, 118, 130

Maduro, Otto, 129
Manuel, 62, 64–66, 171n21
Marco, 101–4
Martell-Otero, Loida, 118, 177n46
Martí, Gerardo, 6, 110, 151, 173n38
Methodist, 6, 8, 14–15, 24–25,
    29–30, 35, 38–41, 53, 57–58,
    62–64, 66, 68, 94, 118, 123, 125,

132–33, 135, 138, 146, 148, 150, 168n20, 169n27, 171n21, 174n17
Miller-McLemore, Bonnie, 8
Mitchell, Henry, 43–44, 151
Moschella, Mary Clark, 8
Mulder, Mark T., 6, 110, 151, 173n38

participant observation, 7, 9, 12–14, 22, 35, 46, 80, 116, 134, 151, 162
Payne, Leah, 119, 133, 176n28
Pedraja, Luis G., 6, 168n19
pentecostal, 1, 6, 15, 20, 31, 33, 35, 38–40, 53, 56–59, 75, 86, 100, 115, 118–21, 123, 125–29, 132–33, 137–38, 145, 160, 167n48, 169n22, 169n24, 169n27, 172n27, 174n9, 175n27, 175n28
Perla, 128, 130–31, 177n40
population, 4–6, 11, 14, 22, 25, 69, 92, 116, 151–52, 158–59, 162, 166n34, 166n44, 169n27
Presbyterian, 27, 57–58
Protestant, 4–6, 8, 13–16, 18, 38–39, 50, 56–57, 73–76, 78, 81, 91, 100, 106, 110–11, 116, 118–19, 130, 137, 140–42, 148, 150–51, 157–58, 167n51, 168n17, 169n22, 169n27, 175n26, 177n46, 178n7

Rafael, 53, 69–70, 167n48, 171n23
Ramírez, Daniel, 26, 75–76, 169n24
Ramos, Aida I., 6, 110, 151, 173n38
Rodriguez, José D., 6
Root, Deborah, 76

Sara, 104–6, 132
Scharen, Christian, 8

Sheppard, Gerald T., 120, 128, 174n13, 174n16, 175n26
Smith, Timothy L., 26, 81, 100, 167n10
social location, 8–9, 37, 75, 118, 148, 164n5
Sullivan, Kathleen, 32

Teresa, 62–63, 70, 71, 132–33
testimony, 20, 33, 39, 83–84, 86–87, 91, 135, 138, 146, 157, 164n5, 168n19, 169n23, 177n40; as authorization for ministry, 16, 35, 115, 122–23, 125–29, 142, 176n28; in connection with migration, 35, 37, 111, 169n24; of ethnography, 8, 146; of healing, 30
Thielicke, Helmut, 43–44, 71, 151

Vigen, Aana Marie, 8
Villoro, Luís, 84–85

Walsh, Arlene Sánchez, 129, 167n51
Weber, Max, 120
wounds (of migration), 15–16, 21–23, 26–27, 38, 41–42, 45, 80, 113, 136, 141–42, 148–50, 153–55